Confederate Spies at Large

ALSO BY JOHN STEWART
AND FROM MCFARLAND

African States and Rulers, 3d ed. (2006)

Broadway Musicals, 1943–2004 (2006)

*The British Empire: An Encyclopedia of
the Crown's Holdings, 1493 through 1995* (1996)

Italian Film: A Who's Who (1994)

*Moons of the Solar System:
An Illustrated Encyclopedia* (1991)

Antarctica: An Encyclopedia
(2 volumes; 1990)

Confederate Spies at Large

The Lives of Lincoln Assassination Conspirator Tom Harbin and Charlie Russell

JOHN STEWART
FOREWORD BY ROY Z. CHAMLEE, JR.

McFarland & Company, Inc., Publishers
Jefferson, North Carolina, and London

LIBRARY OF CONGRESS ONLINE CATALOG

Stewart, John, 1952–
Confederate spies at large : the lives of Lincoln
assassination conspirator Tom Harbin and Charlie
Russell / John Stewart ; foreword by Roy Z. Chamlee, Jr.
p.   cm.
Includes bibliographical references and index.

ISBN-13: 978-0-7864-2868-7
ISBN-10: 0-7864-2868-6
(softcover : 50# alkaline paper) ∞

1. Harbin, Thomas.
2. Russell, Charles Henry, 1833–1919.
3. Lincoln, Abraham, 1809–1865—Assassination.
4. Booth, John Wilkes, 1838–1865—Friends and associates.
5. Harbin, Thomas—Family.
6. Russell, Charles Henry, 1833–1919—Family.
7. Spies—Confederate States of America—Biography.
8. United States—History—Civil War, 1861–1865—Biography.
9. United States—History—Civil War, 1861–1865—Secret Service.
I. Title.
E608.H(Harbin) S+   2007   2006038470

British Library cataloguing data are available

©2007 Stewart John. All rights reserved

*No part of this book may be reproduced or transmitted in any form
or by any means, electronic or mechanical, including photocopying
or recording, or by any information storage and retrieval system,
without permission in writing from the publisher.*

Cover photograph: Charlie Russell (courtesy Tom Kirby)

Manufactured in the United States of America

*McFarland & Company, Inc., Publishers
Box 611, Jefferson, North Carolina 28640
www.mcfarlandpub.com*

For Mike Herring

Acknowledgments

I could not have done this book without Charlie Russell's great-great-grandson Mike Herring.

I would not have gotten into it in the first place if it hadn't been for Helen Ruth Almond, Charlie's great-great-granddaughter.

I was greatly inspired by Roy Z. Chamlee, the author of the brilliantly written *Lincoln's Assassins*, who kindly agreed to my request that he write the foreword to this book.

And I would like to extend my thanks to the many charming and splendid people who have helped with this research:

In Mecklenburg County, Virginia: James Sheppard, the celebrated historian of the county; Buck Russell, of Clarksville, Charlie Russell's great-grandson; Diane Spencer of Boydton Library, and Sharon Wolfenbarger of South Hill Library; Brad Johnson, editor of the *South Hill Enterprise*.

In other parts of Virginia: Mr. Bruce Pencek and Tamara Kennelly of Virginia Tech; Virginia Dunn of the Library of Virginia; Lavonne Markham of Leesburg Library.

In Maryland: Laurie Verge and Sandra Walia, of the Surratt Museum, Prince George's County; Justin Demsky of the Maryland Archives in Annapolis; Anne Ramsey at Upper Marlboro Library; Mary at Frederick County Library; Janet Davis, also in Frederick.

In Washington, D.C.: Jason Moore and Margaret Goodbody at the Washingtoniana Room, Martin Luther King Library; Scott Schulz and Matt Steketee, keepers of the library at Ford's Theatre; Rachel Sterling at Mount Olivet Cemetery; Sandy Hussey, at Christ Church Episcopalian; Mr. William Creech, of the National Archives; Dr. Edward Marolda, Paul Cromwell, Bernadette McMahon, Lucinda Janke, Nancy Metzger, John Franzen.

In North Carolina: the staff of Ashe County Library, my library; Bob

Shar and Jerry Carroll of the Winston-Salem Library, my other library; Zachary Elder of the Perkins Library, Duke University.

In Chicago: Leslie Cakora and Laurie Rubin; the staff of the Chicago Historical Society.

The "Come Retributionists": James O. Hall, for decades the great Lincoln assassination scholar; Dave Gaddy, co-author with Dr. Hall and the late General Bill Tidwell of the controversial book *Come Retribution*; John Stanton, one of the great assassination scholars of today; and my good friend Jane Singer, pioneer in the field of the secret side of the Civil War and author of *The Confederate Dirty War*. Without Jane's input my book would have lost a dimension.

Mike Kauffman, author of the remarkable *American Brutus*, among other works.

The Deacon, Bernie Bernier, archivist of the Archdiocese of Washington.

Beth Watson at El Cajon Library, in San Diego; Sister Eleanor Casey and Bonnie Weatherly of the Sisters of Charity; and many, many other librarians and archivists, names unknown, who helped me, in libraries such as Cincinnati, Los Angeles, Chicago, you name it.

The foremost Harbin family researchers Betty Garbers and Joan Marie Meyering.

Linda Reno, who brought St. Mary's County from the shadows into the light, not just for me, but for the world, with her Genweb page, and who, through countless e-mails and hours of telephone conversations, guided me patiently through the labyrinth of Maryland history.

The descendants and relatives: Tom Kirby of Richmond; Norm Stant; Penny Leese; Jan McMillan; Bob Jensen; Eric Jensen; Chris Jensen; Lisa Bernstein; Peggy Lou Pliscou; Lee Pliscou; Tim Stamps; Dr. Tom Maguire; Joe Maguire; Winston McColl; Jake and Elizabeth Jurney; Mickey Griggs; Edwin Harbin and his wife, Pat; Frank Harbin; Dodie Harbin; Rousby Quesenberry; Bill Quesenberry.

For their generosity and co-operation I would like to thank the *Washington Post*, the *New York Times*, and the London *Times*.

George Alfred Townsend, wherever you are.

As for the two photographs in this book: The one of Tom Harbin is the only known reproduction of his likeness, and that is from a portrait in the collection of Colonel Julian Raymond. It is the same one that has been reproduced several times in different books and articles. Credit goes to James O. Hall and the picture collection of Colonel Julian Raymond, courtesy of Walter Burke, Fort Myers, Florida, and thanks to Dave Gaddy for sending me the best copy I've ever seen.

Photographic credit for the picture of Charlie Russell goes to Tom Kirby.

Table of Contents

Acknowledgments   vii
Foreword by Roy Z. Chamlee, Jr.   1
Preface   3
Introduction   5

I. The Life and Family of Charlie Russell   15
II. The Life and Family of Tom Harbin   97

Appendix A. Graves in the Historic Congressional
   Cemetery, Washington, D.C.   153
Appendix B. More Census Information and Related Documents   155
Bibliography   193
Index   195

Foreword by Roy Z. Chamlee, Jr.

Confederate Spies at Large takes us back to the days of great tragedy which occurred at the close of the Civil War. It provides insight into some of the inner workings of a committed few who connived to avenge what they viewed as the wrongs against an aggrieved South. They were moved forward by a determination to finish the task to which they had dedicated themselves. Many were involved to one degree or another.

John Stewart has made an extensive investigation of those less known in the assassination. This book deals with two of those individuals, Charlie Russell and Tom Harbin. Tom was never put on trial and is seldom mentioned as having had a part in the death of the president. Stewart has brought to light many facts about this Confederate agent. Charlie Russell's activities probably have been mostly unknown among Lincoln scholars until Stewart's investigation.

The first half of the book concerns the life and activities of Russell and the last part contains the story of Harbin. It deals with the families of both men—who, strangely enough, were intertwined by marriages—presenting a comprehensive story of the tumultuous times in which they lived. Stewart's research has uncovered additional information on other little-known individuals, such as Mrs. Quesenberry, Tom Harbin's family and the Confederate spy ring. He adds information on the Mudd, Harbin and Russell families, all of which had strong Catholic ties in and around Southern Maryland. All were associated in some way with Lincoln's death.

This book is a good resource for anyone seeking to understand something of the family life, the social and the religious background of these unrecognized, practically unknown assassins. None of them pulled the trigger, but had their part in the planning and preparations been made known, surely the list of those who went to trial for the assassination of the president would have been much longer. It opens the way to a better understanding as to what motivated them in their villainous plot.

Roy Z. Chamlee, Jr., is the author of *Lincoln's Assassins: A Complete Account of Their Capture, Trial and Punishment* (McFarland, 1990).

Preface

This is the story of Charlie Russell and Tom Harbin. During the Civil War Tom was one of the most wanted Confederate agents. He was also one of the leading lights in the plot to kill Abraham Lincoln. Tom it was who, among other things, left the horse outside Ford's Theatre in Washington—the getaway vehicle for John Wilkes Booth—and it was Tom who helped Booth escape across the Potomac after the assassination of the president of the United States. Tom Harbin, with a big price on his head, went into deep hiding, and was never caught.

Tom Harbin is present in every book about the Lincoln assassination and yet he has been almost totally ignored as a subject for biography. This is an unacceptable omission given that he was such a key character and has such a fascinating story. Until now all the information published on Tom Harbin has amounted to roughly one or two paragraphs. This book sets out to rectify that omission.

The other half of this book presents a brand new Confederate agent: Charlie Russell, a man who never talked, never left a paper trail. Yet all men leave traces, and it was those traces that led to the gradual uncovering of the story of this remarkable spy. Charlie is also important because he represents a group of men and women—and we may never know the size of this group—who, like Charlie, remained silent.

It was only by accident, while I was doing genealogical research into the Russell family of Clarksville, Virginia, that I stumbled across Charlie's activities during the Civil War. From then on the circumstantial evidence just jumped out at me, time after time, and the case against Charlie built and built to such a point that, had he ever been tried in a Federal court of law, the sheer weight of evidence would have hanged him. Of course, if he'd been tried in a court south of the Mason-Dixon Line he would have emerged a hero.

As a bonus, it was while researching Charlie that I ran into Tom. I knew, instinctively, from the first moment Tom sprang onto my horizon, that he and Charlie would be inextricably connected, and I wasn't disappointed.

Wishing to present the stories of both agents, and relying so heavily on genealogical investigation, I chose a book format that would reflect both the wish and the reliance. The first half of the book is about Charlie and the second is about Tom, yet the two characters frequently meet in the middle, partly because they were related by family, and also because by the very nature of their occupation, they would just have to cross paths.

Occasionally I have incorporated relevant census information into the flow of the story in the belief that this information helps carry the story along, and that the census lists tell their own tales which would be hard to improve upon. The bulk of the census information consulted is to be found in Appendix B.

I have also incorporated newspaper articles of the day. In many instances it was better to quote verbatim than to try to paraphrase, it being my belief that a news item, as printed, offers not only authenticity but the flavor of the time. Washington papers predominate because that is where our overall story is mostly set.

The war that lasted from 1861 to 1865 is variously termed "the War of Northern Aggression," "the War Between the States," "the War of the Rebellion," and, only slightly jocosely, "the Late Unpleasantness." The term generally used throughout this book is "the Civil War," because more people recognize that term than any other, and, although it may cause a sense of rebellion in some, it causes no confusion. I am aware that there are many semanticists out there (mostly Southerners) who will not only describe the term "civil war" as inaccurate, but who will define that term for you as two factions of the same political entity both vying for control of that entity. The "War of Northern Aggression," they claim, was a struggle between two separate countries—the United States of America and the Confederate States of America, each with its own capital and congress, and so on. However, on the other hand, and bearing South Carolina's history and more specifically Fort Sumter in mind, there is a distinct case to be put forward for calling the conflict "the War of Southern Aggression."

Introduction

In 1833, Andrew Jackson began his second administration as president of the United States—right in the midst of the Nullification Crisis. South Carolina alone had decided that the United States was a compact of individual units entered into willingly, and that if a particular state didn't want to go along with a certain Federal initiative, then, by heck, it didn't have to. In this case it was a question of the tariff, but the same reasoning could apply also to secession. President Jackson regarded the Palmetto State's stance as treasonous, and promised to meet the threat with force. It was only a political compromise that saved the Union in 1833.

The American Anti-Slavery Society was formed toward Christmas of that year, with good tidings to all men, regardless of color. Sam Colt invented the first revolver that could be used conveniently by a man on horseback. Not as heralded at the time—but as history would later prove, in many ways, just as important—were the births of three boys in Charles County, Maryland: Tom, Sam and Charlie.

Charlie was first out, on February 22—George Washington's birthday. Tom was next, on August 25; and Sam on December 20.

If you dig into the family histories of Tom Harbin or Sam Mudd you'll come across the name Charlie Russell soon enough—provided you are a pretty thorough genealogist, in which case he'll appear on both their trees, hanging from one of the twigs like a peach. But the family connection between Charlie and the other two boys is more quickly and easily arrived at if you approach the research from a different route, if you look through the other end of the telescope, and start digging into Charlie Russell's mysterious past, in which case it's not long before you run up against Tom and Sam.

The three Southern Maryland counties of Prince George's (which this book will sometimes abbreviate as PG), Charles, and St. Mary's (SMC) were all heavily Catholic and completely Secessionist. A case in point: In the 1860 election Lincoln is reputed to have garnered six votes from Charles, and only one from PG. It is said that when the one renegade voter in PG, after a dram too many, bragged about his aberration one evening, he almost got himself strung up on the local oak. That Maryland as a state voted to go Federal for the duration of the war made no difference to the feelings of the Southern Marylanders—their geographical appendage, with its plantation and slave economy, was as Confederate as Mississippi. Because of that, and with Charles County lying just across the Potomac from King George County in the Northern Neck of Virginia, Southern Maryland would serve, during the Civil War, as a fundamental connection in the "Spy Line" running from the Confederate capital of Richmond to Baltimore. It is no exaggeration to say that virtually every home and farm in those three counties was a safe house for Southern agents, a drop point for Confederate President Jefferson Davis's couriers, a meeting place for the hatching of anti–Union plans, or just a haven where a Reb on the run could get a glass of water without getting squealed on. It has often been said that if the Federal authorities had arrested everyone with Secessionist leanings and Southern sympathies, there would have been no one left in Southern Maryland.

The Mudds, Harbins and Russells had been in, around, and all over these three counties of Southern Maryland for generations. In the 1790s thousands and thousands of families from the Eastern United States flocked to the new states of Tennessee and Kentucky. Land and religion had a lot to do with this mass migration, and so did plain orneriness. Anything to get out of sight and out of the clutch of government.

From Southern Maryland alone, various branches of many Catholic families made the trek to Kentucky—the Russells, the Mudds, the Mattinglys, the Jarboes, the Harbins, the Coomeses. All neighbors, related, all close, all Catholics. Charles and William Russell, Charlie's great-uncles, were two of those who went West. One of old Charles Russell's daughters would marry a Mudd man, one of his sons would marry a Mudd girl, and another son married two Mudd girls (at different times). One of old William's sons, William, would marry Sarah Mudd. On top of that, one of old Charles's grandsons would marry a Mudd girl. Mudd everywhere.

In addition, Charlie Russell and Tom Harbin were not only fellow Confederate agents during the Civil War, they were also step-cousins.

This is genealogically interesting in that it connects Charlie Russell to the Mudds and Harbins. Not that the three families needed connecting, as they knew each other for generations; it's just that historically, when it comes down to the role played by Sam Mudd and Tom Harbin in the Lincoln Conspiracy, one might just give Charlie Russell a passing thought, now that one is alerted to his existence.

Sam, Tom and Charlie had a lot in common aside from the year and county of their birth, their religion and background. They were all rabid Secessionists and would all three play a part in the Civil War that would happen soon enough. All had children, and all did well for themselves.

Sam became a regular good ol' boy country doctor, yet they made a big Hollywood movie about him*; Tom was a hotel clerk most of his adult life, yet 150 years later people still talk about him they are still fascinated, still hunting him down. As for Charlie...

Charles H. Russell was a distinguished and very successful Southern gentleman who, for decades, was one of the leading citizens of Clarksville, Virginia. That's the Clarksville in Mecklenburg County down by the Carolina line, a place he had moved to from Washington, D.C., at the outbreak of the Late Unpleasantness. The Russell wagons he manufactured from the 1870s on were famous all along the Eastern Seaboard for years until the mechanized tractor industry finally put an end to businesses like that. But Charlie was dead by the time that happened.

Papa Charlie, the family called him. As an old man he was very handsome—striking; not very tall, and seemingly slight for a former blacksmith, but with a presence you couldn't escape. You could sense that beneath the dignified Robert E. Lee exterior he'd kill you if you crossed him. Even in his eighties he'd kill you. You just had the feeling that sometime in his past more than one man had crossed him.

Sam went through the war deep under cover. Being a doctor helped. But after the war the Federal authorities came down on him like a ton of bricks. He came within one judicial vote of the death sentence.

"All I did was set a bone in this fellow's leg!," he must have wailed. "What could I do? He came to me in the dead of night with a busted ankle. I'm a doctor, for Pete's sake!"

Sam was right, of course. But so were the Feds. Sam was so far up to his neck in the plot to kill Lincoln it's surprising he didn't drown in his own Hippocracy. At least, that's one side of the story. The other side, the stance his family takes, is that he was innocent.

Tom Harbin became something of a folk hero during the Civil War. The most notorious and dangerous of all the Confederate agents, the most fearless, and the most romantic, he was perhaps—to use an anachronistic term—Public Enemy # 1 on the Federals' list. If he was not Number One, he was up there. The Feds wanted him badly, and many times they almost got him. But he was a cunning lad, was Tom Harbin, bold and resourceful. The stuff movies are made of. From today's perspective there is a touch of the movie Custer about Tom, of the movie Robin Hood, of the

---

**The Prisoner of Shark Island* (1936), starring Warner Baxter as Dr. Samuel Mudd.

real-life Errol Flynn. And then, to cap it all off, he was the big fish who got away after the Lincoln assassination.

The war effectively ended on April 9, 1865, at Appomattox Court House, when Robert E. Lee surrendered, forced by military events moving so fast against him that he had no choice. Lee had only recently been appointed general of the entire Confederate army. Before that he had led the Army of Northern Virginia, and that was the army that he surrendered on April 9. That was the army that counted.

With hindsight one is not surprised by Mars Robert's surrender. Richmond, the Confederate capital, had fallen the week before, the high Southern command had fled south, and from our historical vantage point now it is obvious that the South had lost the war. However, at the time—April 9— only those on the Appomattox field knew of the surrender. Communications were slower in those days. The war department in Washington received the news by telegram later that evening, and by 10 o'clock all northern cities which had that facility were celebrating. The newspapers of the 10th were full of it. By the evening of the 10th most communities in Maryland and Virginia had heard the news, one way or another, but word didn't reach some of the farther flung outposts of the fighting until much later, and even then, a lot of die-hard Rebels wouldn't quit. So, the war went on. (In fact it goes on today, as anyone in the South knows.)

Anyway, Appomattox Court House came as a surprise to everyone. The Southerners had already planned their 1865 campaigns and were certainly not prepared for such a quick end to the conflict. At the secret level there were intricately prepared missions afoot that once set in motion couldn't be stopped. One unstoppable plan in particular went ahead, like one of those hit-man jobs you see in the movies where the client tries to call the assassin off but can't get to him in time.

John Wilkes Booth snuck into the presidential box at Ford's Theatre, in Washington, the night of April 14. Just after 10 o'clock he yelled "Sic semper" (or "Sic semper tyrannis," depending on which version you believe), shot Lincoln in the head (or shot Lincoln first, then yelled immediately afterwards), then jumped awkwardly from the box onto the stage, breaking his ankle (or shin bone). He then escaped into the night on a horse that had been waiting at the stage door. Tom Harbin was later to claim he was the one who, earlier that day, had arranged for the four-legged getaway vehicle to be waiting there. Some iconoclasts have even put forward the theory that Booth broke his leg when this horse fell on him.

Booth, in great pain, and at that point now very definitely Public Enemy #1—of all time—thundered down to the Navy Yard, crossed the bridge into Southern Maryland, and rode like the devil, trying to find his accomplice, Dave Herold, who had been scheduled to meet him on the highway to help him get away. About eight miles into Maryland young Herold finally caught up with the actor, and the two plunged on, more and more desperate, toward Sam Mudd's farm. Together Booth and Herold would have a series of adventures that would culminate in Booth being shot and Dave being hanged.

Meanwhile, back in Washington, D.C., another conspirator, bully boy Lewis Powell (alias Payne), attempted, as his part in the "decapitation of the government," to assassinate Secretary of State William Seward, and came very close to succeeding in a ferocious one-man attack against overwhelming odds. Little German George Atzerodt, whose mission was to kill Vice President Andrew Johnson, decided instead to get drunk. One feels sorry for George, swept along in a foreign language, drawn by ruthless individuals into a plot he probably barely comprehended. Nevertheless, even if you chicken out at the last moment, intent to kill the vice president is not going to win you any popularity awards from the police—but it will get you a Public Enemy tag.

Mary Surratt, up to her neck in the plot, was arrested, and became the first woman ever to swing at the insistence of the U.S. government. Her son John Surratt, an important Confederate agent also involved in the plot, was out of town when it all happened, and he managed to get out of the country. A big Public Enemy badge was appended to him in absentia.

Once Dave Herold's part in the whole thing became known he too became a wanted man. Dr. Mudd also made the list, not only for setting Booth's broken bone, but for his major part in the plot in general. The others subsequently tried by the military tribunal for their part in the assassination—Ned Spangler, Mike O'Laughlen, and Sam Arnold—never achieved the notoriety of the others, and were merely jailed.

In the wake of the assassination the Federal detectives nailed a lot of the conspirators. They hanged a few. Sam, just squeaking by with his life, was sentenced to eternity in the Dry Tortugas. However, the way things are in the world, within a few short years he was back home in the bosom of his wife and family in Charles County, and running for political office.

But hundreds escaped the police dragnet. In truth, the Feds let many get away because too many brought to trial simply wouldn't look good. Astonished murmurs of "Gad, that many people wanted to kill Abe!" just wouldn't do.

The Feds never looked for Charlie, of course, but they went after Tom like crazy after the war, even more than they had in the thick of it—not only to bring him to book but because they were afraid of what he, being Tom Harbin, might yet do. With the big conspirators brought to trial, Tom was now very definitely Public Enemy # 1. But they never got him.

Instead, they forgave him, just as they forgave Sam. A year after Mr.

Lincoln's death, Tom was back in the nation's capital, under his own name, living and working with complete immunity, big as life, bigger than life.

Long after it was all over, Tom would hold court in the National Hotel in Washington and tell wild tales about his days as a Confederate agent, about the ten big ones they had on his head—dead or alive; about his flight to Cuba; about the time he took on thirty Feds on his own, a pistol in each hand. And he talked to the press too. Money talks.

But Charlie Russell never talked—partly because the reporters never knew he existed, partly because he didn't need the money, but mostly because he was not that kind of guy. His name has never been linked to the Confederate spy system, and certainly not to the conspiracy to kill Lincoln.

However, it didn't take long in my research into Charlie to find that during the Civil War he was in and out of Washington, D.C., with some frequency, to see the wife and two young children he'd left behind in the capital with his relatives for the duration of the war. Back then—for Charlie, anyway—Washington was the enemy capital.

Not too much need be made of a Johnny Reb sneaking into D.C. during the war. Many did it. It was relatively easy—although no easier, and certainly no less dangerous than an OSS man infiltrating Berlin during World War II. Charlie's getting into the enemy stronghold was made easier by his natural advantages. He had been raised there; he didn't have a thick Southern accent to give him away. And he knew the town like the back of his hand. Moreover, his best plea, if caught, was, "I'm just visiting my wife. You know how it is, fellahs." But the consequences, had he been found, would have been similar to the Gestapo nabbing a Yank—Charlie would have been in big trouble. But Charlie was smart. Not only was he never apprehended, he never talked. Ever. Not like Tom.

There has been so little written about Tom Harbin that he would laugh if he were alive. And there has been virtually nothing written about Charlie, except his obituary. And he would laugh too. On the other hand, the story of Dr. Samuel Alexander Mudd has been so told and retold over the decades that it's almost pointless to regurgitate—yet, now and again, something new comes up.

So, this book is the story of Charlie and Tom. On a secondary level, but only because they are so relevant to Charlie and Tom, this book is also, in its little way, a saga about the Harbin and Russell families, and about the fascinating supporting actors who enter left and exit right. To deny full coverage to the wives, the brothers and sisters, the offspring, the parents, the nieces and nephews, the friends and acquaintances with whom Tom and Charlie were so closely involved, would be to deny access to important facets of the histories of both of our heroes.

As a consequence we have, for example, Tom's illustrious brother,

George F. Harbin, the merchant with a past, one of the leading citizens of Washington, whose tragic swan song was a swan dive in full public view; Tom's son, himself, or at least the elder of Tom's two surviving sons, the brilliant James T., and his valiant but hopeless fight against the demon rum; Tom's wives and his equally brilliant younger son, the celebrated math professor at Georgetown University; Tom's eldest and most tragic brother, Joseph B. Harbin, who, early on, led the family into ruin; Tom's brother-in-law, the notorious Confederate agent Thomas Austin Jones, who escaped hanging only by his extraordinary ability to appear extraordinarily harmless.

We have the tragedies, so many of them, that beset both the Russells and the Harbins: the murders, the divorces, the scandals, the outrageous and very public romantic affairs, the bankruptcy, the mental institutions, the suicides, the pox; but we also have the triumphs, the glorious and romantic days of the Civil War, the social whirl of Washington, D.C., the endless achievements.

On Charlie's side we find his brother, John H. Russell, the ward politician; Janette, the all-powerful step mother; another brother, William Ignatius (why did he go by an assumed name after the Civil War?); Phil Harbin, the cop, Charlie's stepbrother; Charlie's son, Willie, and the shootout on Main Street that doomed a handsome seventeen-year-old to wander in limbo for 50 years. We discover the Arsenal explosion that killed so many women.

The amazing Charles Emmet Joyce, Charlie's nephew by marriage, a relative of James Joyce the writer, a lieutenant in the Union Army at 17, a Fenian terrorist condemned to hang by the neck but who escaped the hangman's noose, only to die at 38 because they couldn't get the clothing out of his lung; his older brother John O'Connell Joyce, in many ways and by many of his contemporaries vaunted as the pride of Erin, until he copped a bullet between the eyes; his younger brother Michael Joyce, accidentally killed by a Gatling gun; Charles Emmet's famous boss General Thomas Francis Meagher, leader of the Young Ireland Movement, who also avoided the devil's noose by the skin of his teeth and who, amid sensational world press coverage, escaped so dramatically from imprisonment in Van Diemen's Land; Charles Emmet's remarkable daughter Daisy Joyce—poet, musician, socialite, reporter, prodigy—and her equally remarkable husband Jackson Elliott, the Associated Press reporter.

In various-sized roles, all vital, we meet other men and women who cross the paths of Tom and Charlie, figures such as Willie Snyder, the D.C. blacksmith—and who knows what he did in the war?—and his baseball catcher brother Charlie M. Snyder; the Milburn brothers from Maryland, spies both, one of whom ended his life plunging 250 feet down a mine shaft in Colorado; General Uriah Forrest, family patriarch and certified hero of two wars; the son of the emperor of Mexico; Robert E. Lee and his cousins, the Lees of Blenheim; Leslie Keeley, the founder of the Bichloride Club of Gold; Admiral William F. "Bull" Halsey's social secretary; George Alfred Townsend, the famous war reporter; top FTC lawyer Robert Brooks Dawkins; and a bunch of very mysterious Catholic priests—well, several of them were definitely priests, but one may well not have a been a priest at all. The Catholic Church, always the Church, it somehow dominates our story, or rather, like the Civil War, casts its immense shadow into all corners.

It was speculated upon, even in the minutes following the assassination, that the Catholic Church had been responsible for the crime. To think that the Vatican might have been behind it is, in fact, hardly thinkable at all. But, as has often been philosophized, where man can think something man can do something. If there was a Catholic involvement, it would surely have been on a local level, and one created by the political sentiments and sensibilities of the day.

The wild story of the Washington Light Infantry and other militia units in the capital at the outbreak of the Civil War, especially the National Rifles and their charismatic leader, Frank B. Schaeffer, is told, perhaps for the first time in succinct summation; as is that of Dem Jack Ass. That venerable institution, the National Hotel, in Washington, is always there too, always, the host of tragedy, comedy, scandal, death, but mostly intrigue. We experience police cappers, slick swindlers, and the congressman who tried to blow his brains out—five times, and still failed.

Then there are the spies and spymasters: the legendary General Thomas Jordan, who initiated the first spy ring in Washington, and who became an even more legendary freedom fighter in the Cuban Rebellion; Rose O'Neale Greenhow, "Rebel Rose," the lady spy, trained by Jordan, who altered the course of the war and was then arrested by the Pinkertons, and who not long afterwards drowned off the Carolina coast as a blockade runner; Allen Pinkerton himself, alias Major E.J. Allen, spy catcher; William Norris, the enigmatic head of the Confederate Secret Service Bureau; Thomas Nelson Conrad, the spy professor, later president of the very same college that Charlie Russell's son attended; and there was Buffalo Springs, the mysterious spy training camp during the Civil War.

Aside from Booth and the Surratts, and the others who were or were not tried, there is the inscrutable William Bryant, and the Widow Quesenberry, and several of the other conspirators and accessories in the plot to kill Lincoln. Many of these figures emerge as real characters for the first time, not just as names in a sentence here and there.

We read of the wars—the Revolutionary War, the War of 1812, the Mexican War, the Ten Year War in Cuba, the Spanish-American War, World War I, and above all else, the Civil War, which changed the lives of all of them. We read of the places—the Southern Maryland counties of Prince

George's, Charles, and St. Mary's; King George County in Virginia; Mecklenburg County, farther south, where Clarksville is; Ireland; but above all the omnipresent Washington, D.C., and most specifically Capitol Hill, where so much of this all happened. As background, but still very much affecting our characters, we read about the menacing Tom Smothers, the Washington rapist who stalked the capital for two years, terrorizing the streets until the boys in blue nabbed him. Then there's Jack the Slasher and his prodigious escapades in the dead of night. And there's the boy who vomited a frog.

This entire story is framed by the census and reports from the newspapers, predominantly the *Washington Post*, and the *Daily Evening Star*, and to a lesser degree by other documentary evidence, such as bounty land claims, personal letters and reminiscences from the families, Bible records, wills, land records, and so on, but it is really the censuses and news clippings that jolly the story along. They tell so many tales of their own.

I

The Life and Family of Charlie Russell

Charlie Russell (courtesy Tom Kirby).

Christopher Russell it was, Charlie Russell's great-great-great-great-great-grandfather, born in England in 1614, who was the first of his family into Maryland, in 1647. All of the individual colonial governments needed settlers back then, to tame the land and the Indian, and some were prepared to pay to get them. When Chris Russell signed the oath of fealty on November 12 of that year—1647—this initiative gained him a headright of 50 dollars and 100 acres on the west side of the Wicomico River, where, in 1651, he built his 75-acre plantation, "Brough," near where Allens Fresh is today, in what was then St. Mary's County but which in 1658 became part of the newly formed Charles County.

On February 7, 1660 the military company formerly commanded by John "Grindingstone" Jenkins was handed over to Captain Russell, but the following year the good Russell fell sick, to such a degree that he was unable to move. They sent for Mary Vanderdonck, the quack daughter of the Reverend Francis Doughty, witch hunter.

"I'll do it for ye for a thousand pounds of tob," said the wily Mistress Vanderdonck.

"A thousand for my soul?" exclaimed an irate Captain Russell, managing to overcome, if only for a moment, his lethargy as he rose on one elbow on his sickbed. "Too much tobacco, not enough soul, Mistress. Five hundred."

"A thousand," repeated the witch hunter's daughter.

And the deal was cut—except that Mistress Vanderdonck, despite her horse-trading skills, failed to secure her payment before she began her tender ministrations. If she had only had her father's insight into the way the Devil works, she could have avoided the embarrassment that followed, when a recovered Captain Russell refused to pay her even an ounce of tob.

However, even the Devil must pay the piper, and in February 1662 Captain Russell's soul, such as it was by his own admission, moved on to a different plane, perhaps as the result of new physic administered him by the vengeful Mistress Vanderdonck. However, the great and final sickness may well have been precipitated by the vast quantities of rum and brandy that he daily consumed. At any rate, on February 20, 1662, the late Captain Russell's company was handed over to Captain Hugh Neale, freshly married to none other than Mary Vanderdonck, and then the creditors began to emerge from not only the woodwork but the masonry too. The hard-drinking captain had left debts of innumerable thousands of pounds of tob to an unreasonable number of persons whose services he had bought but never paid for, including Mistress Vanderdonck—obligations that, now, those owed assailed the administrators and heirs of the estate for satisfaction thereof.

Captain Christopher Russell begat Walter, who begat Luke, who begat Thomas, who begat William, who, by two wives, begat John Baptist, William

Jr. (1747), Ignatius (1748), Charles (1754), and James. This last named was Charlie Russell's grandfather, baptized in the Catholic church of St. Francis Xavier in Newtown, St. Mary's County, Maryland, on December 6, 1755.

Came the Revolutionary War and James's eldest brother William headed west, into the far reaches of Virginia, a territory then known as Kentucky. His brother Charles would follow after the war was over, but Ignatius and James stayed on in the East. James married Maria Graves and begat four sons—William B., Charles Lewis, Jeremiah, and James the younger.

The only one of these four children for whom we have a baptism record is Charlie Russell's uncle Charles Lewis (known as Lewis) Russell—December 18, 1792, in St. Mary's County. The fact that there are no dates or places for the other three sort of implies that they were born in neighboring Charles County. Of Catholic churches operating at that time in Charles County there were four: St. Ignatius (in Chapel Point), the mother church; St. Mary's (in Newport); St. Peter's (in Waldorf); and St. Joseph's (in Pomfret). The three last named were satellites of St. Ignatius and faithfully fed their sacramentals (baptisms, marriages and burials) to that church—no copies. Then St. Ignatius burned in 1866. Some say all that was left of the church after the conflagration was the priest's vest, but, in fact, several sacramentals were saved. Unfortunately, not all.

Although Charlie Russell's 1920 obituary (written by one of his daughters—either Annie or Alice) claims that his father was William H. Russell, that name is incorrect. The census record for 1820 is very clear, as is the 1837 Washington, D.C. license for his second marriage. It's William B. Russell in both cases. "B" may stand for Benedict or, more unlikely, for Benjamin or Baptist.

William B. Russell fought in the War of 1812, enrolling as a private in the Maryland Militia on July 17, 1813, in the 5th Brigade of the 43rd Regiment, Captain Samuel John Maddox's Detachment of Artillery, for an indefinite period (i.e. for the duration). His brother Lewis joined up on the same day, same outfit. They were the only two Russells to serve with Maddox.

Both William B. and Lewis served as matrosses. The word "matross" is also seen as "mattross." This now-archaic term (actually, it was archaic even then) was a German word, from the French "matelot," meaning "sailor"; originally the matross's work was deemed to be that of a sailor. The matross, as a rank, was abolished in the British army in 1783, but revived by the Americans for the War of 1812. The matross was an artilleryman one rank below gunner, really a gunner's mate, and he would help the gunner move the guns, load them, fire and sponge them, and man the drag ropes. Provided with musket and bayonet, he would march with the store wagons, acting as a guard to the wagons and artillery, and assisting when breakdowns occurred. The brothers Russell, with their fellow matrosses, were also there to prevent drivers' running away when the action hotted up.

From July 17 to July 27, 1814, Maddox's men were stationed at Bedlam Neck, St. Mary's County, Md., and the men (but not Maddox himself) were furloughed from the 25th until the 27th. William and Lewis Russell, matrosses, are on the list of furloughed men.

They wound up serving for a total of 50 days, being honorably discharged at Charles County, Maryland, on August 10, 1814. Although they were discharged in Charles County, most men fighting with Maddox were from the Chaptico area of St. Mary's County.

Records show that on February 24, 1816, in St. Mary's County, Maryland, William B. Russell married Sarah Cahay, daughter of Thomas and Mary. This surname is seen in the records variously as Kahoe, Cohoe, Kohoe, Cahooe, Cahill and Cahall. Although Charlie Russell's 1919 death certificate says his mother was Mary Cohill, this information was supplied by one of his children, and is wrong. The name is Cahoe, with the stress on the last syllable. An Irish name. And it was Sarah, not Mary. Mary was the grandmother.

Thomas Cahoe Jr., as he rightly was, enlisted as a Revolutionary War drummer boy on December 22, 1779, which likely puts his birth year at about 1765. He graduated from drummer to fifer, and was discharged on November 1, 1780.

A Thomas Cahall (sic), possibly the son of the drummer boy and brother of Sarah, married an Elizabeth Russell in Prince George's County on May 21, 1822. Looks like it just stayed in the family.

The drummer boy's father, Thomas Cahoe Sr., if the family legend is to be believed (which it shouldn't be), had originally come over from England as part of the British forces and had switched sides, settling after the war in Maryland. This seems an unlikely story, partly because there were Cahoes in Charles County back in the early 1700s. In addition, Tom Sr. was enlisted as a private by Lieutenant William Bond on July 3, 1776 for Captain Uriah Forrest's company, which itself formed part of Colonel Thomas Ewing's battalion for the Flying Camp. However, in his 1819 pension application Thomas Cahoe claims he enlisted on July 4, 1776, in the Flying Camp under Captain Alexander Magruder in the 6th Maryland Regiment. The officer mentioned may be different, but the date is the same. The very method of enlistment is therefore rendered true by the two separate accounts, and doesn't sound like the work of a man who came over from Britain and switched sides.

Anyway, on July 12, 1776, Tom Sr. and his fellow enlistees were reviewed and passed by John H. Briscoe, and on July 26 mustered, passed and examined by Ignatius Fenwick Jr.

Tom Cahoe Sr. reenlisted on July 29, 1777, under Captain Alexander Truman of the 6th Maryland Regiment, 2nd Brigade, for three years, then again under Truman until the end of the war. He was at the Battle of Monmouth, and at Gates's defeat at Camden he sustained a flesh wound. He was wounded again during the action at Guilford Court House in North Carolina. He took a furlough from December 29, 1781, and was soon back again, being present on November 1, 1780, and finally discharged at Annapolis at the end of the war, when Smallwood's Maryland Brigade was discharged.

In 1819, when he made his application for a pension, he was living in clearly distressed circumstances with his wife, Rebecca, who was the same age, at Piney Chapel, near Waldorf, Charles County, Maryland, which is where, on February 15, 1823, he fulfilled the ultimate requirement of his life pension.

William B. Russell and Sarah Cahoe moved a couple of miles from St. Mary's into neighboring Charles County, back to the home county of the original Russells, and had several children.

James Russell the elder, William B.'s father, drew up his will on March 20, 1817, and died in 1820, the will being proved in St. Mary's County on April 4 of that year. William is named as one of his sons and executors, and John H., his grandson, then aged one, comes in for a ewe, a lamb and a custom coat.

1820 Census
Charles County
Maryland

William B. Russell, head of household, aged 26–45
a female aged 16–26 [Sarah, his wife]
a female aged over 45 [we do not know who she is, perhaps William's mother, perhaps Sarah's mother, perhaps none of the above]
a boy under the age of 10 [John H. Russell]
a girl under the age of 10 [Mary Eliza]

There is no birth record anywhere of Charlie or any of his siblings, owing to the 1866 fire at St. Ignatius's Church.

William B. and Sarah's eldest child was John H. Russell, born at the end of 1816 (and not in February 1816, as the 1900 census says; February was the month his parents got married). He is the male under 10 seen in the above census. His 1905 Washington, D.C. obituary confirms that he was born in Charles County, and so does his death certificate.

Then came Mary Eliza, about 1817. She would marry Philip Hezekiah Burroughs. Her own daughter's death certificate says that Mary Eliza was born in St. Mary's County, but this may be an error.

The next child we know for sure was William Ignatius Russell, born around 1824, but there must have been several other children born between Mary Eliza and William Ignatius. They probably all died as infants, as so often happened then.

Because his mother was named Sarah Cahoe, we might have expected Charlie Russell to have a sister named Sarah, and he did. Sarah A. (Sally) Russell was born in October 1828, in Charles County. She would marry Charles W. Brooks.

Charlie Russell was the next, on February 22, 1833, and finally Philip, in or around 1836.

William B. Russell is not in Charles County in the 1830 census. In fact, there is no William Russell at all in Charles County that year, regardless of middle initial. Given the fact that he's in Charles County in the 1820 census, and that all his children seem to have been born there, William B. Russell should be there in the 1830 census, but he's not. However, a Philip Russell is, and he was William B. Russell's uncle. And he is living in Allens Fresh, with exactly the same neighbors as William B. Russell had had in the 1820 census. It must therefore be the same house, or very close to it. So where were William B. Russell and family in the 1830 census? Almost certainly in St. Mary's County, because the 1830 census for SMC (like that of PG) does not exist.

We know from his 1920 obituary that Charles Henry "Charlie" Russell was born on February 22, 1833, at Blenheim (today pronounced locally as "Blen-hime," not as "Blen-um," as it was then). Blenheim was the plantation of the Lee family (Robert E. Lee's cousins), occupying thousands of acres in that neck of land that stretches south from the southern shore by the entrance to Port Tobacco River, in Charles County. The brick mansion itself, by the Potomac, was on land later known as the Laidler Ferry Farm, near to where the Pepco plant at Morgantown stands today. The mansion in Charlie's day was the second one on that site—not as magnificent as the original Lee mansion, which had burned down, but impressive nonetheless.

Although Blenheim would remain in the Lee family for another several decades, the last member of the family actually to live there was Alice Clerklee (there had been a name change to take advantage of a legacy), who left there in 1806, marrying Philip A.L. Contee, who served as the hereditary overseer for her family. The adjoining tenant houses were still rented out, to avoid dilapidation, and William B. Russell became one of the tenants after his marriage to Sarah Cahoe in February 1816. It was in one of these tenant houses that their children, including Charlie, were born. The Lee mansion itself was destroyed during the Civil War.

Although William B. Russell is not in the 1830 census for Charles County, a widow named Jane Harbin was.

1830 Census
Allens Fresh District
Charles County
Maryland

Jane Harbin
two males 5—10 [James and Philip]
one male 15—20 [we do not know who this is]
one female aged 0—5 [Mary Jane]
one female aged 20—30 [Janette]

A Jane E. someone was born in Charles County in 1805. Her tombstone says that she was born on February 8, 1805. However, that same tombstone gives her death date as February 8, 1876. Now, she definitely died on February 8, 1876. It may be that she coincidentally died on her birthday, or it may be that the birth date is wrong. Because she was born in Charles County, the black hole of Maryland genealogy, we'll never know.

Janette had a sister, Catharine A., born about 1810, who later married Charles Oakley (buried October 15, 1842, at St. Paul's Episcopal Church, Prince George's County, Maryland). But despite knowing that, and having run as far as we could with that knowledge, we still don't know the maiden name of the two girls.

In 1820 or 1821 Jane married a Harbin, probably James, son of Naylor Harbin, of Piscataway, in PG County. This Naylor Harbin was originally from Charles County, as all the Harbins were, and was a second cousin to Tom Harbin's father, Walter. Naylor had several sons aside from James— George William and John being two others, and a daughter, Eliza. Young John would be apprenticed in Washington, D.C., in 1811. George William and James would stay on, farming in Piscataway on neighboring spreads, just down the road from old Naylor. Eliza would appear in Washington later, as protector of Charlie Russell's sister Sally.

The 1820 census has only three Harbins in PG County, all in Piscataway: Naylor, George and James, all three heads of separate households, all living very close together. James was then 17, and for a 17-year-old boy to have his own house was very rare, unless he was about to be married. The same was true of the slightly older George, who would marry Elizabeth Frazier, Rezin Frazier's daughter, in 1821.

There is no marriage record for James Harbin and Janette. As for marriage records of that time, in Southern Maryland, St. Mary's County records are intact as from 1797, and this particular marriage is not on the list. Prince George's County is intact from 1770, and it's not on there either. That leaves Charles County, which is the key county because that's where Janette—and the Harbins—came from. However, people moved with great frequency between the three counties, so it's always worth checking the other two.

Charles County did not require its marriages to be registered on a county level until 1867. Before that, records were kept by the individual churches.

Even though, today, the Archdiocese of Washington controls Charles County, and has an archive, it does not hold the sacramentals (baptisms, marriages and burials) for that period—the individual churches do. However, most of the pre-1866 records were destroyed in the above mentioned St. Ignatius fire. So a good run of Catholic sacramentals for Charles County prior to that date doesn't exist as such.

We have to assume, then, because of the lacunae in the records, that Janette married Mr. Harbin in or around 1821, in Charles County.

James Harbin was two years older than Jane. They had two sons and a daughter: James H. Harbin, born in either 1821 or 1822, then Philip W. Harbin, born in 1824 (give or take a year); and finally Mary Jane Harbin, born about 1827. Then Mr. Harbin died, probably about 1829.

Jane always signed herself Jane, although she was known as Janette. She was about 24 when her husband died. She's the widow in the 1830 census above, living with her three Harbin children, in Allens Fresh District, the same district that included the Lee Plantation of Blenheim, where Charlie Russell was born. The male, aged 15—20, living with her and the children could be a male servant, a friend staying over, or another relative, or none of the above.

Anyway, Janette lived on as a widow, in Allens Fresh District, and presumably as a neighbor of William B. Russell and his family. She didn't own this property in Allens Fresh; her name isn't on the land records at all. Her late husband had probably been a tenant on the Lee estate, and Janette may well have continued in that cottage until forced to leave, which she did in 1832, when she made the move to Washington, D.C.

Sarah Cahoe Russell, Charlie's mother, died in or around 1836, as the result of complications giving birth to her last child, Philip. William B. Russell now had to get married again, quickly, for if he didn't, there would be no one to look after the children except Mary Eliza, his eldest daughter.

Soon after Sarah died, William B. Russell gathered some, if not all, of the children and moved to Washington, D.C. We know the eldest, John H., then aged 21, went; he had just finished his seven-year carpentering apprenticeship in Charles County. We know the youngest two went too, Charlie and Philip. We know young Sally made the move. And we assume William Ignatius did. But we're not sure about Mary Eliza, who was about twenty at that time.

On March 28, 1837, at St. Peter's Catholic Church in the Capitol Hill area of Washington, D.C., William B. Russell married Janette Harbin. The ceremony was performed by the Reverend Joseph Van Horsigh. An interesting point is that, although the Washington marriage records say 1837,

Janette always stuck to 1836. Another point of ever so slight coincidence is that Joseph Van Horsigh is the priest who baptized Mary Surratt's children, and Mary Surratt was the woman hanged in 1865 for her part in the plot to kill Lincoln.

We know from later documentation that Janette's three Harbin children and some, perhaps all, of the Russell children were witnesses to the 1837 wedding. We know, from the bounty land claims that Janette made in the 1850s, that a Julia Stansbury was also a witness to the wedding. Julia was not a Stansbury back in 1837. She would have been only 16, but we can't tie her in with any of our players.

Julia Ann something was born in 1819 in Maryland or Washington, D.C. The censuses vary on her birthplace, but her age is consistent. Janette's bounty land claim tells us Julia's age, and that matches the censuses. Around 1841 she married James E. Sansbury, place unknown, but almost certainly Charles County.

A peculiarity about Julia is that in all the censuses she is listed as Sansbury, not Stansbury. Her death notice (she died in 1893 in Piscataway, in PG County, Maryland) lists her as Sansbury. Her husband, James E. Sansbury, spells his name that way on his tombstone. Yet, Julia spelled her name Stansbury in Janette's bounty land claim. One might put this down to error, yet Julia's children, later in life, all referred to themselves as Stansbury in the censuses. It's a strange case. Regardless, it's tempting to think that Julia might be a Russell, especially as she named her eldest son William, yet there's no room for her on the 1820 census.

There is a marriage in Washington, in 1842, between a James Sansbury and a Juliet Tillion, but research into this leads nowhere. This marriage would post-date the birth of Julia's eldest child William, anyway, so it's unlikely that Julia is Juliet Tillion. Besides, Tillion does not really exist as a surname, not really. And Juliet is not Julia.

In addition, the 1850 Washington census shows James Sansbury, his wife Julia, the children, and a seventy-two year old lady named E. Keeling, born in Maryland. Research into this E. Keeling also led nowhere.

More likely is that Julia was a relative of Janette's or of her first husband. She might be Janette's sister, or sister-in-law. Julia's origins remain a mystery.

Van Horsigh, an obscure but remarkable priest, was born in September 1795 in Antwerp, studied theology in his native country and came to the U.S.A. in 1823. He concluded his priestly studies with the Sulpician Fathers at St. Mary's Seminary in Baltimore, where he was ordained. His first station was in St. Patrick's, Baltimore, then down for several years at Portsmouth, Virginia; then in July 1834 he took up his post as pastor of St. Peter's, Washington, where he began fund raising for a new pastoral residence. He proved very popular among his parishioners and died, probably of overwork, in September 1849, at St. Peter's (he had a regular assistant only in the last year of his life). They buried him first under the altar, but he was later removed to the south side of the sanctuary. Coincidentally and strangely, the St. Peter's sacramentals that took place during Van Horsigh's regime have disappeared.

Janette brought into the new marriage household her two youngest children by her (previous) Harbin husband. At that point, her eldest, James H. Harbin, was about 15, and was at the onset of a shoemaking apprenticeship in Washington, D.C., and living with his master. Phil was two years younger, and would soon embark upon a similar apprenticeship. Mary Jane was about 10. With the two Harbin children at home, and the four younger Russells—William Ignatius, aged 12, Sally, aged 8, Charlie, 4, and Philip, aged 2—that made a total of eight people, too many to support. Consequently young Sally was placed in the care of Miss Eliza Harbin, Janette's sister-in-law from her previous marriage. The two ladies, Miss Harbin and Miss Russell, would spend the next fifteen years living in boarding houses in Washington.

However happy his new marriage might have been, it was all too much for William B. Russell, for he didn't long survive his nuptials, flying upwards on August 29, 1839, during a trip back to Charles County.

After William B. died Janette continued to live in D.C., and William Ignatius Russell, now 14 or 15, left home.

1840 Census
Washington, D.C.

Jane Russell
2 white males aged 5—10 [Charlie and Philip]
1 white female 10—15 [Mary Jane]
1 white female 30—40 [Janette herself]

Although no address is given, it's probably the same 11th Street address we find for Miss Jane Russell in the 1843 Washington city directory, just north of the Navy Yard, on the west side of the street between Eye and K streets—or, to put it another way, as the 1846 city directory does, on the north side of K Street, between 10th and 11th streets east. She is not to be confused with the Mrs. Russell who had a boarding house right by the Capitol, on the west side of First Street, between B and C Streets south.

Neither the 1840 census nor the 1843 Directory lists John H. Russell or any of the other Russell children by name, which means they were all lodging somewhere.

James H. Harbin, Charlie's stepbrother, took out a marriage license in Washington, D.C. on December 24, 1842, and married the following day in

Baltimore, to Jane Eliza Bradley. This was reported in the *Baltimore Sun* of December 29, 1842. It's hard to know why they chose Baltimore as a place of marriage, as Jane Eliza was from Virginia. However, the young couple then returned to D.C., where James set up a shoemaker's shop a few minutes walk north of the Navy Yard, on the north side of Virginia Avenue, between Seventh and Eighth streets east, which is where we find him, as a shoemaker, in the 1843 Washington, D.C. city directory. Within a few years he would give up cobbling and realize his true potential as a brass finisher.

James and Jane Eliza had Joanna W. (Annie), born in 1846; Martha V., born in 1848, who died in the 1850s; Eliza Janette (known as Lula), born in June 1850; Katherine M. (Kate), born on October 17, 1852; James Samuel, born on February 8, 1854; John Henry, born on December 27, 1859; and Daniel W., born on July 14, 1863.

On December 17, 1845, John H. Russell took out a license to marry his stepsister, Janette's daughter, Mary Jane Harbin. The happy event took place probably the next day. This is the first time we pick John H. up in the Washington, D.C., records. He leased a new house, a big one, at 523 Eighth Street east, on the west side of the street, between G and Eye streets, in the Sixth Ward, and he and Mary Jane and Janette and Charlie Russell and presumably Philip Russell all moved in, and they took in lodgers or rather a lodger—Marcelano Pariz, a Spanish musician who lived with them there for years.

A thousand leagues away, as the Wild Geese fly, dwelled one Michael R. Joyce, whom the London *Times* of August 29, 1840, referred to as "a respectable builder." Times were not peaceful in Ireland back then—when were they ever? Michael Joyce was a patriot, a young man of thirty, dedicated to the cause of kicking the British overlords out of his country. By 1846, when his wife Lucy produced their fourth child, he was halfway through creating a family many members of which would leave their mark on the other side of the world. Michael spoke Gaelic and, by way of preserving the old ways, made sure his children did too. He was that kind of romantic.

He named his new son—the second son—after Robert Emmet, the great Irish orator and freedom fighter. The first son, John O'Connell Joyce, born in 1840, had also been named after a legendary Irishman, but this one a relative—Daniel O'Connell, the first son of Erin to sit in the House of Commons in modern times and the man who got the vote for Catholics.

Charles Emmet Joyce was born in the summer of 1846, when the Irish potato famine was about to reach its height, and just as Robert Peel was being replaced as British prime minister by Lord John Russell.

The spud was the poor Irishman's staple diet; he ate it for breakfast, lunch, dinner, supper and snacks. That's all there was. The potato was king. However, to his eternal credit, the Irishman could do things with a potato—culinarily—that would make even Escoffier blush from his own lack of versatility. The great famine that began in 1845 was not the first potato blight in Ireland, and it wouldn't be the last, but it was the big one. The population in Ireland in 1841 was 8.2 million. By 1851, a mere decade later, it was down to 6.5 million. They say a million died and that the rest went to the United States. But we know that many more than 700,000 Irishmen left their native shores during this time period, perhaps twice the official number, because the official number is based on U.S. immigration records, and those records never took into account the thousands of little vessels that daily left Kerry and Clare and Galway, headed west on their perilous three thousand mile voyage, to land secretly in coves and inlets on the East Coast of America—that is, if they made it.

It was a bad time for Ireland, or more specifically, for the Irish. The British landlords had it good. The Irishman didn't. But even that was largely a matter of degree. The more educated and better-fixed did comparatively well, people like the Joyces.

The pretty town of Fermoy lies on the Blackwater River in County Cork, 134 miles southwest of Dublin, 38 southeast of Limerick and a mere 23 northeast of the town of Cork itself. Only 50 years before Charles Emmet was born Fermoy had consisted of a few mud cabins and the ruins of the old abbey. Now, half a century later, the town was pretty spiffy. It was owned by Sir Robert Abercrombie, a British absentee landlord, and managed by his agent Matthew Hendley. Fortunately for Fermoy the Abercrombie regime was a benevolent one. The same cannot not be said for so many Irish towns of the time.

In 1841 the population of the town of Fermoy was 6,379. Everyone knew each other. James Joyce's family had once lived in Fermoy but had all moved on by 1830. Joyce the writer, that is—*Ulysses*, *Finnegans Wake*, *Portrait of the Artist as a Young Man*, *Dubliners*—third cousin to young Charles Emmet, who, himself, would become, in time, not a writer but a soldier. Fermoy had a few churches of different types—Methodist, Presbyterian, no synagogues, no mosques, but there was a Catholic chapel, of course, built in 1811 at Laurel Hill. Father Timothy Murphy was the parish priest, ably assisted by his two curates, Mike O'Donovan and Dan Dilworth, amateur pugilists of note. That was Michael Joyce's church.

Of Michael's relatives in Fermoy his cousin and namesake Michael Joyce, the stone mason, same age, would go over early to Washington, D.C.; there was also John Joyce, stone mason on Barrack Hill; there was Fanny Joyce, who ran a provisions store on New Market Place; James Joyce was a feather and skin dealer on King Street; there was Mary Joyce, on William Street; and then there was Michael, the builder and, as he called himself later, engineer, on Sraid Padraig (Patrick Street), which is where young Charles Emmet was born.

They'd had Kate after John O'Connell, then Isabel. After Charles Emmet came young Michael in 1848, then Lucy, then Mary, then Edmond W., and finally Maggie in 1858. It was a normal size Irish family.

One Irishman, neither from Fermoy nor so luckily set up, was Charles W. Brooks, who decided to go east instead, to London, where he gained employment as a coachman. But life was tough for an Irishman in England back then and it wasn't long before the eighteen-year-old had had enough of flogging a dead horse. So, on a hot summer's day on the Thames he walked up the gangplank of the good ship *Westminster*, and on July 10, 1846, arrived in New York. He went straight into the U.S. Army, serving in the Mexican War. Afterwards he remained committed to his new government's pleasure, being based first in Kentucky and then in San Antonio, with the First U.S. Infantry.

In Washington, on June 5, 1847, young Philip Russell, aged 11, died and was buried in the Congressional Cemetery, a graveyard owned by Christ Church Episcopalian Church on G Street southeast. Philip was the first of many Russells to be interred at the Congressional Cemetery. The grave was paid for by John H. Russell, and so was the interment. In that very same grave, 31 years later, in 1878, John H. Russell's other brother William Ignatius Russell would be buried with Philip. Again, John H. Russell would pay for the interment.

John H. and Mary Jane presented to a small but eager world their first daughter, Margaret Alice, in 1846, and their second, Mary Alice (Alice), in July 1848. Margaret Alice died on October 21, 1850, inspiring John H. Russell to buy, that very month, a cluster of several more grave sites in the Congressional Cemetery. In this cluster would be buried over the years John H. himself, his wife and children, his stepmother Janette, one of his grandchildren, two of his nieces, and Catharine Oakley, Janette's sister. John H. paid for all the interments. John H. Russell and Mary Jane would have a third and last child, Janette Alice ("Jennie"), born in September 1851.

In 1847 young Charlie Russell was apprenticed out to Washington blacksmith and wheelwright Nicholas Snyder, a German who had been in the country for years, and who had a house and shop on the north side of B Street north, between 10th and 11th streets west, in the Second Ward. Nick had been married to Martha, by whom he'd had some children, including, notably, William H. Snyder, born in July 1839. On July 17, 1845, Martha had died. On June 18, 1846, Nick had taken out a license in Washington to marry again, to Sarah A. Plant, with whom he started a new family. That was the situation when Charlie moved in to live and study for seven years under Snyder.

In the Snyder household also lodged Willie Speiden (which he pronounced Speeden), now a journeyman (one who has qualified, but does not have his own business), trained by Nick Snyder. Willie Speiden and Charlie Russell became best friends.

On July 13, 1849, in St. Mary's County, Maryland, Charlie Russell's eldest sister married Phil Burroughs, and they set up house at Medley Neck.

Philip Hezekiah Burroughs was the son of Elisha Burroughs and Margaret P. Swann of Charles County, and like Mary Eliza, had been born in Charles County (although his daughter Molly's death certificate says Phil was born in St. Mary's County—an error). He had been married before, on February 23, 1843, in St. Mary's, to Elizabeth A. Sothoron. By this first marriage he had produced one child, Sarah Frances "Sally" Burroughs, born in 1846 in SMC, and he brought young Sally into his marriage with Mary Eliza. On February 9, 1861, Sally would marry Samuel Alexander Owens, son of Alexander Owens by his second of four wives, and she would die in 1906.

Philip Burroughs and Mary Eliza had, between them, a grand total of three children, the first two being William, born in September 1850, and who died young, and was buried at Christ Episcopal Church in Chaptico, St. Mary's County; and Philip Francis, born December 18, 1850 (that's what the record says, but it must be 1851), and who was buried on July 8, 1854, at St. Andrew's Episcopal Church in St. Mary's County. The third would be born later, amid tragic circumstances.

William Ignatius Russell didn't have a trade like his older brother John H., or, indeed, like Charlie himself. Although we can't find his marriage date, William Ignatius must have married Margaret Rebecca someone about 1849, probably in Charles County, Maryland. If the wedding had taken place in Washington, D.C., we would have found it. All we know, biographically, of the early life of Margaret Rebecca is from her death certificate as filled out by one of her daughters—probably Julia—and that is that she was born in Maryland on June 10, 1823, and that her parents were born in Nova Scotia.

On July 6, 1850, the census-taker working the Fifth Ward of Washington, D.C. got around to William Ignatius Russell's house and listed the family like this:

1850 Census
Fifth Ward
Washington, D.C.

W.I. Russell, 24, laborer, born in Maryland
M. Russell, 24, born in Maryland
S.E. Russell, 7 months, born in D.C.

A full 17 days later another census taker, this one working the Sixth Ward, knocked on the door of John H. Russell, William Ignatius's brother, and recorded that household like this:

1850 Census
Sixth Ward
Washington, D.C.

John H. Russell, 35, carpenter, born in Maryland, no real estate, no personal estate
Mary J. Russell, 32, born in Maryland
Mary A. Russell, 3, born in D.C.
Julia Russell, 7 months, born in D.C.
Jane Russell, 45, born in Maryland
Philip Harbin, 26, born in Maryland
Martaland Pearese, 40, musician, born in Spain

Phil Harbin had finished his apprenticeship, thus qualifying as a shoemaker, and had moved in with his mother Janette and stepbrother John H. Russell and family on Eighth Street, and would remain there until he got married later that year.

As for the seven-month-old baby, a researcher really has to be on guard. Each of these two households—William Ignatius's and John H.'s—has an infant Russell, aged seven months and born in D.C., but they have different names. One would assume S.E. was William Ignatius's daughter and that Julia was John H.'s. But that's not the case. S.E. and Julia are one and the same infant, despite everything.

The U.S. Census Bureau, from 1820 to 1870, issued instructions to its enumerators (actually to its assistant marshals) to the effect that the census taker would interrogate the household and record all persons who would normally be living at that address on a specific date (June 1, Aug. 1, whatever date the Census Bureau decided, and the date would vary from one census to the next). So, if a person was absent physically from the house on the night the census taker came around, it didn't really matter. He or she would be recorded as belonging to that household if he or she would normally be living there on the date specified. That way, the Bureau figured, no one would be missed, and no one would be listed twice. That was the theory. It was all done for taxes anyway. Genealogy was not a consideration with these early censuses. The more accurate accounting of how many people were in a particular town or ward would lead to a more accurate amount of funds coming into the local government coffers, one way or another. Naturally, this system led to abuses and errors.

William Ignatius and Margaret Rebecca's daughter Julia E. Russell (which was, in fact, her correct name), aged 7 months, was living at home in the Fifth Ward, with her parents, on the night of July 6, and got listed incorrectly as S.E. Russell.

Perhaps over the course of the next 17 days William Ignatius's stepmother Janette, living over in the Sixth Ward, was on at him, saying, "Bill, you must bring baby Julia over, let her stay the night. Give you two a night off by yourselves. Besides, young Alice would just love to play with the baby"—young Alice being Mary Alice, the three-year-old daughter of John H. Russell.

And perhaps the night they chose for such an r & r was July 23, the very night the Sixth Ward census-taker happened at their door. This taker listed the infant correctly as Julia Russell. But she shouldn't have been listed at all, because it was not her normal place of residence. Nevertheless, listed she was, and therefore twice recorded in the 1850 D.C. census.

We might call this the "Julia phenomenon"—a phenomenon because it's not just Julia we're talking about here. A lot happened in those 17 days in gregarious D.C., where people often went visiting, spending the night with relatives and friends, moving away to another state, winding up in prison or an asylum, traveling one way or another. All contingencies mentioned in the instructions to the marshals, but...

This all brings home a lesson—more than one—to genealogists, if they don't already know it.

One. Don't trust the census-taker. Use him as a guide. Don't set him in stone.

Two. Don't trust the Internet. Ancestry.com, for example, indexes W.I. Russell as W.J. Prussell in the 1850 census, so he's difficult to find. And that's just a symptom. Many, many people are hard to find due to (sometimes really stupid) misindexing on these Internet facilities. One of the many classic cases is HeritageQuest's indexing of the president of the U.S.A. in 1870 as U.G. Grant. That part of the page is very difficult to read, granted, and it does look like U.G., but it is really U.S., of course.* And, it does say—for occupation—president of the U.S.A. The indexers evidently were not alert to the fact that they could look up the name in a reference book.

Three. Beware this: Between 1820 and 1870 the American system of census-taking was not like the British one, say, where census takers blitzed the entire country on one night and one night only, so that every human being was captured, and captured once only, regardless of his or her normal place of residence. With the U.S. system many, many persons escaped the census net because they missed the taker, for one reason or another, despite instructions to the census enumerator that only those persons ordinarily living in that household were to be included. This instruction, in reality, led to far, far too many errors. Many people figure on a census twice, often in the same city. Hence the Julia phenomenon. So, if one is looking for some-

---

*Which, for that matter, is not even his "real" name. He was born Hiram Ulysses Grant, changed his name later to Ulysses Hiram Grant, and enrolled as West Point as Ulysses Simpson Grant, the name by which he was evermore known.

one in a census, they may be in it twice, or even three times, and possibly in very different localities. Or, they may not be in at all.

It is worth remembering that those early censuses were about households and statistics, not about individuals. However, the U.S. system for that period, 1820—1870, is uniquely useful in that a researcher might be able to get two bites of the same cherry, as it were. In 1880 the U.S. changed over to a system more similar to the British system.

Charlie Russell's stepbrother, Phil Harbin, married Sarah Nesmith on November 14, 1850, in Washington, D.C., and they moved to 393 G Street south. Philip opened up a shoemaker's shop at 543 Eighth Street east, near to his mother's house. They had Mary Isabelle in 1851; Sarah A. "Nannie" in 1852; and Samuel Philip in 1856. Philip and Sarah would have another son, Mitchell, but Mitchell didn't survive; he died on August 19, 1865, and was laid to rest in the Congressional Cemetery in Washington.

Phil moonlighted as watchman at the building occupied by the Fifth Auditor of the Treasury, but he left in June 1855; his replacement, Thomas J. Luxon, was announced in the *Evening Star* of June 14, 1855.

Charlie Russell's brother William Ignatius and his wife Margaret Rebecca would have other children, including one, name unknown, who died on April 17, 1856, in D.C., and who is buried in the Congressional Cemetery.

About the time Charles Emmet Joyce was an infant Thomas Francis Meagher was one of the leaders of the Young Irish movement. Tom Meagher was captured and tried by the British for his seditious activities against the queen, and sentenced to dangle; his last and famous words were "Within the shores of Ireland the English never shall have rest." But his last words turned out not to be his last words at all, for his sentence was commuted and he was transported in 1849 to Van Diemen's Land. But they couldn't hold Thomas Francis Meagher for long. In 1852 he escaped and made his way to Pernambuco, and thence to New York, his getaway being covered every inch of the way by an avid press. By the time he struck America's shores the "escaped convict," as he was always referred to, was already quite a celebrity in his new land. He then proceeded to go quite far, did Thomas Francis Meagher.

In 1852 Janette Russell began her "widow's claim for bounty land." For years now the Federal government had been awarding western land in the public domain to men who had served in the War of 1812. An 1850 act of Congress offered the same deal to their widows. Janette was such a widow— "Jane Russell, widow of William Russell, War of 1812, with certificate of Service."

She had her lawyer, John Johnson of Washington, D.C., look into the matter, so he sent away to the Treasury Department for an official statement about William B. Russell. On December 15, 1852, the Third Auditor's Office at Treasury returned to him their findings: "William Russell, a private in Capt. Samuel Maddox's Company, Maryland Militia. Entered the service 17 July 1813 (indef) and served to 27 July, 1813, from 16 June 1814 to 29 June 1814, from 17 July 1814 to 10 August 1814. Examined Dec. 15, 1852, W. Gallaher, for 3rd Aud."

Armed with this, on December 20, 1852, Janette and Johnson took the short stroll through the raspberries to the office of the Magistrate of the Sixth Ward, James Crandell, on the east side of Seventh Street east, between G and I streets, the back yard of Crandell's office abutting the back garden of Janette's house. This application is given in full in the sources at the end of this book.

Janette was awarded 40 acres on March 25, 1853, and duly sold it.

A vehement Democrat, John H. Russell, Charlie's eldest brother, went into local ward politics (Abraham Lincoln was a Republican) and soon became a well-known figure in the Sixth Ward. In 1853 D.E. Kealey, assessor for the Sixth Ward and a letter carrier by occupation, decided not to run again, and John H. Russell's friends pushed him into it, on the Workingmen's ticket. His advertisement, which ran in the *Evening Star* on May 28, 30, and 31, and again on June 1, was subdued but effective: "The friends of Mr. John Russell (understanding that Mr. Kealey declines a re-election) present his name to the voters of the Sixth Ward as a suitable person for assessor at the approaching June election. Many Voters."

It was effective, because he won, on June 5, 1853, with 166 votes, as against 139 for Mr. Beers, 87 for George R. Ruff, 43 for carpenter Israel Wayson, 40 for Mr. Mohun, and 3 for Mr. Little. John H. Russell duly took his seat on the D.C. Board of Assessors for a two-year term.

In 1854 Charlie turned 21, ended his apprenticeship to Nick Snyder, and became a fully qualified blacksmith and wheeler. He went to work as a smith at the Navy Yard, at a key period in that institution's history, when it was exponentially expanding its ordnance section. Indeed, that very year, 1854, was when the iron foundry was established and the production of ordnance became the principal function of the Yard.

The importance of the Navy Yard as a guidepost to cultural change during this period of Washington's history cannot be overstated. By August 1855, for example, the Yard employed over 1,300 workmen supporting five or six hundred families, and a "faux bourg"—a village—was created nearby to accommodate them. In short, the Navy Yard, more than any other single factor, including the Capitol itself, "made" the area known as Capitol Hill.

In a few years' time the Washington Navy Yard would be a major point of interest for the Confederate spy ring, for various reasons. It was an extremely important part of the defense of the capital, and, later, during the war, Lincoln would often visit it. Indeed, in the early stages of the John Wilkes Booth plot, when that conspiracy merely involved kidnapping the president, it was from the Navy Yard that Booth planned to snatch the great man.

With the coming of the Civil War the commandant of the Yard, Franklin Buchanan, would resign his commission to join the Confederacy, and the new commandant, John Dahlgren, the engineer, would assume command on April 22, 1861.

Also working at the Washington Navy Yard, as long-time chief clerk at the Navy Storehouse there, was Adam G. (George) Herold, who lived at 636 Eighth Street east, just down the road from Janette Russell's boarding house. One of George Herold's sons, living with him then, was the teenage Dave Herold. It would be extraordinary if Dave hadn't known Charlie Russell.

Charlie moved in with his brother William Ignatius and family at the latter's rented house at N Street South, near ½ East. William I. was still a watchman at the Navy Yard.

Their sister-in-law and stepsister Mary Jane died on December 13, 1854. Her tombstone says "In memory of Mary Jane, wife of John H. Russell, who departed this life December 1854, aged 27 years. Also her mother, Mrs. Janet Russell, born Feb. 8, 1805. died Feb. 8...."

John H. never remarried. He just lived with Janette, who helped raise his two daughters. After all, Janette was only ten years older than her stepson/son-in-law.

A new congressional act gave 1812 widows like Janette Russell a further chance to cash in on bounty land claims. Congress now said that such widows could get as much as 160 acres, grand total—no more. If they hadn't received that much already, they could make another claim, and get the balance.

Janette moved fast. She was soon back at lawyer Johnson's office. Then, armed with her claim for an additional 120 acres—"Jane, widow of William Russell, Pvt., Capt. Saml Maddox, Md Mil. War 1812. Claim No. 44431"— Attorney Johnson duly took her through the raspberries again to Magistrate Crandell's office on the very day the new act became law—March 3, 1855.

In front of Crandell she filled out a form entitled "Declaration for Widow, who has heretofore received bounty land less than 160 acres." This form contains some new information.

She is described as "Jane Russell, formerly Mrs. J. Harbin, aged 55 years [which is odd, and wrong], a resident of the county and district aforesaid [Washington, D.C.]." She states that William Russell, her late husband, served in the company commanded by Captain Saml Maddox (which is true) in the regiment of the Maryland Militia commanded by Colonel Ashtone

Fotherg (should read Colonel Henry Ashton). It goes on to say that William Russell was in actual service for at least 14 days, and was honorably discharged at Ch. Co., Md [Charles County, Maryland] on the [blank] day of [blank] A.D. 1814. Janette sticks with her marriage year of 1836, and William B. Russell's death date of August 29, 1839, is confirmed. She is still a widow. She further declares that she has heretofore made application for bounty land under the act approved September 28, 1850 (to which she now refers for the particulars of her said husband's service, and for proof of her marriage) upon which she obtained a warrant for 40 acres, No. 85.533, which she has legally disposed of and cannot now return. She makes this declaration for the purpose of obtaining the Bounty Land to which she may be entitled, under the act passed the 3rd day of March 1855. She also declares that she has never received nor applied for Bounty Land under this or any other act of Congress, except as above stated. "John Johnson [lawyer], of Washington, D.C., is duly authorized to prosecute this my claim, and to receive any warrant which may be issued hereon. [signed] Jane Russell."

Then there is an affidavit of two witnesses. "Personally came Wm B. Robertson and Wm S. Venable, residents of the County of Washington in the Dist. aforesaid, who, upon oath, declare that they are personally well acquainted with Mrs. Jane Russell and saw her sign (or make her mark) to the foregoing declaration, that they know her to be the identical person therein represented, and that she is now a widow, and that we have no interest in this claim. [signed] Wm B. Robertson and W.S. Venable."

Then comes the Magistrate's Certificate: "The foregoing declaration and affidavit were sworn to and subscribed before me, this third day of April, 1855; and I hereby certify that I believe the claimant to be the identical person she represents herself to be, that I know the witnesses are credible persons, and that I have no interest in this claim. [signed] Jas Crandell, J.P."

On April 6, 1855, she got it: Land Warrant No. 16785, for 120 acres of Iowa countryside for which she had absolutely no use—the west half of northeast half and northeast quarter of Northwest of Section 28, in township 93 North of Range No. 19 West. This warrant entitled her to apply for the land patent, and it was the land patent that gave her actual ownership. Again, she turned around and sold it to land speculator Horatio J. Olcott, of the National Central Bank in Cherry Valley, Otsego County, N.Y., who in turn, factored it out through the Land Office at Ford Dodge, Iowa, on December 15, 1855. This boosted Janette's income.

In 1855, with his term as assessor up, John H. Russell chose not to run again, and returned to civilian life. His daughters, Alice and Jennie, went to Primary School Number 4, in the Third School District, as did their stepcousins the Harbin girls, Joanna and Martha. On July 28, 1856, Alice was awarded her diploma (*Evening Star*, July 29, 1856). Then she moved up to the

Third District High School, in the Navy Yard portion of the city, in Capitol Hill. The *Evening Star* of July 16, 1858, tells us that the female department of this school was examined on July 15, and in attendance were several local politicians and other dignitaries, including Dr. Samuel McKim, former secretary of the board of the school. The teacher, Miss Mary A. Myrick, had been sick for a couple of weeks, and wasn't expected to attend, Miss Moore having stood in for her. Yet Miss Myrick was there, much to everyone's surprise, to see her girls pass the tests—which they did, including Joanna Harbin and Alice Russell. The young ladies wore black crape as a tribute to a former assistant teacher who had died only a month before, and, after singing "One Sweet Flower," they conducted a series of tests in reading, geography, grammar, history and arithmetic. "Sweet Music is Falling" followed, then more examinations, then "Thoughts of Home," followed by yet more exams. Finally "Sister, Thou Hast Gone" (in honor of the deceased teacher) and then the conclusion, more tests. It was a successful day.

Charlie Russell was not called to the bench as a character witness in the celebrated case of the May 15, 1856, murder of fireman John Rufus Nally, and that's surprising, given that he and the murderer worked side by side in the Navy Yard, and that the killer had introduced Charlie to his cousin, who, before not very long, would become Mrs. Charles H. Russell.

The blacksmith shop in the Yard consisted of rows of "fires," as they called them—individual smith stations—where Charlie and his colleagues would pound away on the anvil all day, supervised by Samuel Champion, who, in turn, came under the overall direction of James Tucker, the head of the department, who reported to Capt. Montgomery C. Meigs. Working side by side with Charlie were his fellow smiths, James Thomas Boisseau (pronounced Bossoo), James Keeley, Daniel W. Jarboe, Bill Tait, James Coleman, Bill Gaddes, Stanislaus "Stan" Edelin, and Nicholas G. "Nick" Sanderson, to name but a few.

There were, in those hot and troubled days immediately prior to the Civil War, many and varied goings-on in the blacksmith shop, especially in the field of politics. Smiths and watchmen were appointed by Captain Meigs, with a keen view to their politics, Meigs being obliged to balance the Democrats with the Know Nothings in order to give the outward appearance, at least, of seeming unprejudiced. Mr. Champion had been Meigs' smithy foreman ever since both of them came on board a few years before. Champion was a good man, honest, reliable, but had recently been infected with Know Nothingism—the American Party, kick out the foreigners, the Catholics, anyone not one hundred percent Hail Columbia. As a consequence Champion's work suffered as he insistently toured the Yard, electioneering, pamphleteering, spreading the Know Nothing word. Largely as a result of this tireless labor, tensions began building within the blacksmith shop.

Several lads working at fires in the shop back then would one day leave a mark on the world. One such was J.T. Boisseau. An Alexandrian by birth (December 20, 1818), he had been in the nation's capital from the age of six weeks, and was the first person ever to be baptized at St. Peter's Catholic Church on Capitol Hill, a church he would remain strongly identified with until his death on April 7, 1906.

J.T., a virulent Anti–Know Nothing, felt that Sam Champion should be replaced as ramrod of the blacksmith shop—by none other than himself. He lobbied, he curried favor, he parried and riposted in his duel with Champion, but to no avail. Captain Meigs, the power, liked Champion personally, despite his aberrant headlong rush into Know Nothingism, and disliked his opponent. However, it was the small beginning of a political career for J.T. Boisseau.

Meanwhile, blue-eyed Mr. Jarboe would soon become the center of legal attention. Dan Jarboe, aged 22 when it all happened—when he became a star—was the son of Navy Yard blacksmith turned Navy Yard guard Benedict Jarboe, a Marylander who had been a resident of the capital for years, and who now patrolled the inner and outer grounds of the Yard's smithy with Charlie Russell's brother William Ignatius Russell.

Dan addressed himself one day to his workmate Charlie Russell.

"Charlie, I have just the girl for you."

"You do?" replied Charlie, his ears pricking up.

"Mary Ann, my cousin."

And so, Charlie met Mary Ann Jarboe.

Seems Fireman Nally, who toiled to extinguish conflagrations—either naturally occurring or manmade—on behalf of his employer, the Anacostia Fire Company, had done anything and everything in his power to win the heart— and more—of Danny Jarboe's sister Mary Jane, including hinting to everyone, especially the young lady, that he had honorable plans—eventually. These plans, however, did not precede the "criminal intimacy," and soon the young smith Jarboe found himself to be a prospective uncle, a disturbing prospect. On his way to work at the Yard that fateful May morning in 1856, young Dan demanded an accounting from the loose and insincere Nally who was perambulating to his own place of employment, his cock o' the walk swagger not only evident but altogether too much for the defender of maidenly virtue.

Mr. Jarboe demanded satisfaction, as it were, but John Rufus Nally was not as forthcoming and honest as young Dan desired, whereupon voices, most notably that of Dan Jarboe, were raised in a loud and heated fashion, all this in front of several entranced—"horrified" was the term they would two days later use in court—witnesses.

Not necessarily in this order, but close, the epithet "You d—-d son of a bitch" was applied by Mr. Jarboe, and the subsequent hand movement, although so fast it was somewhat blurred, would remain in the minds of those present etched indelibly, at least until the trial a few days later. The ball from the five-barreled revolver passed through Mr. Nally's breast and, befitting a fireman of Nally's caliber, he was not only put out, he was extinguished.

Anyway, the good Jarboe did not swing for his crime. Not even close. Amid general rejoicing, the avenger of his sister's honor was acquitted by a jury that had taken precisely fifteen minutes to adjudge him a hero. Dan became a cop, produced a family, left the police force and went back to smithying, and finally wound up in Topeka, Kansas, where he died on March 14, 1913.

The power tussle between J.T. Boisseau and Sam Champion in the Navy Yard's blacksmith shop reached a deadly climax on the morning of May 25, 1857, when the champion of Know Nothingism keeled over, with us no more. Despite pressure from on high, Captain Meigs refused to consider Boisseau and instead plucked Bill Tait from his fire.

It has been rumored in the Russell family that Charlie was working on the Washington Monument in the period immediately prior to the Civil War. This rumor must be dispelled, as there is no basis for it in fact. The monument employed no blacksmiths at that time, and besides, construction was halted long before the outbreak of hostilities.

In 1857, John H. Russell was back in politics, running for assessor again on the Anti-Know Nothing ticket, but he didn't get it. The Anti–Know Nothings were just that: they were against the Know Nothing party. The Know Nothings wanted America for the Americans, and were not above taking extreme measures to assure their victories. On June 1, 1857, the day of the municipal elections in the nation's capital, forty or fifty Plug Uglies from Baltimore were hired by the party fathers to come into Washington to assist the citizens in their election decisions.

Herbert Asbury, in his classic book *The Gangs of New York*, gives the reader a wonderful picture of the Plug Uglies, one of many gangs running riot at that time in New York City and, as cadet satellites, in other towns of note. They wore plug hats (top hats), tails, and stuffed shirts and carried all sorts of astonishing weapons into uninhibited street battles—revolvers, clubs, lead pipes, even blunderbusses, and the ever-present brickbats and slungshot, these last two now thankfully extinct not only as words but as delivery systems of pain and mayhem, pieces of brick and stone wrapped up in socks, underwear, or some other such garment, or indeed, even uncovered pieces of stone, and wielded or thrown mercilessly into a crowd.

The Baltimore gang who descended on Washington on the first day of June was the Maryland branch of this illustrious New York organization. Although they lacked the charisma of late New York leader Bill "the Butcher"

Poole (only recently departed on a one-way ticket for the real Hell's Kitchen) they had acquired enough of the late Mr. Poole's skills to wreak havoc that morning.

After floating around for some time without effecting anything of note, the Plugs pitched upon the Fourth Ward's first precinct as being the most eligible scene for their operations. There they espied a long line of voters, mostly Anti–Know Nothings, waiting at the polling station. Although their first attempts to disrupt the line failed, they were soon back with the able assistance of large numbers of Chunkers and Rip Raps from Washington's own gangland. It wasn't long before jostling and bullying were replaced by stark physical violence and shootings. People were trampled, killed, and maimed, and the polling booth was turned over and wrecked. An outraged citizenry demanded that the mayor (Magruder) call out the Marines, which he did, and the Plug Uglies then went off in search of fresher wards and precincts. Finally the Fighting Leathernecks caught up with them and a pitched battled ensued. Violent days.

The 1858 Washington, D.C., city directory lists William Russell's home (as opposed to business) at N Street south near ½ Street east, a mere sixty seconds' vigorous walk from the western edge of the Navy Yard, where he was a watchman. Also living at that address was Charles Russell, blacksmith. This 1858 directory reflects summer–fall 1857 information, and shows that Charlie was living with his brother at that point.

Mary Ann Jarboe had been born Jane Jarboe on April 22, 1838, in Virginia, but like so many young Catholic girls of the time (including Mary Surratt, incidentally) she adopted her confirmation name. Her father, George, was a tailor in Alexandria, but it looks as if he left his family and went to Baltimore. Anyway, he was dead by October 1857. Mary Ann's mother, Ann, died, aged 42, in Alexandria, on April 27, 1851, and was buried at 3 o'clock on the 29th, the funeral starting out from the home of Ariel D. Collinsworth of Duke Street.

This Ariel was a scion of Shakespearian-minded Alexandrians and was a well-to-do cordwainer. In Washington, on April 20, 1840, he married Rebecca Dixon and produced a string of issue—Charles, Frank, Julia, Laura, James, Mary, Emma—and then, immediately before the Civil War broke out, he moved to Washington, D.C., where he opened a shoe store in the Fifth Ward. From there he expanded into real estate. He lived next door but one to Navy Yard blacksmith James Coleman, one of Charlie Russell's colleagues and best friends. It was here, in the Fifth Ward, that A.D. Collinsworth would produce his last child, Horace, in 1861.

On the death of her mother, Mary Ann Jarboe (then only just 13), her sister Elizabeth and her brother Horace, were all put up with relatives in Washington, notably Benedict Jarboe. Mary Ann's first Catholic communion in D.C. was at St. Peter's on April 19, 1857. The Reverend E.A. Knight was pastor (1853—61). By that time she had met Charlie Russell.

Charlie took out a marriage license on October 27, 1857. The actual certificate of marriage from St. Peter's Church says: "This is to certify that Charles H. Russell and Mary Ann Jarboe were lawfully married on the 29th day of October in the year of our Lord 1857, according to the rite of the Roman Catholic Church and in conformity with the laws of the District of Columbia. Reverend Edward A. Knight officiated in the presence of William P. McNeir and Sarah Ann Hefferman [sic]."

After the ceremony Charlie and his new bride moved to 527 E Street south, in the Sixth Ward, next door to his old blacksmith friend Willie Speiden. Mary Ann's sister, Elizabeth Jarboe, then 14, came to live with them. William Ignatius, Margaret Rebecca and the children also moved—to 525 Eye Street south, in the Fifth Ward.

In early June 1858 John H., still with the Anti–Know Nothing party, ran for the position of city councilman for the first time. Each of the seven wards that comprised Washington had municipal elections every year, sending one alderman to what was called the Higher Board and three city councilmen to the Lower Board of the District of Columbia government. Georgetown had similar elections. The three Anti–Know Nothing candidates for city councilman were the three winners—George Bohrer with 444 votes, John H. Russell with 441, and Franklin H. Ober with 439. The losers were "the opposition"—John Sessford Jr. with 403, William Hutchinson with 401, and James A. Gordon with 399.

In the 1850s the James H. Harbin family moved in to the house next to Janette and John H. Russell and their family, and the eldest daughters went to the Third District Primary School, with the Russell girls. Joanna later attended the Third District High School with young Alice Russell.

The 1860 census gives us one of those lucky breaks, when an actual address appears on a pre–1880 census. By the side of James Harbin's family it says, quite distinctly, "525 8th Street east." As we know from city directories that Janette lived at 523 Eighth Street east, we have the picture: two separate houses, next to each other. The widow Krafft was living at 521, on the other side of Janette's house.

This address of 523 Eighth Street east is also confirmed by the 1860 D.C. city directory, which, incidentally, refers to James Harbin as a machinist. The 1870 city directory tells us that the Harbins were still at 521 (this should say 525—Catharine Krafft was still living at 521) Eighth Street east, and still lists James Harbin as a machinist.

Tragedy was just around the corner for Philip Burroughs and his family. Philip's boss was one B.L. Hayden. Bernard Lafayette Hayden had a checkered past, and an even more checkered future lay ahead. His first wife had died within a year of their marriage, and his second wife would divorce him in 1862, which was a rare achievement back then. In between divorces he managed to shoot Philip Burroughs in the knee in May 1858 [the *St. Mary's Beacon*, May 27, 1858], just at the time Mary Eliza was five months pregnant with her third child, Molly. Surprising everyone, Phil died on June 22, at his home at Medley Neck. He was 41 [*St. Mary's Beacon*, June 24, 1858]. The following day he was buried in St. Andrew's Episcopal Church.

Mary Eliza moved to Washington, D.C., immediately, and set up as a seamstress at First Street east near M Street south, and had her new child in the nation's capital on August 11, 1858—Mary E. Burroughs, Charlie Russell's niece. In a way things turned out well. Mary Eliza's younger sister, Sally, and her step-aunt Eliza Harbin, had been lodging for over a decade in the Second Ward with New Yorker O.J. Preston and his New Jersey wife Rebecca. However, with the Civil War looming and ravage on the horizon, O.J. sold up, headed out to San Francisco, and became a merchant. Sally Russell moved in with Mary Eliza and joined her in the seamstressing business. Miss Eliza Harbin moved into Mrs. Downer's boarding house on North D Street, between 13th and 13 ½ Street, and would die there on March 30, 1862, aged 70, being buried the next day at Mount Olivet Catholic Cemetery, Washington.

Never in the Armed Forces during the Civil War, B.L. Hayden died in 1862. His divorced wife, now a widow, took the children to Omaha, Nebraska.

Charlie and Mary Ann had their first child, William Horace Russell, on January 29, 1859. This birth date is not noted in the St. Peter's registry, but it is in the family documents. We assume the Horace part of his name came from Mary Ann's brother, Horace Jarboe, a cooper living in D.C. It might also have come from Horace Harbin, who may have been a relative of Janette's first husband. William Horace Russell, son of Charles Henry Russell and Mary Ann Jarboe, was baptized on April 3, 1859, at St. Peter's, by the Reverend E.A. Knight. Young William's godmother was Sarah Russell (later Brooks), his aunt Sally.

On August 8, 1860, Charlie and Mary Ann's second child was born— Annie Alice. She was also baptized by the Reverend Knight at St. Peter's, on September 10, 1860. Her parents were listed as Charles Henry Russell and Mary Ann Jarboe. Her godmother, who signed her name as Ann Virginia Smoot, was actually Mrs. Ann Virginia Coleman; earlier that year (June 12), at St. Peter's Church, she had married blacksmith and future prison warder, and Charlie's very good friend, James Coleman.

Although consisting of a mere five letters, Smoot is a big name in Southern Maryland. The Smoots and the Russells had been neighbors in Charles County long ago. Ann Virginia Smoot was born on March 17, 1837, in Washington, D.C., daughter of George Arthur Smoot and his second wife Ann

Mitchell, formerly Ann Jenkins (the same last name as Mary Surratt before she married, coincidentally), whom he married on July 23, 1833. George Arthur Smoot had fought in the War of 1812, under Colonel George Magruder, First Regiment, D.C. Militia.

John H. Russell's carpentering skills led naturally to the profitable business of coffin-building, and it was as an undertaker that he ran again for the city council in June 1859, again as an Anti–Know Nothing candidate from the Sixth Ward. His party cleaned up in their ward, he and Frank Ober and James T. Boisseau (Charlie Russell's boss at the Navy Yard) each garnering 371 votes, and the opposition a grand total of 50.

The Philip W. Harbins left the capital in 1860 and headed out to Beltsville, in Prince George's County, Maryland, to stay with Sarah's aging English mother, Mrs. Sarah Nesmith. They wouldn't be there long. They moved back to Washington's Sixth Ward just before the Civil War, to 529 E Street south, the house right next door to the one at that moment being vacated by Charlie Russell. Phil become an officer with the Metropolitan Police, a job he would hold until his death in 1890.

Missing the 1860 U.S. census because they were not in the country yet were Michael Joyce and his family over in Fermoy. But they would arrive soon enough. In dock at Liverpool were two ships bound for America: the *Europa* and the *Edinburgh*. For whatever reason, Michael sailed on the *Europa* and Lucy—claiming to be a widow—and the nine children on the *Edinburgh*. The *Europa* made land first, at Boston, on September 21, 1860, and the *Edinburgh* hove into New York Harbor on the 29th of September, by which time Michael was waiting for them at the dock.

Unfortunately, poor old Michael was asthmatic and rheumatoid at the same time, a dangerous combination, and as a result he couldn't get work in the New World. So it was up to John O'Connell, the eldest son, to be the breadwinner—and he did win the bread, getting whatever jobs a sub-human Irishman could get in New York City at that time. But then the Civil War happened and John O'Connell—and Charles Emmet—proved to the world that an Irishman is as good as any other human being, maybe better.

At that point Michael and Lucy took the daughters and the younger sons to Washington, D.C., where Michael's cousin Michael had already set himself up at 467 N Street south, between 11th and 12th streets west, right at the eastern perimeter of the Navy Yard. The new arrivals established a home near the Chain Bridge.

In June 1860 John H. Russell ran on the Democratic ticket with Frank Ober and J.W. Robinson. The three lads won, Ober with 421 votes, Russell with 125, and Robinson with 116. The losers were Charles W. Davis, John H. Peake, and William Talbert, all with about 112 each.

This situation was reversed in the June 3, 1861, elections, when Peake

(374), Thomas McGrath (371) and Bill Talbert (372) wiped the floor with John H. Russell (112), Frank Ober (111) and J.H. Roberts (110).

On July 1, 1861, President Lincoln appointed the defeated John H. Russell one of the five inspectors and measurers of lumber, a post for which he was qualified by his carpentering skills, and he didn't run for political office again until three years after the Civil War ended.

William Ignatius continued to patrol the Navy Yard's perimeter on a nightly basis until, midway through the war, he became a boilermaker.

In 1861 former Irish Potato Famine refugee Charles W. Brooks was posted with his regiment to his new nation's capital, fought in the opening rounds of the Civil War, and then met Sally Brooks, making a married woman out of her on November 6, 1862. He and Sally would have their first child, John Russell Brooks, in 1863, and their second of two, Charles W. Brooks Jr., in 1866.

In the couple of years just prior to the Civil War, it was plain to everyone that events were about to change dramatically the lives of Charlie Russell and many others in the nation's capital. The closer it got to the lighting of the tinder box the more this presentiment became evident, so much so that it rapidly mutated from a vision of the future into an established fact. The momentous day for Charlie was April 10, 1861.

The District of Columbia—which comprised the cities of Washington and Georgetown and a few other small communities—was not very well prepared to defend itself if an invasion of Secessionists should ever take place, and as the nation drew closer to the outbreak of war, the threat of such an invasion became greater and greater. The winter of 1860–61 was especially tense in the District.

When Brigadier General Charles P. Stone took over as inspector general of the District of Columbia on Jan. 1, 1861, he assessed the local militia situation minutely, if not totally accurately, and found that the District's preparation for a possible invasion was quite woeful. His book, *Washington on the Eve of the Civil War*, tells us not only about his research at the time, but of his thoughts too. Although his book, detailed reports in the newspapers, and other documents vary in their details, these sources can be combined for a reasonable summary of the situation.

In a nutshell the District of Columbia did not have many men to defend it if there were to be a Southern raid. The regular United States Army had a presence of 984 men in the capital, and in addition to that force were the local militia units, or companies as they were generally termed, formed from volunteers living in the various parts of the District, each unit with its own local armory, each with its particular uniform and drill and parade specialties. All were armed and, to some extent, trained for warfare, their purpose being to defend the capital in time of need.

One of the principal units was the Washington Light Infantry Battalion, comprising lads from the Capitol Hill area, with their new arsenal on Pennsylvania Avenue, between Ninth and Tenth streets south side—an arsenal including, among much else, about 161 rifled muskets. The battalion had been formed on August 21, 1836 (or September 12, 1836, depending on which source one believes). Charles H. Russell was a member of this group.

The Washington Light Infantry, Colonel James Y. Davis commanding, at that time consisted of three companies—A, B, and C. Company A was the original, going back to 1836, and now commanded by Captain Levi Towers, with 70 men. Companies B and C had both been formed in June 1860, and both had about the same number of men as Company A. Captain Peter M. Dubant and Captain R.C. Stevens commanded B and C respectively. So the total number of men in the Washington Light Infantry, on the eve of the war, numbered about 210.

At least that was the figure quoted on Valentine's Day, 1861. Inspector Stone, in early January 1861, had numbered them at about 160, "all old volunteers, Washington people, loyal almost to a man," said Stone. He was wrong. By April 10 the strength of the Washington Light Infantry was down to 90.

The boys got to wear the fancy Washington Light Infantry uniform of black plush headdress of the then popular "shako" pattern, with plume and gilt ornaments; a skirted, silver-braided coat of dark blue, with three rows of buttons, in "plastron," or bellboy effects; "winter pantaloons" of sky blue with double stripes of "white cassimere"; and summer trousers of white. A fatigue uniform, described as "Kentucky jeans," consisted of a single-breasted pea-jacket and trousers of blue-gray, and a cap of French kepi type in dark blue. This uniform differed substantially from the one re-designed for the re-formed, post–Civil War Washington Light Infantry.

Another militia company was the National Guard Battalion, "a small organization," according to General Stone, but a very active corps, recently much improved in skill and discipline. It comprised three companies—A, B and C—commanded respectively by Lieutenant Lloyd, Captain P. King, and an unknown third commander. Total number of men: 140. The National Guard would subsequently grow.

There was also, and not to be overlooked, the President's Mounted Guard, about 75 cavalrymen, under the command of Captain S.W. Owen. These lads had been parading recently, and presented a very soldierly appearance.

There were the Metropolitan Rifles, commanded by Captain Nalley; the Tenallytown, D.C., Rifles, led by Captain H. Blount; the Anderson Guards, led by Captain Foxwell; and the Turner Rifles, Captain Gerhardt. Captain Balback led the Washington Rifles; Captain Thistleton the Putnam Rifles; and Captain Rutherford the Mechanics' Union Rifles.

In Georgetown, on the eve of the Civil War, also stood ready the Potomac Light Infantry, with one company. These boys were fairly well drilled and well armed, and most, but not all, could be depended on (from a Union point of view). Georgetown also sported their own Mounted Guard, presided over by Captain Stewart.

And then there were a few other, scattered and historically anonymous, volunteer units throughout the district. All in all, there to defend the District of Columbia in case of emergency were about 10 corps in Washington, averaging 60 men per corps, and eight corps in Georgetown, with a total of 400. So, including the 984 regular U.S. troops at the ready, 1,984 men prepared to defend the nation's capital.

And then there were the National Rifles, probably the most famous (or notorious) of all the D.C. Militia companies. The National Rifles were an ultra–Secessionist unit, formed on November 22, 1859, by Captain Frank B. Schaeffer, a Marylander of unequivocal political persuasion. The one company they had comprised mostly Marylanders, with three lieutenants commanding under Schaeffer: L.D. Watkins, A.D. Davis, and Henry Noe.

Schaeffer was a former Regular Army lieutenant from the Second United States Artillery, who had fought in the Baltimore Company during the Mexican War of 1846–48. An excellent drill master, Schaeffer enjoyed nothing more than getting his Rifles out on the streets of Washington, duded up in their fancy uniforms, weapons and artillery gleaming in the sun, performing the most spectacular drills, some of them never before seen by humankind. The boys loved it, and the crowds went wild. A National Rifles parade was always a grand occasion in Washington, D.C. The other militia units, including Charlie Russell's Washington Light Infantry, all enjoyed the same sort of day out, only their own individual uniforms and flourishes differentiating one group from another.

By January 1861 Schaeffer had about 100 men in his National Rifles, and he was enlisting new men every day. By February 14, 1861, the number was computed at 117. When he took over as Inspector General, Charles Stone was astonished to find that the Rifles had not only an overabundance of weapons (Minié rifles, revolvers, saber bayonets), equipment and ammunition (200 rounds of ball cartridges per man), and even two mountain howitzers, but also unlimited access to the Arsenal, a written, signed and official privilege accorded Schaeffer by the late secretary of war John B. Floyd. Although times had, perhaps, changed since Floyd had issued that privilege, they had not changed that much. Floyd must have been a very, very good friend of Schaeffer's, and was later to come under much censure for these and similar favors—but that would be while he was commanding Confederate armies in the west.

Stone was aghast when he talked to Schaeffer, who bragged openly about his Southern leanings and about the invincibility of the Rifles, and about how he could take Washington any time he chose to. It is easy to imagine the confrontation, with a horrified Stone declaring, "I can't allow you to have all that stuff," and a proud Frank Schaeffer responding, "Too bad. I've got it, I've got it legally, and that's that."

And Stone: "No, it's not. You've got to be mad if you think I'm going to let a unit with such Southern sympathies roam about the streets of Washington armed to the teeth, and with howitzers, for Pete's sake! Hand 'em back."

Frank refused and stormed out. He called all his men together and told them that from now on they were to take their arms and equipment home with them, instead of depositing them in the Arsenal, which was no longer safe for them. Code words were issued, so that, if need be, the men could muster quickly and be ready for action.

Inspector Stone knew he was in a bind, because he didn't have the men to take on the Rifles, and if he tried to exercise his authority it would lead to a blood bath in the streets of (still) peacetime Washington. Worse, March 4 was coming up, Lincoln's inauguration, and Stone had the gut feeling that something bad was going to happen unless he acted fast.

And act he did. On Monday, March 4, the very day of the inauguration, just hours before Companies A and B of the Washington Light Infantry held a gay inauguration soirée at their arsenal, Inspector Stone fired Schaeffer—or rather, Schaeffer offered his resignation, and on March 8 it was accepted. On March 20 his replacement, Union man John R. Smead, of the 2nd U.S. Artillery, finally took over active command.

There had been a bit of a scene before Schaeffer was dismissed. The George Washington's Birthday celebrations in the capital were, as usual, magnificent. The local militia groups all turned out to parade, forming at 11 o'clock that morning on Pennsylvania Avenue in the following order: the President's Mounted Guard, the Washington Light Infantry (including Charlie Russell—whose 28th birthday it was—and precisely 99 other muskets in line; they made a superb appearance, cried the *Evening Star*), the National Guard Battalion, the Washington Rifles, the Turner Rifles, the Metropolitan Rifles, Company A of the Union Regiment, the Georgetown Mounted Guard, the Potomac Light Infantry, the new company the Carrington Home Guards, of Georgetown (named for General E.C. Carrington), the newly formed Scott Rifles, Company A of the Anderson Rifles (Company B couldn't make it), the Zouaves and the Junior Potomac Rifles. Seventy National Rifles men under Schaeffer refused to march with everyone else, and had their own parade. This gesture of independence, bordering on insubordination, was noticed.

It has been said that when Schaeffer left the Rifles so did his men. That is simply not true. The men of the National Rifles were still a big worry for Stone, even after Schaeffer's dismissal. This situation had to be handled carefully.

By April the specter of a Rebel invasion had hardened into the shape of Ben McCullough, a Texas Ranger rumored to be amassing a large force in Virginia with the express intention of marching on, and seizing, the nation's capital. This invasion never materialized, but, for a short while, McCullough was a bogey man as real as Napoleon had ever been in Europe.

Considering this McCullough threat, compounded with the imminence of the war itself, and also with the Secessionist sentiments of a good portion of the District's population, and, most immediately, with the reality of Rebels within the militia companies, General Stone had no option but to take measures. He had been gathering his forces and formulating his plans, and, on the morning of April 10, 1861, he went into action.

For the past few days it had been more than a solid rumor that the government had selected the morning of April 10 to muster the local militia units into United States service. No one, however, knew exactly what was about to happen—how long the term of service would be, or where the companies were to serve. No one, that is, but Stone and his men.

Using the National Rifles as an example to illustrate what transpired with all the companies that day, including the Washington Light Infantry, we can form a clear picture of events on the morning of April 10th.

The N.R., 67 of them under Smead (or 54, or 150, depending on which report one believes), were, with one hour's notice, ordered to parade again through the streets of Washington. The well-attired lads turned out gleefully—another parade! The crowds thronged the streets, as always. With newly polished guns and ammo boxes, freshly scrubbed and sparkling howitzers, they all proceeded toward the War Department building, where they were formed in line in front of the building and given a choice—muster in and take the oath or get out of town.

Inspected by General Stone, the men, with right hand ungloved and raised, were required by his man, Major McDowell, to take the oath: "I, _____, do solemnly swear that I will bear true allegiance to the United States of America, that I will serve them honestly and faithfully against all enemies or opposers whatsoever, that I will obey the orders of the President of the United States and of the officers appointed over me, according to the rules of the armies of the United States. So help me God." In other words, just the usual army oath.

The north side of Pennsylvania Avenue was extemporaneously allocated to the use of the "willing spirits" and the south side to the "unwilling." The "unwilling" were marched double-time back to their armory, hissed by crowds along the way, and once at their destination, were dispossessed of their arms, stripped of their uniforms and accoutrements and drummed out. Allowing for slight variations of procedure, the same thing happened to all the units that morning.

Charlie Russell's 1920 obituary says that he was "stripped of his uniform and accoutrements" and drummed out of town at an hour's notice. Although he had considerably more than an hour, the story is essentially true.

A *New York Times* report, filed from Washington on April 11, says, of events the day before, that all public buildings were guarded, and that in one unit sixteen refused to take the oath of allegiance to the Union and twelve of those were employees of the Navy Yard and one a Post Office clerk. Although the *Times* does not name this unit, it was, in fact, the Washington Light Infantry, and one of the twelve Navy Yard lads was Charlie Russell. We know that Charlie was a Navy Yard man right up to the very end, until he was forced to leave Washington.

The *Evening Star* of April 11, 1861, also reported on events of the previous day: "On the administration of the oath to the Washington Light Infantry the following men refused to take it, and were ordered out of the ranks: Philip J. Ennis, Joseph Reynolds, J. Cahill, Charles Murray, Chas. H. Russell, John McNamee, Sergeant McDermott, Jack Yates, M. Wallach, John Hands, F.A. Siler, H.J. Ebbs. Subsequently they were placed under the command of Lieut. Lord and marched back to their armory and their arms taken from them."

The following day, April 11, the government was still weeding out Secessionists from the volunteer outfits. An example: Only fifty National Rifles men had stayed on (or was it twenty, as other reports say?) and taken the oath. Anyway, twenty men from the National Rifles had resigned on the day of April 10, and another two resigned in the evening. Or was it 32 in toto? On April 11 over forty new (Union persuasion) recruits were added to the N.R., and they formed the nucleus of the new Rifles, the first unit to be ordered into the Union Army. The rest, the Secessionists who had been booted out, left to disperse back to their homes, and to plan.

Also on April 11 Colonel Davis, the commander of the Washington Light Infantry, resigned, but on the 12th he reconsidered. On the night of the following day another 15 National Rifles boys seceded, but 21 new recruits were found to take their place. This was a trend that would spill over into the other companies as well—two steps back, three forward.

Everyone knew the war was upon them, and Charlie, knowing it was just a matter of time before he would have to leave the capital, made arrangements for his wife and two children to stay with Janette and John H. The latter, realizing that three more people in the Eighth Street house wouldn't work, made a tactical decision. They would have to split up. But it wasn't much of a split. They all moved out of the big house, and John H. and his daughters Alice and Jennie leased another house at 138 East Capitol Street, between Fifth and Sixth streets north, on the northwest corner of Sixth Street, while Janette and the newcomers leased the house around the corner, at 518 Sixth Street east. That's where Mary Ann Jarboe and her two children spent the duration of the war.

By April 12th all the companies who had taken the oath were guarding their respective arsenals, with the exception of the Metropolitan Rifles, who were on guard at the Patent Office, and the Mechanics' Union Rifles in the south wing of the Capitol. Meanwhile, in South Carolina, Confederate artillery opened fire on the Union-held Fort Sumter, and the Civil War began.

On the night of April 13, 1861, the dismissed members of the National Rifles, under Frank Schaeffer, met to celebrate the reduction of Fort Sumter and to reorganize their corps. Earlier that day the formation of the (new) District Militia, i.e. the new and loyal militia, was completed after two days. The new District Militia was composed of the Andrew Johnson Guards (the first volunteer militia group to be officially formed for the war anywhere in the country—on April 11), the newly re-formed National Rifles, the new Potomac Light Infantry, and the President's Mounted Guard. Then, on April 15, 1861, in the wake of Fort Sumter, Lincoln declared war, and Charlie Russell, suddenly but not unexpectedly, found himself an enemy in his own town.

For four days nothing happened. A typical phony war, in that while hostilities had been officially declared no one really believed it—they couldn't take it in—and so an inertia lingered. But all inertia breaks eventually, and with a suddenness that is in direct proportion to the external pressures applied.

There existed a Secessionist organization of Marylanders with the quaint name of the Democratic Jackson Association—lampooned by its Union detractors as "Dem Jack Ass," which after Lincoln's election in 1860 became virtually a secret military order. Dem Jack Ass raised an army and marched on Washington. Between April 10 and 25 Dem Jack Ass posed a real threat, as great but more geographically immediate than Ben McCullough. Fortunately the jack ass only reared its head; it didn't bite.

Dem Jack Ass didn't die with the Civil War, it just changed its name— to Jack Dem Ass. One of its members, certainly in 1880, would be Tom Harbin.

On the night of April 19 the first casualties of the war were sustained— in Baltimore. That day Southern sympathizers cut the telegraph wires and bridges to Washington. The Sixth Massachusetts Regiment happened to be passing through the city and were attacked by local Seceshes. The Boston boys fought back, shooting into a crowd, killing three soldiers and a civilian.

This so enraged the old—dismissed—National Rifles and Washington Light Infantry boys that the following day they got word to each other to rendezvous at Alexandria on the morning of the 22nd.

On the afternoon of April 21, 1861, the disenfranchised militia lads headed south for Alexandria—some by wagon, some by boat, some by horse, and some on foot. We know, from his obituary, that about this time Charlie Russell left the capital and walked to Alexandria. It was never explained in this obituary, and it never came down through the generations, why Charlie should have walked to Alexandria after leaving Washington, but here was the reason: so he could be present at the huge meeting of Seceshes planned for Alexandria on the morning of the 22nd. That meeting was duly held. They all felt, as departing soldiers do when embarking on most wars, that it would all be over in 90 days. However, in the back of their minds, they knew they might never return. They grouped around Schaeffer, who then and there formed the new Southern outfit called the Beauregard Rifles. Actually this was only one of three separate and distinct units with the name Beauregard Rifles, the other two being in Blacksburg, Virginia, and Mississippi.

Charlie Russell being a skilled blacksmith, was sent to Richmond to work in the Artillery Harness workshop, a section of the Confederate Ordnance Depot better known as the gun shops. So, in actual fact, he never donned a Confederate uniform in time of war—something worth bearing in mind.

Going forward several years, after the war, on May 10, 1871, the Washington Light Infantry would be re-formed, as many of those old regiments would be. These new groups had balls, countless dinners, big anniversary get-togethers, and similar festive reunions throughout the decades following the Civil War, and the newspapers usually reported them, at least the big ones, and sometimes with the names of those attending. We do not have any complete rosters of these parties for the Washington Light Infantry. But we do, on occasion, for the National Rifles, which was re-formed amid much celebration on June 9, 1880.

At the time war was declared Thomas Francis Meagher was an officer in the 69th New York Militia, a regiment that would later become the Fighting 69th, also known as the Fighting Irish. Among those who fought under him at the first major engagement of the war—Manassas (Bull Run to the Yankees)—was Sergeant John O'Connell Joyce, then 19 years old.

When Meagher conceived and put into action his plan to form an Irish Brigade, composed of the 69th, the 63rd and the 88th New York Volunteers, John O. Joyce joined Company C of the newly formed 88th New York Volunteers, as a sergeant, and his brother, Charles Emmet, joined the same company on November 5, 1861, as a private. Charles was only 15 but lied about his age, said he was 18. Younger brother Michael would later join the Artillery in 1864.

The 88th was organized at Throg's Neck, New York, and the men enlisted from early September until mid–November, 1861. The Irish Brigade became a reality on December 6, 1861, when the New York regiments marched down to Washington, D.C. The 88th would serve as the 5th Regiment of the Irish Brigade, Sumner's Division. The Irish Brigade, a celebrated crack outfit, highly decorated, saw action everywhere and sustained huge losses during the Civil War.

Charles Joyce and his regiment patrolled the area of D.C. until March 1862 when the brigade became part of the 1st Division, 2nd Corps of the Army of the Potomac. Joyce served under McClellan in all the Peninsular battles, including the Seven Days Battles. On Sept. 14 he took part in the battle of South Mountain, Maryland, and then on the 17th was at Antietam, where he was in the thick of it. It was here, at bloody Antietam, that the soul of his brother, John O. Joyce, left the battlefield.

The *Irish-American* of October 18, 1862 describes John O'Connell Joyce in rather flowery terms: "A young man who was just twenty-one, with a fair complexion, bright, beaming blue eyes, and hair the color called auburn. His height was medium, his figure burly, his step firm and determined." Then he got shot between the eyes.

On December 13, 1862, Charles Emmet was in the melée at Fredericksburg. Chancellorsville was next, on May 3, 1863, and then General Meagher, who had commanded the Irish Brigade from February 3, 1862, resigned on May 14, 1863. Lieutenant Colonel James Kelly assumed command.

Around Christmastime 1861 Charlie Russell's wife, Mary Ann, up in Washington, conceived. The infant, Henry Jackson Russell, was born on August 28, 1862, but didn't survive, dying in D.C. in February 1863. In order for the conception to have taken place Charlie must have been in the enemy capital nine months after the war broke out. And he would be there again in 1864 for similar reasons, i.e., the conception of his daughter Alice.

It is unthinkable that these two children of Mary Ann's, conceived during Charlie's four-year absence from Washington, were another man's. She was living in an almost cloistered environment, with Janette, her stepmother-in-law, John H. Russell, her politician brother-in-law, and the rest of the family—all in the same two neighboring houses. There was a war going on, and there were the social and moral restrictions of the day to think about. Besides, the most important point is that Charlie thought they were his children. He even named them—or someone did, and he didn't object. Which means he must have had something to do with the procreation process, and that process took place twice during the war, when he was in enemy territory. So, the two children were his. No question. Thus we have proof that Charlie Russell was in and out of D.C. during the War. If he was there twice during the conflict, then the chances are that he was there more often than that. That's the law of averages, especially when one is talking about conception.

We know there were hundreds, maybe more, of Confederate agents, spies, couriers, during the war—male and female. Although they were amateurs by today's standards, and although it was pretty easy to get in and out of Washington in those war years, it still required nerve, because capture might mean death by hanging. Charlie was strong enough, fit enough, bold enough, and clever enough to be a spy. It would make more sense that he was than he wasn't.

Even before the war the South had agents, or spies. For decades it had been obvious that the Civil War was both inevitable and imminent, and, perhaps as early as 1850, certain Secessionist intelligence gathering units were in place in the nation's capital, taking notes on anything and everything that might be useful to the South when the war broke out. Certainly by 1860 a spy ring was in full operation, headed by Captain Thomas Jordan.

This ring had been ordered into place by the governor of Virginia, Honest John Letcher, who realized the need for such an organization. He couldn't have picked a better man than Thomas Jordan to run it. Jordan's spies included government clerks, widows, businessmen, doctors, you name it. It wasn't hard to find willing men and women.

Jordan was born in Page County, Virginia, in the Luray Valley, on September 30, 1819, son of Gabriel Jordan and his wife Elizabeth Ann Sivert. He was admitted to West Point in 1836 and graduated four years later, 41st in a class that included his roommate William Tecumseh Sherman. He went into the 5th U.S. Infantry as a second lieutenant, then transferred to the 3rd, garrisoned at Fort Snelling, Minnesota.

He fought against the Seminoles in Florida, 1841—42, and was part of the unit that surprised and captured Chief Tiger Tail in November 1842, near Cedar Springs. Garrison duty in the South and West followed, and then came the Mexican War. On June 18, 1846, Jordan was promoted to first lieutenant, and from 1847 to 1848 was assistant quartermaster at Vera Cruz, where, on March 3, 1847, he achieved the staff rank of captain. He took part in the battles of Palo Alto and Resaca de la Palma.

He was up against the Seminoles again, 1848—50, then spent six years as assistant quartermaster at Fort Miller, in California, and at Fort Dalles, in Oregon. He was a golden boy, was Jordan, a man to watch. He introduced steam navigation on the Columbia River, above Fort Dalles, and provided a lot of help to the pioneers out west. Then he came to Washington, D.C.

This, then, was the man who organized the first recognized Confederate spy ring in Washington. A ring means people—spies—and it is reasonable to assume that Charlie Russell was one of them.

Jordan resigned his United States Army commission on May 21, 1861, and headed south, becoming a lieutenant colonel in the Confederate Army. General Lee himself made Jordan adjutant general to General Beauregard. However, before he left Washington, Jordan left behind an agent in place in Washington: Rose O'Neale Greenhow, a socialite who had access to high places. The "most persuasive woman that was ever known in Washington," remarked Colonel Erasmus D. Keyes, a Union soldier. And he knew, first hand. Allen Pinkerton, a Scotsman with awesome powers of self-restraint, would later grant that Rebel Rose had "almost irresistible seductive powers."

Born Maria Rosatta O'Neale, this formidable seductress was from Maryland, and came to Washington, D.C. at 17 with her sister. Their aunt ran a fashionable boarding house in the Old Capitol Building (that later became the prison). On May 23, 1835, in D.C., Rose married an older man, Dr. Robert Greenhow from Virginia, and they lived in D.C. for seven years, having four daughters. In 1850 they headed west, where Dr. Greenhow died in San Francisco. Rose returned to Washington.

Then the war started. The first real engagement was the First Battle of Manassas (Bull Run), which the South won, with thousands of civilian spectators watching the spectacle from the comfort of their picnic chairs. Without Wild Rose's intelligence supplied to Jordan in 1861, the outcome of First Manassas might have been very different.

The Pinkertons (Allen Pinkerton himself, no less) nabbed Rebel Rose in July 1861, after her triumph, and jailed her. In 1862 she would be deported to the South, and go overseas, dying in a blockade running attempt in 1864.

Jordan was present at Manassas, directing Rebel Rose's spying activities and also acting as adjutant general for Beauregard. Later he went to Tennessee as Beauregard's chief of staff; from that point on he drops out of the spying picture. He fought at Shiloh, was promoted to brigadier general on April 14, 1862, then was with General Braxton Bragg for a while. He was at the defense of Charleston, and, when the war ended, was paroled on May 1, 1865, at Greensboro, N.C.

Back to Charlie Russell. Early in 1862, with the Union threatening the Confederate capital of Richmond, it was decided to move the harness works down to Clarksville, in Mecklenburg County, Virginia, close to the North Carolina line. This made sense for another reason: most of the leather that supplied the harness works came from North Carolina. Charlie Russell went with them, and the works opened up for operation on June 14, 1862, under the superintendency of Captain Henry Pride. The call for a blacksmith at these new works was due to the fact that other things aside from harnesses were being made there—harness accoutrements such as bits, bridle pieces, anything metal, as well as cartridge boxes.

The land containing Clarksville was originally owned by one William

Royster. The Roysters were the bosses of Mecklenburg County. There was a town called Roysterville, but that's long gone, disappeared into history. William Royster had a son named Clarke, and when a new town was built in 1818 it was named Clarkesville. They subsequently dropped the "e." One of the Royster descendants, Captain Charles, fought in the Civil War, and his granddaughter, Elizabeth, married Brown Averett. Brown and Elizabeth had a son, George Washington Royster Averett, on September 20, 1822. In 1850 G.W.R., by inheritance a rich landowner, by profession an auctioneer, and by avocation a slave trader, also became a policeman. But, despite what would have been a full enough life for ten men, there was still a gaping lacuna in the life of Constable Averett. That missing something was two very young wives. In 1857 he married Mary Williamson, and then, after she died, he married her sister, Rosa, in 1862. He and Rosa had at least one son, Courtland P., who, much to the gratitude and pleasure of his father, would, as he conquered puberty, become the paragon of Clarksville handsomeness. However, this gratitude wouldn't last forever. In 1883, thanks to the dazzling Courtland, G.W.R.'s police career would come to a violent and sudden end, as would his life.

In the years immediately prior to the Civil War the area in and around Mecklenburg County had been the focus of a concerted industrial drive. It was ideally located for businesses, for many reasons, geography being one of them. The war put a stop to that, and then Reconstruction, so that by the 1880s time had passed Clarksville by, and big business had chosen other sites.

On June 12, 1863 Charles Joyce, now a sergeant, was transferred from Company C to Company A, of the 88th. Then came Gettysburg, where he couldn't fail to be inspired by General Winfield Scott Hancock. None of the boys could, and none of them did. The continual and awesomely withering fire coming from the Confederate enemy had such a demoralizing effect on the front line of Union soldiers that at any moment it appeared they all might turn and flee; but the general, alone on his horse, rode slowly and calmly up and down in front of his troops, completely exposed to the unworldly fusillade, never sustaining as much as a scratch (well, he finally got one in the thigh). Only George Washington had ever possessed such divine invincibility, and the men heartened and came out like banshees. It was a wonderful moment.

Charles Emmet fought like a demon and was promoted on the field to lieutenant—an officer now, and only just turned seventeen. He was hit that day, July 2, 1863, in the wheat fields, and had to be pulled out of the battle. He shared an ambulance with a wounded and thoroughly exhausted General Hancock. A bullet had passed through Charles's right lung, but they successfully extracted the offending projectile. However, pieces of young

Joyce's clothing, pushed into his lung at the insistence of the bullet, remained in his body, an inconvenience which would later in life cause phthisis and consumption problems.

Down in Mecklenburg County Charlie Russell set up residence in a two-story house on Virginia Avenue, next to what would later be the Chappell's Insurance building. Never in a regular Confederate army unit, he became one of the Home Guard, or Local Defense Troops, better known as the Clarksville Volunteers, composed mostly of men working at the Confederate harness works. Organized on Nov. 9, 1863, this unit was commanded by Captain Henry Pride. In January 1864 Captain Henry was forced to swallow what pride he had in his good name when he was replaced by Captain John Kane. By that stage, owing to the difficulties that the South was experiencing as they began to lose the war, output at the harness works was irregular, to say the least.

Laid up, Charles Emmet Joyce missed the experience of the New York City draft riots in July 1863. His next action was at Bristoe Station on October 14, 1863, and on February 1, 1864, he was transferred back to Company C. On May 5 of that year he was at the Wilderness, followed immediately by the Virginia engagements of Spotsylvania Courthouse, Po River, North Anna River, Landron House, Totopotomoy Creek—a back and forth series of battles that culminated in Cold Harbor (June 1 to June 11, 1864). On August 2, 1864, still in Virginia, he transferred back to Company A, in time for the various battles at Deep Bottom Run, Strawberry Plains, and Reams Station, and on September 1 was promoted to full sergeant.

This promotion might seem, on the surface, to be a demotion, given that Charles Emmet had been a sergeant before Gettysburg and was then promoted on the field to lieutenant, but that's the way the Army works. Given the speed these boys were moving, and the slowness of Army administration, his first promotion to sergeant had finally been made official. The paperwork making him an officer and a gentleman wouldn't catch up with him until after the war had finished.

On June 17, 1864, there was an explosion at the U.S. Arsenal in Washington, D.C.—not foul play, just an accident. Several women were killed and given a state funeral at which Abraham Lincoln appeared as chief mourner. Mary Burroughs was one of these ladies, but because she was one of those so completely charred, she was unidentified at the time of the funeral. Mary's death left her young daughter Molly an orphan, well and truly. Both parents killed.

Of the state funeral of these ladies on June 19, the *Evening Star* had this to say the following day:

> Yesterday afternoon, as the funeral of the unfortunate victims of the Arsenal explosion was in progress at the Congressional Cemetery, Officers Harbin and Shelton, who had just cleared a space around the graves in which the mourners

and pall-bearers could stand, found that a young man named Henry Greenfield had placed himself right in the road, and the first named [Harbin] requested him to leave. This Greenfield refused to do and replied with an oath, and the officer arrested him. Greenfield resisted him and Officer Shelton went to Harbin's assistance, when some of the prisoner's friends attempted to rescue him, and he also made an attempt to escape, when the officers drew their revolvers and intimidated the party and succeeded in carrying the prisoner to the station, where Justice Cull fined him $21.58 for being disorderly in the graveyard, and held him to security for appearance at Court to answer the charge of resisting the officer.

The Officer Harbin who tackled Greenfield was Charlie Russell's stepbrother, Philip W. Harbin, no longer a cobbler.

Young Molly Burroughs couldn't very well stay at the First Street house by herself, so her uncle William Ignatius Russell, now a boilermaker, and his family left their house on Eye Street and took over the First Street house. For some reason they had to place young Molly in St. Vincent's Orphan Asylum in Washington, D.C., which is where we pick her up in the 1870 census, listed as Molly Burrows, aged 11, born in D.C., under the care of Sister Blanche, first cousin of Father Francis E. Boyle, pastor of St. Peter's Church on Capitol Hill. In 1873, aged 14, she would leave the orphanage and move back in with William Ignatius and his family, at their new house, 1005 G Street southeast.

In June 1864 General Lee was desperately defending the city of Petersburg, in Virginia, relying, as he did, on supplies coming up on the railroad from the South. The Union Army had to cut those lines, and they did, pressing ever south and west, ripping up track, heading for the key bridge over the Staunton River, over which the Richmond—Danville Railroad ran. This was a long, covered bridge in Charlotte County, just north of where Charlie Russell lived, and its destruction by Union forces would be a devastating blow to the South.

A force of 5,000 Federal cavalrymen under the command of brigadier generals James H. Wilson and August V. Kautz descended inexorably upon their desired target, the only thing to repel them being a force of 296 Confederate reserves and six pieces of artillery under Captain Benjamin Farinholt. This was not enough of a bulwark, not by the longest shot imaginable.

On June 23, 1864 Farinholt sent out an urgent appeal for local home guard units, from surrounding counties, to rally to the bridge. Two mornings later 150 regulars formed from different units and 492 "old men and boys," as they were called, showed up at the Staunton River Bridge. The Mecklenburg lads were there, under the replaced but still irrepressible Captain Pride, and including Charlie Russell. These irregular units were placed under Colonel Henry Eaton Coleman on the west side of the bridge for the impending battle.

On that day, June 25, 1864, at the Battle of Staunton River Bridge—more popularly known as "the Battle of the Old Men and Boys"—although outnumbered five to one, the local lads won the day through a series of clever maneuvers and bluffs, prevented the enemy from destroying the bridge, and forced the Union forces to withdraw. Charlie Russell was shot in the head and was not expected to live. But he pulled through.

So much so that shortly thereafter his wife, Mary Ann, conceived again in Washington, this time with her daughter Alice, who would be born in late April 1865. Take nine months from April 1865 and you have July 1864. That means Charlie was up there again in July 1864, head buzzing, but otherwise obviously unimpaired.

On October 6, 1864, at Petersburg, Charles Emmet Joyce mustered out of Company A. His time was up, and aside from that, his father was dying in Washington, the old man's health having been somehow damaged during Jubal Early's raid on Washington in June. Michael Joyce died on October 12, 1864, at his home, the one near the Chain Bridge.

So Charles Emmet missed the October engagements at Petersburg, but he reenlisted on March 25, 1865, with Company D of the 88th, just in time for that day's battle at Petersburg. On April 1, 1865 he was promoted again, to full sergeant first class, and then to full lieutenant second class on May 31, 1865, an official confirmation of his Gettysburg field promotion. This was long after the war was over. Mustered out on June 30, 1865, with Company D, near Alexandria, Virginia, under Lieutenant Colonel Denis F. Burke, he went to Washington to stay with his family for a while.

Other, more sinister things may have been happening in Mecklenburg County, Virginia, during the war—at Buffalo Springs, four and a half miles west of Clarksville and eight from Charlie Russell's house. In the 1990s General Bill Tidwell, now deceased, one of the leading experts on the Lincoln assassination, formed a theory that the British were funding a Confederate spy training camp at Buffalo Springs during the Civil War. He was one of those scholars convinced that the British were more involved in the Civil War than has ever been let out, and from that perspective he was able to see certain events and documentation in a different light from those scholars who believe that the oh, so respectable and dignified United Kingdom could not possibly have had such an involvement.

Tidwell based his theory on a diary written by two young Confederate brothers from St. Mary's County, Maryland, named Milburn—Charles W. and James R., who went down to Buffalo Springs during the war, arriving there on July 31 and staying a month. Extracts from this diary were published by the chief of the Detective Force of the War Department, Federal sleuth Lafayette C. Baker, in his 1867 book *History of the United States Secret Service*. It was considered worthy of publication, this diary, mainly because the Milburn boys described in it certain activities of the ring headed by Confederate spymaster Captain John W. Hebb.

Buffalo Springs, with its beautiful, rustic hillside setting and its natural lithium springs, was used as a health getaway as early as the 1790s. Just after 1800 it became a resort, with rather strange-looking guest rooms built in step formation on the hillside. Other amenities such as a ballroom, soon grew up alongside. But Buffalo Springs was used only during the warm weather; this we know because many of the guest rooms did not have fireplaces. By the 1840s Buffalo Springs was famous, and not long before the Civil War two important guests stayed there, although not at the same time. On July 19, 1851, the resort was graced by the presence of General Winfield Scott, former military hero of the Mexican War, later presidential candidate, and soon to be first (albeit briefly) supremo of the Union Army in the Civil War; and on September 9, 1854, by that of his old opponent Santa Anna, the Mexican general most notorious for his Alamo activities.

By 1861 the resort had been owned for several years by an aging local Clarksville doctor named David Shelton. By 1863 Dr. Shelton's health was failing, and on December 1 that year he sold Buffalo Springs to a Pennsylvanian named Timothy Paxson, who had recently been in Maryland, of all places. Certainly regular Southern civilians were tripping to Buffalo Springs during the war, the place being a safe retreat from the advancing Union armies and the havoc they wreaked. As soon as Paxson bought it he began advertising it in the local papers in Richmond and Petersburg, and places like that. If Tidwell's theory is to be believed, then Buffalo Springs was more than just a spa, more even than a safe haven for fleeing Rebels: It was a training camp where young Confederates learned how to write secret messages, to adopt disguises, to bluff and counter bluff, to use signals, and so on. It may or may not signify anything, but the resort did not open to the public in 1864, the first year it failed to do so. What was happening there that year is unknown.

Paxson stayed on after the war, improved the place and then faced a lawsuit from the Shelton heirs. He hired a lawyer, Colonel Thomas F. Goode (not pronounced as "good"), who settled with the heirs, making Paxson finally the sole and undisputed owner. In 1873 and 1874 Goode made deals with Paxson whereby, in lieu of unpaid legal fees and with an additional $13,400 paid, Goode became sole owner. Goode it was who really made the place famous, adding a new big ballroom and other glitzy devices, as well as marketing the spring water. It became a local hangout, people going there from Clarksville on a Sunday night to dine in the famous dining room, and local teenagers, like Charlie Russell's son Willie, hanging out there. With the coming (or rather, the return) of the railroad to Clarksville in 1890 the place really took off.

Stonewall Jackson's widow visited the resort in 1870 and 1877, but perhaps Buffalo Springs' major claim to fame is a Hollywood connection. During World War I one of the somewhat itinerant dancing teachers there was a German named Christian Ebsen who ordinarily lived in Belleville, Illinois, but who brought his family down to Mecklenburg County for the duration. That family included his son, Rudolph, then only a little lad, who, even back then, went by the nickname "Buddy."

Buffalo Springs wound down in the 1930s and the individual guest rooms and other buildings, including the ballroom, were sold off for lumber and masonry. Finally the Corps of Engineers bought the land, it being part of the flood plain connected to the John Kerr Lake that was finished in the early 1950s.

Whether General Tidwell jumped to conclusions or not, many other experts dismiss his notion of a spy camp. However, what makes it interesting is that there is no way that Tidwell could have known anything of Charlie Russell.

Knowing that John Baptist Russell, Charlie's father's first cousin, had married a Milburn, it is just a matter of genealogical detective work to make the connection. The Milburn lads were sons of Robert Nelson Milburn, whose aunt was Nancy Milburn, the girl who had married John Baptist Russell. Thus the Milburn lads were second cousins once removed of Charlie Russell.

To make it even more intriguing, the captain who ran the Milburns, John Wise Hebb, was born on April 1, 1839, into a long standing and prosperous family of St. Mary's County, Maryland. Hebb had been a student at Charlotte Hall Military Academy (as had John Wilkes Booth and Dave Herold), then gone on to study as a doctor at the Medical College of Maryland (as had Sam Mudd), and graduated as a very young physician in 1860. He then went into the Confederate Army, and in 1863 into the Navy, as a spymaster. Hebb would not die until 1910.

A curious genealogical fact or two about Hebb. One of his cousins, Benedict Wise, married Jane Eliza Russell, one of Charlie Russell's second cousins, and another of John Wise Hebb's cousins, George William Hebb, married another of Charlie's cousins—Mary Elizabeth Russell. The Hebbs and Russells were as closely connected by family as were the Russells and the Milburns. And John Wise Hebb was running the Milburns in and out of Buffalo Springs, where Charlie was living throughout the war.

Was Charlie tied in with the Buffalo Springs spy camp? Of course he was. The Confederate spying system, subsequent to the capture of Rose O'Neale Greenhow by Allen Pinkerton in 1861, had developed as the war progressed. Thomas Nelson Conrad had started a new Washington spy ring from scratch, and the Confederate War Department in Richmond initiated a Secret Service Bureau, headed by William Norris. The operation became more unified; operatives became more and more skilled, daring, outrageous, and, as the war came to a close, desperate. A desperation that would result in the assassination of Abraham Lincoln.

William Norris was yet another Marylander, a Baltimorean, with an adventure-packed background. He had studied at Yale, then ventured to New Orleans as a lawyer, to San Francisco as one of the Forty-Niners, to Chile, and then back to Maryland, produced a large family, and then when war broke out, became a signals officer for the Confederates. Finally, in 1862, he started the Secret Service Bureau. He rose from captain to colonel, masterminding the entire Confederate spying system, a system that included, among others, Charles H. Cawood, Tom Jones, Tom Harbin, William Bryant, and maybe, just maybe, Charlie Russell.

If Charlie was a spy, he would have worked for Norris, perhaps later for Hebb. If Charlie wasn't a spy, then how could he possibly have obtained that all-important travel pass, printed on brown paper, that would enable him to travel through Confederate territory with the frequency that he did? In other words, how could he have gotten through his own—Confederate—lines if he wasn't under orders? And then, what occurred when he got back to Clarksville? It's inconceivable that his superiors wouldn't have said, "Now, Charlie, when you were up in Washington…"

Thomas Nelson Conrad bears a close examination if only because of an extraordinary coincidence that took place in the 1870s, long after the war was over.

Conrad was born in Fairfax County, Virginia, in 1837, and became a teacher and headmaster at the Georgetown Institute in the District of Columbia. In June 1861 (i.e. after the war had started) he allowed a band to play "Dixie" at the commencement exercises and was jailed briefly at the Old Capitol Prison. After his release he became a rabid Confederate, if he wasn't one already, and obtained the position of chaplain in the Third Virginia Cavalry, a post that he soon quit for that of "scout," or "agent" as we would call it today. He would ride around enemy territory dressed as, and posing as, a clergyman. He found people trusted him in that disguise, and that they talked freely. His next assignment was to be "chief agent in place" in the enemy capital itself—Washington. He set himself up in the Van Ness mansion, backed financially by secret Confederate supporters in D.C., and began spying and setting up his ring. By 1862 this ring was well underway, the successor to the Jordan—Greenhow ring which had fallen into disrepair.

In those early days Conrad basically reported to either the Confederate War Department direct, or to Jeb Stuart, his titular military superior (Jeb was 16 days older than Charlie Russell). His activities soon came to the attention of Union detective and spymaster Lafayette Baker. Forewarned by one of his own agents, whom he had, with fortunate foresight, planted on Baker's staff, Conrad barely escaped from the capital with his life. After another year of intense spying, Conrad burned out and became one of the heads of Confederate counter-espionage, catching Union spies. After the war he went back to teaching, and in the late 1860s was president of Preston & Olin College in Blacksburg, Montgomery County, Virginia.

In 1872 the state of Virginia created a new land-grant school (one of two in different parts of the Commonwealth) on the site of Preston & Olin. One of the movers and shakers—the main mover and shaker—who pushed this deal through was Thomas Nelson Conrad. The new school was called the Virginia Agricultural and Mechanical College (VAMC), and would later become Virginia Tech. Conrad wanted for himself the post of president of this new institution, and went for it, only to be defeated by one vote by former Virginia cavalryman and ordnance captain Charles L.C. Minor II.

Conrad stayed in Montgomery County and remained strongly affiliated with his baby (the college). In 1877, he was head of the English department and adjunct professor in charge of the preparatory department.

This is the coincidence: In 1875 Charlie Russell, in Clarksburg, sent his son Willie to college at VAMC. This may be just a coincidence, or it may be that he was recommended the new school by Thomas Nelson Conrad.

Anyway Conrad did, indeed, finally become president of VAMC, from 1881 to 1886, when he was ousted. He wound up as a statistician at the Census Bureau in Washington, D.C., and died on January 5, 1905, at 2150 Florida Avenue northwest, of acute indigestion.

If there was a spying relationship between Thomas Nelson Conrad and Charlie Russell, then it never came down either as rumor or in any other way. However, we know Charlie never talked, and presumably, at least about Charlie Russell, Conrad didn't either. But again, maybe there was nothing to talk about.

Old Nick Snyder, the blacksmith and wheeler, Charlie's former master, died of consumption on October 10, 1862, aged 52:

> Farewell, dear wife, my life is passed,
> My love for you until death did last,
> And after me no sorrow take,
> But love the children, for my sake

His widow, Sarah, taking the advice of the epitaph, remarried, to John Kennedy, a New Yorker who took over Old Nick's business. The Kennedys continued to live in Nick's Second Ward house for years, along with an ever-decreasing number of Snyder issue. They even had their own son, Edgar, in September 1864, and it would have been neat to report that Edgar Kennedy was the father of the famous Hollywood actor of the same name, but he wasn't—no relation.

Nick's eldest son, and Charlie Russell's old friend—almost a brother, in fact—was William H. Snyder; what he did during the war we don't know. Willie was 21 when the war broke out, a blacksmith, footloose and fancy free, obviously fit as a fiddle. Even if he had suffered from hypertension, flat feet, wonky vision in his left eye, or some such ailment, he would have been in—unlike today. He was just the type of boy the Federals—or the Confederates—would have snapped up for service. Yet, there seems to be no record of him in either army. Did he just stay in Washington, D.C., as a blacksmith? It's possible. Yet...

The backdrop is this: Richmond, the Confederate capital, was taken by the Federals on April 2 and 3, 1865. On the 4th Lincoln came down from Washington to cast his giant shadow across the defeated enemy stronghold. On that very day Colonel Edward H. Ripley, Ninth Vermont Infantry, one of the conquerors first into Richmond, was—believe it or not—approached by a young enemy soldier named Snyder who maintained that he was there purely to warn Lincoln of an impending assassination plot. This lad claimed to be a member of the Confederate terrorist organization known as "The Torpedo Bureau," the very unit that was charged with the assassination ("torpedo" was the then current word for a mine). Ripley was impressed by young Snyder, and took him seriously. Lincoln didn't. Ripley lived to write his memoirs. Lincoln died.

The Ripley memoirs, entitled *The Capture and Occupation of Richmond, April 3, 1865*, were not published until 1907, over forty years after the event, and therein the Snyder story was told for the first time. In other words no one had even known about Snyder until Ripley's memoirs were published. The Snyder episode was news to everyone, at least those who cared. Ripley says that he ordered his aide, Captain Rufus P. Staniels, to take Snyder's statement, which Staniels did, according to Ripley.

What is terribly disappointing for Late Unpleasantness buffs is that Ripley just happened to forget to mention Snyder's first name in his book. Ah, but the Archives would have the Staniels statement. That would be bound to give Snyder's first name. This is not to suggest that Snyder-hunters rushed to Washington, D.C. to consult these archives the moment Ripley's memoirs hit the streets in 1907, but by and by the subject did come up. Actually, there couldn't have been many Snyder-hunters, if any at all, because as late as 1988, when Hall, Gaddy and Tidwell came out with their book *Come Retribution*, these three top scholars had failed to find Snyder's first name. They stated that the Staniels document was not yet found, i.e. it was not where it was supposed to be.

However, in 1995 Bill Tidwell published his book *April '65*, in which he finally named William H. Snyder.

What had transpired in those seven years between the time *Come Ret-*

ribution was published and when *April '65* came out was that General Tidwell had found the Staniels document, or rather, as he says: "The statement dictated to Staniels ... has not been found, but another statement made by him [i.e. Snyder] on April 12, 1865, has been" (then a footnote says "Union Provost Marshal File on Confederate Citizens [alphabetical], RG 109"). Tidwell goes on to say:

> In this statement Snyder describes how he had been recruited by Captain Leitch [this is Samuel Gooch Leitch] and passed on a mixture of gossip and facts that he had learned about the Confederate Secret Service during his two-month service in the Torpedo Bureau. He mentioned that Leitch had told him that the Confederate Congress was in secret session considering a bill to create a secret bureau that would include a corps to carry on a systematic crusade against the enemy's shipping, arsenals, magazines, powder mills, hotels, etc. He described several other Confederate operations as well as speculation about a raid on a seashore resort like Providence, Rhode Island.

All this from Tidwell's book *April '65*, published in 1995.

We have to assume, then, that Snyder's first name was William H. The reason for the excitement among Snyder-hunters when Tidwell broke this news in 1995, is, of course, that William H. Snyder is the very name of Willie Snyder, the lad Charlie Russell had lived with for seven years in D.C. back in the forties and fifties.

It's easy to say that William H. Snyder is a common name. Simple enough to enunciate the words, but not so easy to swallow, not when you already know the name from Washington, D.C.—from another life, as it were; then the name jumps out at you.

By 2005, in Jane Singer's book *The Confederate Dirty War*, the name William H. Snyder is set in stone, and, one supposes, given the provenance (as they say in the art world about the history of a painting), William H. Snyder it is. Jane Singer was the first, aside from General Tidwell, to do research on William H. Snyder, even to care about Snyder. This shows that, after all, there probably aren't too many Snyder-hunters out there.

Despite Jane Singer's research into young Snyder, from Confederate Army records, he remains a shadowy figure. Ms. Singer's investigation came up with a particular William H. Snyder, but whether this is the man who tried to warn Lincoln or not is debatable.

The suspect in the Army records (for that is all he can be, given the evidence available—a suspect) has a record which, in itself, looks horribly confused, to such a point that one believes one is reading about two separate men. To wit: he enlisted on May 23, 1861, at Amherst Courthouse, in Amherst County, Virginia, as a private in I Company (later research reveals that it is, in fact, Company E) of the Second Virginia Cavalry (his date and method of discharge are not known). He claimed to be a clerk, aged 25, which would put him at being born in 1836. He may have been from Bedford

County, Virginia, but then again, he may not have been. He was hospitalized on July 15, 1861, and returned to active service on Oct. 15, 1861. These dates are estimated, and the places are not stated. This Snyder was "detached Ordnance Department, Gen. Longstreet's Corps," on January 15, 1862, then taken prisoner of war at Gettysburg on July 5, 1863 (estimated day), and then promoted to ordnance sergeant in Longstreet's Corps, on July 15, 1863, then interned by the Union Army in Harrisburg, Pa., on July 22, 1863, and finally "detached Aug. 6, 1863, Ordnance Dept., Gen. Longstreet's Corps."

Unless there are mistakes in the dates, and there may be, then there are clearly at least two William H. Snyders here. One is the boy who enlisted at Amherst in 1861, and he may well be the one taken at Gettysburg and dumped into a camp in Harrisburg, and the one some other archivists think may have later lived in Lexington. If the dates are correct on these Army records, then the Amherst boy is certainly not the Ordnance boy—the dates don't fit, don't even come close. If he was taken POW on July 5, 1863 (albeit an estimated day), promoted to ordnance sergeant under Longstreet on July 15, confined in enemy Harrisburg on July 22, then he was a busy boy, an impossibly busy boy. No, unless the dates are fouled up, there's more than one William H. Snyder here. There's the Amherst boy, and the Ordnance boy, to name but two.

Now, which one of these boys, if either, tried to warn Lincoln? The Amherst boy was probably still languishing in Harrisburg, unless he'd been exchanged. What about the Ordnance boy? Ordnance means a certain skill with guns, metal, and such. After all Charlie Russell spent the entire war in the Confederate Ordnance Depot, and he was a blacksmith. It's looking better and better for D.C. Willie.

But again, as we all know, there were lots and lots of William H. Snyders alive at that time. What makes one so sure that the D.C. blacksmith was the Ordnance Boy? Just because he had the same name? Yet, by the same token, what makes one so sure that the Amherst private and the Ordnance Sergeant were the same man? Just because they had the same name. And impossibly conflicting dates, to boot.

There are several questions here. How many William H. Snyders are we talking about? The 1861 Amherst private, the 1863 Ordnance Department sergeant, the lad who tried to warn Lincoln, and the blacksmith from D.C. Are they all one and the same? Unlikely. Jane Singer firmly believes that the D.C. blacksmith is not in any way involved, and she's probably right. Yet...

Now, this is not to say that Willie Snyder, the D.C. blacksmith—just because a William H. Snyder had already crossed our path—is the same man who tried to warn Lincoln. Yet, it is an amazing coincidence of names. After all, we don't even know what D.C. Willie did in the war. So, what did you do in the war, Willie?

We know what he did after the War. He was a blacksmith in D.C. In the 1870 census we pick him up in the Seventh Ward, married to Susan (aged 23 and born in Maryland) with children, Mary M. Snyder (aged 3) and William N. Snyder (aged 1). The fact that Willie is listed as 35 in this census is interesting in that this would put his birth year as 1835. However, he wasn't born in 1835—he was born in July 1839. It's just that Jane Singer's Amherst boy also claimed to have been born around 1835.

Incidentally, and for pure amusement, Willie Snyder's half brother Charles M. Snyder would become a semi-pro baseball catcher with the Cincinnatis. This is not the more famous Charles Snyder, the pro ball player (a catcher also) who died in 1901, and the team is not the more famous professional team, the Reds. The 1880 census describes our Willie Snyder's brother as a baseball catcher. That's what it says! In May 1883 Charlie dislocated his thumb, a painful injury for a catcher.

Susanna [Susan], Willie's wife, died on November 11, 1912, and Willie Snyder himself died on December 27, 1916. They are buried together in the Congressional Cemetery, in Washington, D.C.

Charlie Russell was in Washington on the very day John Wilkes Booth assassinated Abe Lincoln. This is not to suggest in any way that Charlie had anything to do with the actual assassination, but it is, nonetheless, a curious coincidence of timing. Lincoln was shot on the night of April 14, 1865. The imagination revolts at Charlie being anywhere else aside from the capital on the 14th. He had to have been right there when it happened. It's almost as if it happened because Charlie was there. But, of course, thousands of people were in D.C. when Lincoln was shot.

Immediately after Appomattox Court House, with the war now at an end, or rather, as soon as he heard the momentous news—news he had been eagerly awaiting for what seemed like an eternity—Charlie Russell left wherever he was to return to Washington to pick up his pregnant wife and his two young children, Willie and Annie. We know from family records. that "as soon as the war was over he went up to Washington to collect his wife and children and bring them back to Clarksville."

We don't know where Charlie left from, where he was at the very moment he heard the news of the surrender, but it must be presumed that it was Clarksville. If it was Clarksville, which is on the North Carolina line, then it would have been sometime late in the evening of the 9th, or at the latest during the morning of the 10th, that he heard news of the surrender. Even if he left as late as the morning of the 11th, he would have been in Washington by the morning of the 13th, or thereabouts.

But he may just have been in D.C. itself when Lee surrendered on April 9. Or he may have been anywhere in between D.C. and Clarksville, or none of the above. He might have guessed that the surrender was imminent, as the week before Jeff Davis had fled south from Richmond to Danville, which is very close to Clarksville. Either way, or any way, Charlie had to have been in the capital on the day Lincoln was killed; or, to rephrase this, at the precise moment Charlie was back in the District of Columbia, the assassination took place.

We also know that on April 29, 1865, the very pregnant Mary Ann delivered young Alice Lee Russell—in Clarksville. Incidentally, the Lee part of her name came from the general, and from Charlie's old neighbors—same family—up in Charles County, Maryland.

Anyway, no matter which way you cut it, there were only twenty days between the time of the surrender and the time Alice was born in Clarksville, so in that precise space of time, the following sequence of events took place: The news of the surrender traveled to Clarksville, Charlie left for Washington, Charlie arrived in Washington, Lincoln was shot, Charlie stayed a while with his family, then Charlie headed back to Clarksville, at the very time Booth was fleeing for his life in Charles County, Maryland, Charlie's old home.

Charlie wouldn't just have picked Mary Ann up and said bye-bye to his brother John H. and his stepmother Janette and the rest of the family. He would have stayed a couple of weeks to visit, to see the livery stable that John H. had started with a fellow named Davis—the Metropolitan Livery stable at Sixth Street west, south of Pennsylvania Avenue, where they hired and sold horses and buggies.

In Clarksville, at some point soon after the war ended, Charlie opened a blacksmith's shop near First Street, on the river low grounds, just below where the Best Western Motel stands today.

In the spring of 1866 (or 1867, but most likely 1866) Mary Ann went up to Washington to visit the Russell relatives with whom she'd lived during the war. She took Annie and Alice with her, and Willie stayed back at Clarksville with his father. We have a fascinating letter from Mary Ann to Willie, dated "Washington, May 26" (unfortunately there is no year):

> My dear little boy. I suppose you are getting very impatient for my return home, but you will not have to wait very long now, for I want to see you so very much that I cannot enjoy myself from you any longer. I hope you have been a very good boy while I have been away and said your prayers every night and I hope you and Miss Molley get along without having any falling out. I suppose you love her as much as ever. Your sister Annie wants to see you very much. All of your little cousins send their love to you and say that they want to see you very much. Your Aunt Sally sends her love to you and says you must make haste and learn to write for she is very impatient to receive that letter from you. She wants to see how well you can spell and your cousin Janie is very anxious to go home with me. Wouldn't you be delighted to have her come see you? She sends her love to you. I have some very pretty books and marbles for you and a knife also. I have nothing more to tell you now but I will soon be home with you, so I will say

goodbye. You must be a good boy until I come home. I have got a marble for you with a bird in it. No more at present. From your ever-loving mother.

The Aunt Sally mentioned was actually Mrs. Sarah Brooks, Willie's aunt and godmother. The cousin Janie was Jane Russell, William Ignatius's daughter, the future Mrs. Jane Stant. As for the "Miss Molley," Good Golly! we don't know who she is. If it's Molly Burroughs, Willie's cousin born the same year as him, then what is she doing in Clarksville, when she should be in the orphanage in Washington? But then, Miss Molly may be a little girl-friend of Willie's. It's impossible to tell, at this remove.

Colonel Thomas Jordan, erstwhile spymaster, went to Memphis where he edited the *Memphis Appeal*, then to New York where, with J.B. Pryor, he wrote his second book, *The Campaigns of Lieutenant General Forrest*, published in 1868. Soon afterwards, he was offered a mercenary job by the Cubans.

Spain owned Cuba at that time, and the Cubans, of course, resented that fact. A rebel force was gathered together and the Declaration of Cuban Independence was signed on October 10, 1868, and the Republic of Cuba declared in April 1869, a new polity immediately recognized officially by most of the Latin American countries. The first military engagements took the Spaniards by surprise and were gloriously successful for the revolutionaries, but they needed a general of experience to take on the mighty Spanish forces which were daily shipping in from Europe. Jordan left New York on the good ship *Peril* in May 1869, bound by a one-year contract to be chief of the General Staff of the Rebel Cuban Army, and with a small but well-trained army of ex–Feds and ex–Rebs he landed at Mayan, and then marched into the interior.

After some successes, notably his momentous defeat of 1,200 Spanish troops at Las Menas de Tana with only 300 of his own Cubans, Jordan realized that the jig was up. Despite Jordan's having been promoted to commander-in-chief in December 1869, and despite another major success at Guimaro, supplies and reinforcements were simply not coming in, and it was just a matter of time before the Spanish authorities got Jordan. The price on his head was $100,000. By September 1869 rumors were flying around Cuba and the United States that Jordan had approached the Spaniards with a deal. For a very generous consideration he would surrender himself and his army, and get free and unmolested passage back to the States. This rumor was, of course, instigated by the Spanish, who, in the course of the spreading, added that they had plainly and bluntly informed General Jordan as to what he could do with his offer, and even where he might put it.

Jordan resigned in May and fled Cuba in a most dramatic longboat escape, managing to achieve Nassau. From there he arrived back in New

York on the *Morro Castle* on May 6, 1870. The Ten Year War, as it's sometimes called, would deteriorate into a miasmatic series of guerrilla encounters, and in the end would peter out, having achieved little.

Jordan, back in New York City, was arrested at his Ninth Street boarding house on December 7, 1870, by two policemen led there by A.W. Davis, the "Spanish Spy." The charges: violating neutrality laws, hiring mercenaries to fight in a foreign "filibustering" war, and offending a foreign power with whom the United States was at peace. All serious charges, and, without question, true. General Jordan was allowed to go free after posting a $10,000 bond, and then he waited for his trial—and waited, throughout all of 1871, and waited, until finally he was acquitted through lack of evidence. Lucky Jordan.

In New York General Jordan wrote several magazine articles about the Civil War and took on the job of editor of the *Financial and Mining Record*, a position he would hold for the rest of his life. Lung trouble, it was, that caused his death on Nov. 27, 1895, at his home, 124 East 25th Street, aged 76, and he was buried two days later at St. Francis Xavier's Church on West 16th. He had been a Catholic for a year. Old soldiers and comrades, both from the Confederate Army and from Cuba, flocked to the funeral. He left a son and daughter, his wife having died in 1884.

At some stage young Charles Emmet Joyce—not so young anymore, he was almost 19 at the end of the Civil War—had joined the Fenian Movement. This was as natural a thing for him to do as for his father to have named him Emmet, the Fenians being yet another—the latest—brotherhood in the long list of such leagues throughout Irish history formed to expel the British from the Emerald Isle.

In Ireland it was called the Irish Republican Brotherhood, and had been formed in Dublin on Saint Patrick's Day in 1858 by James Stephens, a veteran of the Young Ireland movement of the 1840s, the same '48 Movement that had died with the transportation to the Antipodes of Thomas Francis Meagher. Stephens swore in Thomas Clarke Luby and Luby swore in Stephens, and so the movement began.

Just after that, in America, John O'Mahoney and his partner Michael Doheny, both old Forty-Eighters, came up with the name "Fenian," after the Fianna, Finn McCool's legendary army of Ireland's ancient days. It took a while to catch on, but soon Fenian was the word, a word that attracted money and supporters from the Irish exiles all over America. But not Meagher. Thomas Francis and many of the old brigade, both in Ireland and America, refused to have anything to do with the new band, despised it for its upstartness. They were wrong to thus shun this movement, a movement which caught the Irish imagination more than any other had ever done, and which, arguably, turned out to be the first of the last straws for the British, an exasperating and costly straw that, with subsequent last straws, persuaded the British to begin the long, long evacuation.

With incredible energy Stephens and his boys in Ireland stumped the country, and America too, raising funds and inducting members. What really got the Fenians moving, though, was the death in San Francisco in 1861 of Terence McManus who, like Meagher, had been a Forty-Eighter, transported to Tasmania and escaped to America. The Fenians decided that McManus should be buried in Ireland, so they brought him—slowly, by train—across the continent to New York, a public relations triumph that gathered momentum with every stop until, finally, on the East Coast, the reception given the dead lad was as great as for any conquering general. And thence to Cork and Dublin, where the reception was equally enormous. Some 250,000 attended the funeral, among them 50,000 soldiers of the Fenian Brotherhood, newly inspired by McManus's famous last words, "Is there any hope?"

As the vast crowd—which by sheer numbers would have formed a large city—passed in its procession by St. Catherine's Church, they all remembered it was here that the great Robert Emmet had dangled from the gallows in 1803, his ultimate struggle for the Irish cause. To a man, they removed their caps. And then it was on to the funeral, with Bishop Moriarty railing that Hell was not hot enough nor Eternity long enough to mete adequate punishment to such as the Fenians.

This one single publicity stunt—the McManus affair—attracted more thousands of members to the Fenian cause than any amount of labor could have. The Brotherhood went from strength to strength. The Brits stamped down pretty hard on the movement in Ireland, yet people still flocked to it. The American government was tacitly supportive for a while, on principle mostly, and the Fenians flourished openly in the United States, without let or hindrance.

In the Irish autumn of '65 the British rounded up the leaders and threw them in jail. James Stephens escaped in a manner that left all Ireland, and England, thrill-struck. They talked about nothing else. It was as if he had walked through walls. What had happened was that Fenianism had extended its reach to within the government, and what seemed like magic had, in fact, been a metal key opening a metal lock. Stephens escaped to America, where he led the abortive Fenian invasion of Canada.

Col. John Kelly had taken over from Stephens in Ireland. More and more men came from America. The recent Civil War had thrown up a lot of what, at this moment, the Brotherhood needed most: experienced officers, and Lieutenant Joyce was one of them.

"I, Charles Emmet Joyce, do solemnly swear, in the presence of Almighty God, that I will do my utmost, at every risk, while life lasts, to make Ireland an independent democratic Republic; that I will yield implicit obedience, in all things not contrary to the law of God, to the commands of my superior officers, and that I shall preserve inviolable secrecy regarding all transactions of this secret society that may be confided to me. So help me God! Amen."

For Charles Emmet the following several months were occupied by constant meetings of the Brotherhood in Ireland and Liverpool, back and forth trips between Ireland and the States, and skirmishes with the Constabulary. A detailed London *Times* report on the Fenians, written (later) in the April 29, 1868, edition, tells us that "Fenian meetings were held in Liverpool in January and February 1867.... All the American officers were present—Captain Beecher, Captain Dohaney, two Captain O'Briens, Lieutenant Joyce, and about twenty in all."

The big new Fenian rising in Ireland was planned for March 5, 1867, with Charles Emmet in the thick of it. But two things really militated against the success of the grand insurgency. The first was the weather. On March 6 came a snowstorm the likes of which no one had ever witnessed in Ireland, and it went on and on, for two weeks. All movement ground to a halt. The second was the informer, John Joseph Cullen, more commonly known by his alias of Corydon, or by the suitable epithet given him by Irishmen of all leanings: Corydon the Bastard.

This from the London *Times* of April 17, 1867:

> Charles Edward King Joyce [sic], a respectable-looking young man, was brought up in custody of Acting-Inspector Smollen, charged with having been connected with the Fenian conspiracy. Much interest was felt concerning the case, as it was known that Lieutenant John Joseph Cullen of the Federal Army, formerly of the "Fenian Brotherhood," and now one of the informers who had offered their services to the Police, was to give evidence. The informer is a dapper little young man with rather a florid face, sharp nose and thin lips, and wears a profusion of red-brown curly hair. He was most carefully dressed and appeared to be quite indifferent to the curiosity his presence excited. On the arrival of Mr. C.J. O'Donel, at half past two o'clock, the prisoner Joyce was placed in the dock, and the informer entered the witness box, while Mr. Kelly, Assistant Clerk of the Crown, read over the information he made which was to the effect "that he [the informer] was in America [from] 1862 up to a recent period and had served in the Federal Army. Saw the prisoner attend and take part at Fenian meetings in America. Also saw the prisoner at Fenian meetings at Carey's City Mansion Hotel, Bridge-street [Dublin]. The prisoner went back to America and then returned. Saw him in Liverpool at a meeting with Captain Dunne, McCafferty and others and he (witness) believed that the prisoner and those who accompanied him from America, came to levy war against the Queen." The witness having deposed that all contained in the information was true, Mr. O'Donel addressed the prisoner, and said that he was committed for trial at commission.

In fact Charles Emmet was thrown into the notorious Mountjoy Prison with only one thing to look forward to, namely a bewigged gentleman in a black cap looming over him tolling the words no prisoner wishes to hear: "Mr. Joyce, you are to be taken from here to a place of execution, and there to be hung by the neck until you are dead."

As that great Irish writer and patriot Seumas MacManus says in his masterpiece *The Story of the Irish Race*, "Fearful indeed was the life—the living death, rather—that Irish political prisoners had to face in English jails." Hands chained behind backs for weeks on end, a prisoner would have to "feed himself as a dog would, by lapping it up." They would be starved, systematically, so that "prisoners would snatch a candle-end out of the garbage" when the keeper was not looking, "and save it to feast upon." The air in their awesomely vile cells was so fetid that they would be reduced to lying down by the door and sucking in through the crack the "vitiated air of the corridor," which tasted so good in comparison. They would be put in with common criminals and lunatics, and stripped naked several times a day and insulted, struck and otherwise violated, herded along by shouting, truncheon-wielding over-zealous prison officials. And if they got sick, tough. It was not a cozy life in Mountjoy.

However, God was on Charles Emmet's side. The U.S. authorities bailed him out, as they did several American Fenians who had served the Union so well during the Late Unpleasantness. He and Patrick Connolly were summarily taken to Queenstown, County Cork, and on July 31, 1867, thrown on a steamer heading for the United States. At that point this particular round of the Fenian uprisings was at a virtual end, yet such was the fear that the movement struck in the hearts of Englishmen, notably Gladstone the prime minister, that changes began to take place almost immediately, and those changes eventually led to freedom. Charles Emmet Joyce had not fought for nothing.

On his return to the States in late 1867, Captain Joyce (the Irish apply the term "captain" as Southern Americans apply "colonel," i.e. willy-nilly) moved back to D.C., to a boarding house at 324 G Street, and obtained a job as a clerk in the adjutant general's office of the War Department, and became a respectable citizen of Washington.

Just as important, in early 1868 he joined John A. Rawlins Post # 1 of the Grand Army of the Republic (G.A.R.), named for a Civil War general, the first G.A.R. post to open in Washington, D.C., on Oct. 13, 1866. Charles Emmet would remain with the post for the rest of his natural life, achieving the highest posts within the G.A.R. Another member of the Rawlins Post was Union veteran Charles W. Brooks, husband of Charlie Russell's sister Sarah, and uncle by marriage of Charlie's niece, Alice Russell.

In 1869 Charles Emmet snagged a personal favor from General Grant (actually President Grant at that stage, but old Union boys would always know him as "General"), or perhaps from someone in Grant's office: a "U.S.

at large" appointment to West Point. In the summer of 1869 he moved to New York for a while, staying with his guardian P.J. Clarke at 45 Bleecker Street, in Greenwich Village. He was due to be admitted on Sept. 1, 1869, but was rejected by the Academic Board due to deficiencies in arithmetic, grammar and geography, and not due to his bad health (as his obituary would later claim). Disappointed, he made his way back to Washington, and took up residence in a room on Seventh Street southeast, between B and C streets.

He then lodged with insurance agent (and Washingtonian Fenian leader) James P. Ryan and his family, and finally got his own place in 1870, at 509 Eighth Street southeast.

On June 1, 1868, John H. Russell, back in political harness, was the big winner in the city councilman elections in the Sixth Ward, running on the Conservative ticket. He got 927 votes, G.W. Miller got 926, and J.L. Dalton got 921. The opposition was M. Davis (780), E.A. Adams (710) and C.E. Lathrop (702). That year was a big year for the Conservatives in Washington.

In 1869 John H. Russell retired from the city council, his friends having nominated him for the higher position of alderman. Unfortunately for John H. it was the year of the Republicans, and he didn't stand a chance. That was his last shot at politics.

On July 29, 1869, Charlie Russell's last child, Charles Henry Jr., was born in Clarksville. There were complications with the birth, and Mary Ann died a week later, on Aug. 7, 1869, in Clarksville. She was buried at Oakhurst Cemetery. The infant, Charles Henry Russell Jr., died in Sept. 1869, aged 6 weeks.

In the late 1860s Charlie went into the farm wagon–making business. He definitely did not do so in the 1850s, as the 1977 book *Life by the Roaring River* claims; the author of that book was misled by an article written by John Kline that appeared in the *South Hill Enterprise* of March 10, 1876, headed "C.H. Russell and Son Closes After 120 Years" (reproduced in Appendix B).

On Aug. 19, 1869, Clarksville came out with a new newspaper, the *Roanoke Valley*. An ad for C.H. Russell appeared on page 1, complete with an anvil logo. He ran this ad for months without changing it. It said: "Wheelwright and blacksmith. Has on hand three new two-horse wagons, one four-horse wagon, one spring wagon; all of first-rate material and workmanship, which he will sell cheap for cash or produce. He is prepared to do all kinds of work in his line on the most reasonable terms, in the best manner. All work warranted. Horse shoeing and repairing of all kinds done promptly."

The Roanoke Valley of Jan. 26, 1871, has this to say: "We have wagon making and blacksmith and wheel wright work by Mr. C.H. Russell, who is an ingenious and practical workman himself, and has good mechanics under him. His one, two and four horse wagons will bear comparison, as to real substantial work, ease in running, and durability, with any others, no matter where made. Northern made wagons have more fancy work on them, and make a rather more favorable impression on that account. But Mr. Russell's will, in almost every instance, outwear them." The Russell wagons became so popular that Charlie decided to go into regular wagons. He manufactured them and sold them, and his son Willie painted them, and helped in sales. In 1888, as a wedding present from his father, Willie would become a partner in the business.

Given a blacksmith's wages it's interesting to speculate on where Charlie might have managed to get the capital to start his business. He had no inherited money, and neither did Mary Ann. Some—later—injection of funds may have come from Jennie, his second wife, but that's not the question. Charlie was up and running as a wagon maker before he married Jennie.

The point is, the money may have come from old Confederate funds seeded away during the war. We know Charlie never talked about his spying activities, so there's no reason why he would have blabbed about a secret hoard either. This hypothesis of such a secret stash is quite reasonable, as there are many similar instances recorded in the wake of the Civil War (and every other war as well).

1870 census
Sixth Ward
Washington, D.C.

R. Ignacious, 46, boilermaker, born in Maryland
Margaret Ignacious, 46, born in Maryland
Julia Ignacious, 18, born in Virginia, married Feb. 1870
Jane Ignacious, 17, born in Virginia
Martha Ignacious, 11, born in D.C., at school
Agnes Ignacious, 6, born in D.C.

This is William Ignatius Russell, for some reason posing as R. Ignacious. The annotation beside Julia's name saying that she married in February of that year should have been assigned to the next line down, as it was Jane, not Julia, who married in February 1870, to John Wesley Stant. Jane was the only one of William Ignatius Russell's children to marry.

Five doors down from R. Ignacious lived

Richard Wood, 42, Marine, born in D.C.
Mary A. Wood, 36, born in D.C.
John W. Stant, 20, laborer, born in D.C., married Feb. 1870
Jane Stant, 17, born in Virginia, married Feb. 1870
William E. Wood, 18, Marine, born in D.C.
George W. Stant, 16, born in D.C., drummer in garrison
Virginia A. Stant, 14, born in D.C., at school

Mary S. Stant, 11, born in D.C., at school
Rosella Stant, 9, born in D.C., at school
Ida E. Stant, 7, born in D.C.
Ellen M. Stant, 6; born in D.C.

So Jane appears twice in the 1870 census, same night even, once as Jane Stant and again as Jane Ignacious. This is the "Julia Phenomenon" at work, double-time.

Another 1870 peculiarity, similar in many ways to the Stant—Ignacious case, is that, in the census listing that year for the family of James H. Harbin (Charlie Russell's stepbrother), taken on June 9, Jennet Harbin is listed, aged 16 (should say 20). Jennet's nickname was Lula. Odd in that she had married the previous October 2 (1869) in D.C. to Joseph Steiner. In the very same census we duly find Mr. Steiner, a musician, 28, born in Hesse, Germany, living in the Sixth Ward with Lula, his wife, aged 20, born in D.C. And the census says they were married in October 1869. The census taker got around to them on July 14, five weeks after he had censused "Jennet" at home with her parents.

Lula would have three or four children (depending on which census you believe), only one of whom, Alie, survived. What became of Alie we do not know. Lula and Steiner seem to have been absent from Washington for years.

Charles Emmet Joyce married, on November 7, 1870, at the Christ Episcopal Church on the corner of St. Paul's and Chase streets, Baltimore. Often in those days a Catholic couple would marry in an Episcopal church, but the priest and the ceremony would be of the Papist variety. His bride was John H. Russell's daughter Alice, and young Joyce would begin his life of married bliss by moving in with his wife, his new sister-in-law and father-in-law at 138 East Capitol Street.

It was at the adjutant general's office in the early 1870s that he met another young man working there, John Paul Simonton, who would become not only his brother-in-law, but also one of the great Lincoln assassination scholars. John Simonton would marry Charles Emmet's youngest sister, Margaret, in D.C., on October 15, 1879, and they would have thirteen children, ten of whom would survive into very interesting adulthoods—Charles (alias Carl) and Vincent became Prohibitions agents, Charles was murdered by the mob in October 1942 and Vin, some say, became deputy attorney general under Roosevelt.

In the early 1870s Charles Emmet's younger brother Michael, who had stayed in the Army after the war, married an Irish girl from Illinois, Bridget, and they had Belle, born in 1873, and Katie, in 1879. Those were the nice things. But bad things were to happen to Michael. Very bad things.

Their sister Lucy Joyce married an Irish rigger at the Treasury Department named, coincidentally, Patrick Russell, and had a daughter Mary

("Mamie") in 1870 and a son Edward in March 1873. Paddy Russell died in the 1870s, still in his twenties, but Lucy would live into the 20th century as a trained nurse, running large boarding houses first at 1124 Eleventh Street and then at 1205 M Street.

Charles Emmet's sisters Kate and Isabel died suddenly, we know that; but we do not know how, when or where, or if they were married. That Mary and Edward lived on into the 1880s we do know for certain.

In the 1870s Charles Emmet made a transfer to the Navy Department, then to the contract division of the Post Office Department, where he would stay for the rest of his life. His wife Alice would do good works, such as managing the confectionery table at the St. Peter's Church Fair on October 30, 1879 (her cousin Mary I. Harbin would manage the Sunday School table at the same function)—this according to the *Washington Post of* October 30, 1879.

In Washington, Joanna (Annie) Harbin, James H.'s daughter and Charlie Russell's step-niece, married James Buchanan Silcott, son of Norval and Margaret Silcott of Loudoun County, Virginia, on August 6, 1873, in Washington. The Rev. Charles Andrews officiated.

James B. Silcott was born on August 4, 1841, in Loudoun County, and was in the Civil War, enlisting in Company E of the Eighth Virginia Infantry on May 29, 1861, as a private. On October 15, 1862, he was court-martialed for going AWOL, and fined ten days' pay. He was soon back in the thick of it, only to be captured at Gettysburg on July 3, 1863, and sent to Point Lookout, Maryland, as a prisoner of war on October 26, 1863. He was exchanged on February 13, 1865, but unfortunately, along the way, he had contracted consumption, and this was to be his undoing, just as it was to cause the death rattle of so many veterans of that war.

The happy couple, James and Annie, moved back to Silcott country, but then Annie died seven months after the wedding, on March 3, 1874. That she does not show up in the Loudoun death register indicates she died elsewhere, perhaps Washington, as she was buried in the Congressional Cemetery in August (sic) 1874. James B. Silcott married again, in 1876, to Emma V. Bradfield, but then he too died, in Loudoun County on September 17, 1878, aged 37. Despite the brevity of his second marriage it was extraordinarily fruitful, producing two children, Bromma and Marion. Emma, his second wife, died in 1912, and was buried with her husband in Ebenezer Cemetery, Loudoun County.

Another of James H. Harbin's daughters, Kate, married James Charles (J.C.) Robinson in Washington, D.C., on May 27, 1874, and they lived at 1521 Eighth Street southwest. However, Kate died of heart disease on September 25, 1878, with no issue. She is buried in the Congressional Cemetery with her husband, who died on April 26, 1895.

Officer Philip Harbin's daughter, Nannie, would soon marry Alexander McKenzie of the auditor's office. Son of David McKenzie, a Scottish ship's carpenter, by his wife Elizabeth, Alex had been born in Baltimore in 1848, had arrived in the nation's capital in 1862 and on July 10, 1868, had begun working for the government. He and Nannie had a son, Alex Jr., born in 1876, and then Nannie passed away, aged 24, at three in the afternoon on August 9, 1877.

The funeral took place on Sunday, the 12th, at 5 o'clock, from Phil Harbin's home for the last seven years, 724 Seventh Street (although the *Evening Star* of August 13, 1877, says it was from 726 G Street northeast). Services were conducted by the Rev. A. Floridus Steele, of St. Mary's P.E. (Protestant Episcopalian) Church. She was buried in Congressional Cemetery.

After Nannie's death Alex McKenzie went back to live with his parents at 1005 Pennsylvania Avenue southeast, but he finally married again, in 1885, to Alice Guinand, an American girl of Swiss parentage (or so she said; actually her father was from New Orleans, and Alice had grown up in D.C., only six doors down from John H. Russell's house on Eighth Street), and they would have a son, John Vincent McKenzie, in May 1887. Alice's sister Grace came to live with them and never left, not even when Alice died. Alex continued to live with Grace, until, just before he died, in the 1920s, he married her.

Alex Jr. didn't last long, dying at high noon on February 29, 1896, aged 20, and was buried on March 3, at 2 o'clock, from his father's house, 1004 East Capitol Street.

J.V., the son by Alex's marriage to Alice, is probably best remembered for his 1911 prank which involved going away to Baltimore for several days with Josie, the daughter of Livingston Vann of the Interstate Commerce Commission, and while there hoaxing a marriage with her, a hoax that backfired. Nevertheless he and Josie did marry, and they had two children — Alex in 1915 and Alice in 1917 — and then they moved to Brooklyn, where J.V. worked as a bank clerk. J.V. later became a salesman.

Phil's brother, James H. Harbin, his wife Jane Eliza, and their family moved in the 1870s to 750 Seventh Street southeast. Son James S. Harbin, now a brass finisher like his father, married Miriam S. (Midie) Worthan on May 4, 1878. Midie, born in May 1856 in Washington, D.C., was the daughter of engineer William Worthan and his wife Mary, of L Street southeast. James and Midie moved in with her parents and would have one child, Lelia Elizabeth, born on December 7, 1888, in D.C. Jane Eliza died in the morning of August 5, 1878, aged 54. She was buried in the Congressional Cemetery in Washington, D.C. James H., still a machinist and brass finisher, and his youngest son, Daniel, now a clerk in a store, moved into a smaller house at 704 I Street southeast. The next to youngest son, John H., had gone away to be a skipper on river boats.

Papa Charlie (as he would later be known) married again, on October 12, 1871, in Clarksville, to Virginia Price Moss (born on September 10, 1840, in Clarksville), but they would have no children. It brings a glow to the cheeks to learn that Jennie (as she was known, or, to a later generation, "Grandma"), really became the mother to Charlie's children, not just a replacement stepmother.

Young Willie's education, not long after the prompting of the "Dear Little Boy" letter, took a turn for the better. In 1867 he came under the instruction of the Rev. Mr. Whaley in Clarksville, and in 1875 he would set out for Blacksburg to be a freshman at the newly-formed (Oct. 1, 1872) Virginia Agricultural and Mechanical College, the very same institution that had been pushed into existence by former Confederate spymaster Thomas Nelson Conrad. Interestingly, this institution was built on the site of a former college, of which Conrad had been president: the Preston and Olin Institute, named partly after Dr. Stephen Olin, the founder, in 1832, of Randolph—Macon College in Mecklenburg County, Virginia. Willie completed his second year, as a sophomore, in 1876, but then dropped out and returned home, never graduating. The college would go on to become the famous Virginia Tech. Willie would go on to spectacular things too, even making the *New York Times*.

A frequent member of the Board of Visitors of VAMC during the time Willie was there was a former Confederate congressman named D.C. DeJarnette. A Virginian, Daniel Coleman DeJarnette had a first cousin, Elliott, whose son, Joseph Spencer DeJarnette, would become arguably one of the most sinister and evil men ever to run a Virginia asylum, a Heinrich Himmler look-alike and act-alike. It would not be long before Willie Russell—in an indirect way, perhaps—would encounter the bizarre Dr. DeJarnette.

Charlie's two daughters, Annie and Alice, were educated at the very reputable and strictly Presbyterian Sunnyside Academy for Girls, situated less than a mile from the center of Clarksville. Sunnyside, run by sisters Isabella, Mildred, Emily and Agnes Carrington, was a boarding facility, but it took a few day boys too, from the local area, and Willie may well have gone there too before he went off to college in Blacksburg. The academy would not close until 1908.

At 5 o'clock in the morning of February 8, 1876, at her home, 518 Sixth Street east, Janette Russell, Charlie's stepmother, aged 70, died of asthma after a five-month illness. She was buried at the Congressional Cemetery, in D.C., on February 9, at 3 o'clock in the afternoon. Her death certificate says she was 71, born in Charles County, Maryland, and that she had lived in D.C. for about 43 years.

Janette had been converted from Catholicism to Protestantism sometime in the 1860s, and began attending Christ Cuurch Episcopal, on G Street. Sometime between May 12, 1867 and February 8, 1870 she became a communicant there [between those dates, and only those dates, Christ Church didn't record confirmation dates].

At noon, on September 4, 1878 William I. Russell died at his home, 1005 G Street southeast, in Washington, D.C., aged 54, and was buried two days later at the Congressional Cemetery, in lot r37/93, in the same grave where Philip Russell had been buried on or around June 5, 1847. William Igantius, like his stepmother, had become an Episcopalian, and like her had been, toward the end, a communicant at Christ Church.

After his death his widow, Margaret Rebecca, and the daughters and niece moved to 909 Eye Street southeast, where the girls set up an industrious tailoring beehive.

Martha was the first of the three remaining spinster daughters of William Ignatius to die, on December 19, 1881. She was buried in the Congressional Cemetery. The rest of the ladies moved again, in the early 1880s, and in July 1883 Molly Burroughs left to get married to Richard Aloysius O'Brien.

Captain Joyce was junior vice commander of the Rawlins G.A.R. post on October 13, 1879, when the post celebrated its thirteenth year in business, and on November 20 of that year General Winfield Scott Hancock, the old hero of Gettysburg, came to town. About 150 of his former officers and men lived in D.C., including Captain Joyce and his buddy Michael Emmet Urell, both of whom went along to the meeting to see the general. On December 16 General Grant himself, (i.e. former President Grant) came to town, and Joyce, as standard bearer and secretary of the joint committee of all the G.A.R. posts in D.C. went to welcome him. After the meeting with Grant, they all went off to Philadelphia for another Grant welcome, and more Grant booze.

The *Washington Post* of January 10, 1880, tells us that Charles E. Joyce was elected commander of the Rawlins post the day before. He was succeeded on January 14, 1881, by Mike Urell.

Joyce was also a mason, belonging to Lafayette Lodge # 19. He was very active in East Washington affairs, and sat on committees with George F. Harbin, the dry goods merchant brother of Tom Harbin.

In late 1880, John H. Russell, now in bad health, moved, with his daughter Jennie and the Joyces, down the street from 138 to 224 East Capitol.

Then the awful thing happened to Michael. The best way to tell the story is to reproduce the article published in the *Washington Post* of September 19, 1880, with annotations in brackets:

Killed by a Gatling gun. A shocking incident occurred at the Arsenal yesterday [Sept. 18, 1880], by which two men lost their lives. The day previous, Battery B, Second United States Artillery [Major Breckinridge's Battalion], was put through the regular semi-annual firing exercise with the Gatling guns. One of the guns was stationed down close to the river and yesterday morning the order came to move it up the bank farther and clean it. Sergeant Mason was placed in charge of the work and six men assigned to the duty. Four men were behind the gun, dragging the trail, and two men, Michael Joyce and John Berry, pushing at the muzzle almost directly in front of it. When the trail was dropped the crank, by which the gun is fired, is supposed to have been moved by the jolt and to have discharged the gun which, by some fatality, had been left with two charges remaining. The two men, Joyce and Berry, fell, the shot, an eight-ounce one, passing through the right breast of Berry, hitting Joyce, who was standing by his side, just in the rear, in the left breast, just over the heart. Berry lived but about half an hour and Joyce about one hour and a half dying at 11:45 A.M. Post surgeon Bayne attended the sufferers, but could do nothing. Father A. Bokel, of St. Dominic's Church, arrived in time to administer the last consolations of the church to the dying men. Mr. C.E. Joyce, brother of one of the deceased, also arrived in time to see his brother alive. After death the bodies were dressed in the Artillery uniform and placed on ice in the ward of the hospital where they died, and will remain there until they are removed for burial. The deceased will be buried with military honors Monday morning. The joint funeral will take place at 9 o'clock from the Arsenal, and will be attended by Battery B and the band of the Second United States Artillery. Private Joyce, who was about 32 years of age [he was, indeed, 32], entered the United States Army in 1864, serving in the Third Artillery, Ordnance Corps, and to the battery to which he was attached at the time of his death [he had transferred to Breckinridge's Battalion at Fort Foote a few years previously]. He leaves a widow and two children, one an infant and the other about six years old. He was the son of M.R. and Lucy Joyce. His father was well-known in this city and died here in 1864. His brother, Captain Joyce, Eighty-Eighth New York Volunteers, was killed at the Battle of Antietam, September 17, 1862, while gallantly leading his company. His aged mother resides on K Street [she was living with Michael and his family at 2120 K Street northwest], near Twenty-Second [also near the Western Market], and she was completely prostrated yesterday when she heard of her son's terrible fate, he being the fourth of her children who have died suddenly.

The *Post* then says that "Coroner Patterson will hold an inquest at 11 o'clock today."

At the inquest First Sergeant Moore, whose responsibility it had been to clear the Gatling guns of ammunition, tried to throw the blame on some mythical kids who might have come along and slipped cartridges into the weapon while the soldiers weren't looking. The commission of inquiry also found that Joyce and Berry were partly responsible because they stood in the line of fire.

According to Dr. Bayne, the ball entered Michael Joyce where they said it did, in close proximity to the armpit, passed through the body without penetrating the lungs, heart or large vessels in the armpit, and came out the body. Pvt. Joyce died from the shock.

Capt Charles E. Joyce was called, and said:

I believe it to be my duty to defend my dead brother and repel the charges made by one who is really responsible for this and young Berry's death, that they (the dead) or some careless child were to blame for the fatal explosion of the cartridge in the Gatling gun. My attention was attracted to this individual yesterday morning by the desperate manner in which he was endeavoring to accept his theory of cause which led to the shooting. I immediately asked, "Did this man have charge of the gun on Friday?" and was answered "Yes, after Lieutenant Hubbard." I then commenced an investigation on my own account, and for thirty-six hours, with the exception of five hours spent to sleep, I have devoted my time to hearing the statements of every person who had any knowledge on the subject, reading the affidavits of the witnesses before the military court of inquiry, listening to the testimony given before the coroner's jury, and I have come to the conclusion that First Sergeant Moore, of Battery B, Second United States Artillery, is alone responsible for the presence of the charge in the gun. Lieutenant Hubbard, in his testimony before the jury, stated that when he got through firing he ordered Sergeant Moore to see that the gun was freed from all charges and cylinders. This order Sergeant Moore disregarded and convicted himself by his testimony before the coroner's jury [*Washington Post*, September 20, 1880].

When the Joyces moved to 626 East Capitol Street, John H. and his daughter Jennie moved next door, to Number 628, but in the same building.

In early July 1883, in Washington, Molly Burroughs, Charlie Russell's orphaned niece, married Richard Aloysius O'Brien. Richard A. O'Brien was born in May 1859 in Martinsburg, Virginia (the part of Virginia that would become West Virginia in 1863), the son of Irishman Michael O'Brien, a stonecutter, and Mary Kennedy. Richard Aloysius became a plumber, moved to Washington, and became a member of the District National Guard. He and Molly had six children, all born in the area of Capitol Hill known as Swamp Poodle (or, more correctly, Swampoodle), in Washington, D.C. Five of the children survived:

Louise R. O'Brien, born in April 1884. She married C. Ernest Colliflower, and died a widow on June 11, 1964, leaving four children: Mrs. Mary Louise Grimes, Charles Colliflower, Joseph Colliflower, and Mrs. Gertrude Walton.

Gertrude Kennedy O'Brien, born in October 1885, who married J.J. Murray, and had issue.

Ralph B. O'Brien, born in December 1887, who moved to New York.

Howell Vincent O'Brien, born in March 1890. He became a Washington architect, and died, unmarried, on June 3, 1960. He was buried at Arlington on June 7, 1960.

Richard Aloysius O'Brien Jr., born in September 1895. He fought in World War I, and died at the Veterans Administration Hospital in Washington on July 14, 1973, leaving a son, Ralph Vincent O'Brien, of Bethesda. Several of his descendants are alive today.

Young Willie, after returning from college, had some problems for a while, until he straightened out. He was a hard drinker, was Willie, a wild partier, and he packed a gat. But handsome he was not, and everyone knew it.

On July 14, 1883, in downtown Clarksville, just having issued forth from a drinking establishment, Constable Averett's son, Courtland—who, following the style of a Southern gentleman, was known as "Seepee" (from his initials), and who although only seventeen truly was handsome—brought, in a most tactless and forcible manner, Willie's lack of good looks to his attention, as if Willie needed this reminder.

"Hey, Willie. You ugly son of a bitch," he said—or words to that effect.

This was C.P.'s first mistake.

"Smile when you call me that," said the Virginian.

Now came young Courtland's second mistake. He repeated the insult, word for word, joy and amusement failing to light up his countenance to the degree desired by Willie Russell, so Willie hit him.

What followed next is hard to determine, because there was a subsequent cover-up. But Constable Averett happened on the scene at that very moment and tried to break up the melée before something serious happened. At that point the Constable's son, emboldened by booze and by the presence of his blue-clad father, felt sufficiently encouraged to pull his iron and plug Willie in the back. As Willie went down, he snatched his own angel from the back of his trousers, pointed it in the general direction of the offensive Averett, and squeezed the trigger. The missile struck the policeman instead. Willie's injuries were insubstantial, and it would have been almost funny, except that the constable died the following day.

The *Tobacco Plant*, Clarksville's newspaper, relayed this gem to its reading public, "Last Saturday a terrible tragedy was enacted in Clarksville. During an affray between Mr. G.W.R. Averett & Mr. Willie Russell, Mr. Russell was shot from behind by someone. He received a wound that may terminate seriously. Immediately after Mr. Russell was shot, a second shot was fired which struck Mr. Averett & from which he died on Sunday morning."

The *Torchlight*, of Oxford, N.C., reported, "A shooting affray occurred in Clarksville, Va., on Sat., the 14th of July 1883, between Deputy Sheriff G.W. Averett & his son, a young boy, & Wm Russell. Pistols were freely used, G.W. Averett was probably fatally shot in the region of the stomach & Wm Russell received a wound in the back, not considered dangerous. We didn't learn particulars. Later, just before press time, Deputy Sheriff G.W. Averett died Sunday morning, July 15, 1883."

Several other local literary organs produced facsimiles of the already much-discussed sensation. The *Charlotte Gazette* (Charlotte County, Virginia) of July 19, 1883, for example, referred to the incident in the following manner, the haphazard writing of the correspondent indicating the tremendous excitement and stress that he was under as he put his pen to paper, so much so that he couldn't, for the life of him, remember from one sentence to the next the names of the principals involved: "A serious difficulty occurred at Clarksville on Friday last between the son of C.H. Russell and the son of a constable of the place called Averett. The latter shot at Russell, who retaliated, inflicting mortal wounds upon the elder Avery [sic] from which he died the next day. There were a number involved in the affray. George W. Royster Averett died July 15, 1883; he was 61 years, 9 months and 17 days old."

The *New York Times*, in their July 18, 1883, edition, picked up the story (it was too good to miss): "An altercation took place at Clarksville, Mecklenburg County ... last Saturday, between G.W.R. Avereth [sic] and a man named Russell, which resulted in a resort to pistols. Avereth was mortally wounded. Russell was shot in the shoulder and his condition is critical. Avereth is stated to have said something derogatory to the good name of Russell, who went after the former for satisfaction." The *Times* had it quite wrong in detail, but they were rushing to print at the time, and had only the bare bones, little more than rumor.

Anyway, Willie was charged: "Bond of Wm H. Russell, Mecklenburg Co., Va. Wm H. Russell do & shall personally appear before me, John W. Spencer, some other justices of said County on Sat., 21st day of July 1883, in the town of Clarksville at the Hotel. Then & there to answer the Commonwealth concerning a certain felony by him committed, shoot with a pistol with intent to kill one W.G.R. Averett. The said Wm H. Russell stands charged, and shall not depart thence without the leave of the said justices."

Willie was tried on July 21, 1883, but having the services of that great trial lawyer, R.E. Kennon Harris, he was acquitted on August 8, 1883—self defense.

This from the *Richmond Daily Dispatch*: "Wm H. Russell, charged with the murder of G.W.R. Averett, was tried before 3 justices of the peace at Clarkesville [sic] last Thursday. The evidence tended very strongly to show that he acted entirely in self defense & he was unanimously acquitted on Aug. 8, 1883."

The *New York Times* could not, in all faith, leave its eager readers hanging, and reported the sequel to the fracas on September 2: "Acquitted of murder. W.H. Russell, who has been on trial at the August term of the County Court of Mecklenburg County, for the killing of G.W.R. Averett at Clarksville ... in last July, has been acquitted. His trial lasted three days."

The shootout had a profound effect upon the Averetts. To a man they left town, never to return. After all those decades, centuries even (if measured with a certain amount of latitude), the once great family of Clarksville disappeared into the night as the result of the shootout on Main Street. In 1892 the Averetts' property on Main Street (i.e. Virginia Avenue) was sold at auction. The buyers were—C.H. Russell & Son, Wagon Makers.

More specifically, the effect fell heavily upon C.P. Averett himself, which, because he started it all by calling Willie an ugly son of a bitch, had about it a sense of heavenly justice. After the unpleasantness (not to be confused with the Late Unpleasantness), and after C.P., along with his tribe, had vanished from the warm bosom of Clarksville C.P. wandered aimlessly, alone, never marrying, living a life of abject obscurity.

He found employment wherever he could, whenever the urge struck him, but he was a doomed man, condemned to wander like Cain. He would be seen now and again, working in a bank, as an accountant, not too far from home, but far enough. At last his brain snapped—how he held on so long was a wonder—and he wound up as an inmate at the Western State Hospital, in Staunton, Virginia, an institution that until 1894 had been called the Western Lunatic Asylum. Under the not so tender care of the frightening eugenicist and sterilizer Dr. Joseph DeJarnette (first cousin once removed of Daniel Coleman DeJarnette), C.P. withered out the last decades of his miserable life, dying there on September 21, 1937.

The shooting and trial by themselves, of course, had a dramatic effect on the formerly wayward 24-year-old Willie Russell, an epiphany as a matter of fact. He saw the light—a Methodist light, which would illumine his path for the rest of his days. No less important, and in some ways more amazing, was that Willie began to lose his bad looks. By April 30, 1888, he was good-looking enough to be able to take out a marriage license, and two days later, on May 2, to marry Zed Griffin's daughter Kate in Clarksville. (Kate had been born on January 15, 1862, in Clarksville.) The older he got, the better looking did Willie become, so that by the time he was an old man he was very striking. In his natty three-piece white suit and still sporting most of his hair, he might have been a predecessor to Douglas Fairbanks Jr. Strange how things work out.

Willie and Kate had the following children:

Charles Henry Russell II. Born on March 6, 1889, at Clarksville. Died at 9:30 A.M., on September 9, 1970, at South Boston Hospital, Virginia. He married, on June 14, 1919, Ella Louise Watkins.

Carrie Moss Russell. Born on March 13, 1890, at Clarksville. She married, on June 14, 1919, Thomas E. Kirby.

Minnie Price Russell. Born on March 13, 1890, at Clarksville. Died on December 29, 1981, in Pitt County, N.C. She married, on November 12, 1917, R. Sidney Koonce, and had issue.

Sarah "Sallie" Katherine Griffin "Katie" Russell. Born on January 18,

1892, at Clarksville. Died at 5:20 A.M., on June 16, 1949, at Valdosta Hospital. She married, on November 20, 1920, Arthur Lee Davis, and had issue.

John William Russell. Born on December 9, 1893, Clarksville. Died at 6:15 A.M., on March 17, 1972. He married, on March 20, 1917, Frances Gallyon.

William Horace Russell Jr. Born on April 29, 1897, Clarksville. Died on November 26, 1979, at Henderson, N.C. He married, on September 2, 1925, Elizabeth Hunter.

Arthur Davidson Russell. Born on March 12, 1899, in Clarksville. He married, on September 18, 1930, Evelyn Howerton.

Thomas Joseph Russell. Born on February 7, 1904, in Clarksville. Died at 9 A.M., on March 18, 1982. He married, on August 23, 1934, Dorothy Latane, and had issue.

By late August 1883 Captain Joyce was confined to his bed and got worse. By December they didn't know if he would live, but he pulled through, and by Christmas time was active adjutant of Rawlins Post.

Charles Emmet's mother, Lucy, died at 8:15 in the morning of February 16, 1884, at her home, 2120 K Street northwest. She was 66, and had had enough pain; she had seen her husband and more of her children die abruptly and before their time than a mother should. She left a will.

On March 15, 1884, Charles Emmet was presented with a solid gold badge for 16 years' service with Rawlins Post # 1 (*Washington Post*).

In Washington, D.C., Charlie Russell's brother-in-law, Charles W. Brooks Senior, dropped dead at 3:30 in the afternoon of February 17, 1884, at his home, 1105 New Jersey Avenue southeast. The doctor, Bayne—the same Bayne who attended Michael Joyce in his last remaining moments after being hit by a bullet from a Gatling gun—was summoned, but failed to make it in time.

Sally and her progeny moved into 18 Seventh Street southeast, were they would live for several years, often renting out a room to relatives. Charlie Russell's daughter Annie stayed there for a while just after she moved to Washington in the late 1880s, and then Sally's cousin Lydia replaced Annie as Annie moved on to other relatives.

This Lydia Russell living with the Brookses was Lydia Rose Russell, born in 1857 in Maryland, the daughter of John Alexander Russell, himself the son of Charles Lewis Russell, the son of James Russell who died in 1820. In other words, Lydia Rose was Sally's (and Charlie Russell's) first cousin, once removed.

It was the 17th of December, 1884, and Captain Joyce lay dying at his home, 224 East Capitol Street. He was 38. He had obviously suffered from consumption for years, probably as the result of exposure to the elements during the Civil War and in Ireland, not to mention the pieces of clothing floating ominously in his lung. Dr. Frank Donohue of 1134 Eighth Street northwest said he died of phthisis, which he had had for about nine months.

But the captain remained conscious and alert to the end, giving instructions as to how he wanted the funeral to go, naming his pallbearers, and so on. At 1:30 in the early afternoon the Wild Geese flew by and carried him home.

He was buried by undertaker James Bellew at 3:30 P.M. on the following day in lot number r72/328 of the Congressional Cemetery. His pallbearers were a mixture of old Rawlins Post buddies—Irishmen all—and colleagues from the Post Office. There was Mike Urell—Major Michael Emmet Urell—a clerk in the surgeon general's office, but before that a Medal of Honor winner and later a general in the U.S. Army; there was Dennis O'Connor, a stonecutter; John Keogh, a clerk in the adjutant general's office; and Napoleon Fithian, who had been a drummer boy in a New Jersey regiment during the Civil War. From the Post Office Hanson Weaver, old Colonel Stanley T. Trott, Joe Porter, and G.M. Severing helped the Irishmen bear Captain Joyce to his last resting place where members from all the Washington G.A.R. posts came to pay their final respects. Post Commander Dennis O'Connor made the speech for the G.A.R.

His tombstone reads: "In memory of Charles E. Joyce, 1846—1884, 1st Lieut. 88th N.Y. Vol. May he rest in peace. Alice R., his wife, 1848—1930; daughter Alice O. Joyce, 1870—1939."

James H. Harbin married again, on December 23, 1884, in Washington, D.C., to Sallie Cochran, a girl almost twenty years younger than him, and moved to Philadelphia. His son James S. Harbin and his wife moved into 712 Eye Street southeast.

On December 29, 1884, six days after his father's marriage, John Henry Harbin, the river boat captain, married Mary Ann Skinner, at the Metro Presbyterian Church in Washington. He would leave the river boats and, following a long family tradition, would settle down as a machinist at the Navy Yard. He and Mary Ann moved to 715 Virginia Avenue southeast, and would have five children, including the notorious James Wilbur Harbin. They would all later move to 1328 Eleventh Street.

On January 14, 1885, widow Alice R. Joyce, of 224 East Capitol Street, filed for an Army pension in Washington, D.C. By that stage she was closely associated with St. Stephen's Church.

Captain Joyce and Alice had two daughters—Alice in 1871 and Isabella (known as Daisy) in December 1873. After Captain Joyce's death Alice and the two girls continued to live on Capitol Street, but in the 1890s they moved to Number 623 and then to Number 626. Alice's father, old John H. Russell, now ailing and an invalid, along with his teacher daughter Jennie, who never married, moved from their house at 518 Sixth Street to 628 East Capitol Street, next door to Alice. Finally, in August 1888, they moved in with her, while Congressman John J. O'Neill of Missouri moved into 628. Years later Alice and her sister Jennie and her daughter Alice would all move back into Number 628.

Margaret Rebecca Russell, William Ignatius's widow, died of rheumatic arthritis, aged 61 years 11 months and 9 days, on May 19, 1885, at her home, 916½ Eighth Street southeast, Washington, D.C. She was buried at 4 P.M. on May 21, 1885, in lot r8/238 of the Congressional Cemetery, but not with her late husband William Ignatius. Edward M. Boteler was the undertaker.

Julia and Agnes, now left alone in the world, moved to 444 Q Street northwest, still seamstressing. Julia was the first to submit to the temptations of a promised better life, dying at 11:30 A.M. on December 19, 1893, at her home; she was buried at the Congressional Cemetery, on December 21, at 2:30 P.M., in lot r136/227.

Agnes couldn't last much longer, and didn't. She breathed her last at precisely 2 o'clock in the morning of Sunday, December 8, 1895, and was laid to rest at the Congressional Cemetery at 3 P.M., on December 10, in lot r8/238, with her mother. One of Mrs. Jane Stant's daughters would be buried in the same grave in 1918.

James H. Harbin's son Daniel W., now an engineer, sometimes in the notions business, other times a machinist's helper, married Elizabeth Gaskin in 1888, and they moved to 1831 Sixth Street northwest, and in 1890 to 1314 Eleventh Street southeast. By the turn of the century they were at 915 Eighth Street and only a little later at 1109 N Street southeast. This marriage, their peripatetic wanderings and the lives of both parties, would all end in great tragedy at N Street. What led up to the awful denouement was also far from happy.

But, in the meantime, the father, James H. Harbin, came back to D.C. from Philadelphia, to spend his last days with his son James S. at 712 Eye Street, and died on Monday, November 13, 1893, at 9:40 P.M., aged 71. The death notices told Philadelphia papers to cover the story. The funeral was from his home, 712 Eye Street southeast, on Thursday, at 2 P.M.

James S. Harbin and Midie and their daughter Lelia moved into a new house at 505 L Street, between First and Second streets.

By 1900 Lula Steiner, James H. Harbin's daughter and Charlie Russell's step-niece, was back in town, at 22 Jackson Street, a widow, with no occupation, lodging with Tennesseean Winfield A. Bunn and his family. In 1910 she was living alone, a widow, dressmaking. She died on October 28, 1911, and is buried in the Congressional Cemetery in Washington, D.C., with her parents. We haven't got a clue what happened to Mr. Steiner, but one senses something dreadful.

Charlie's daughters were very pretty. The elder one, Annie, left Clarksville for Washington in the 1880s. She stayed first with her aunt Sarah Brooks at 18 Seventh Street southeast, and became one of the first women typists in the capital. She ran classified ads in the papers to get typing students.

In 1890 she moved to her uncle John H. Russell's place on Capitol Street. Her place in the spare room at Sally Brooks's place was taken by Lydia Russell, her second cousin.

On September 10, 1891, at St. Joseph's Church, Washington, D.C., Annie married William J. McGee, a clerk at the General Land Office.

William James McGee had been born in Marshall, Michigan, on April 12, 1862, the son of Edward McGee and Isabella Hogan. Edward McGee's parents had come over from County Monaghan, in Ireland, in 1825, to New York City, then on to Rochester; then in 1855 Edward and his wife moved to Marshall, Michigan. Edward McGee did well, becoming mayor of Marshall on April 1, 1878. He had nine children. William James was one of them.

William J. McGee moved to D.C. and became an active member of the Democratic Party and president of the Michigan Society. He and Annie lived at 636 C Street, Washington, D.C., and later, for a much longer time, at 1810 Lamont Street. They had the following children:

Charles Russell McGee. Born September 12, 1892, D.C. Married December 24, 1940, D.C., Florence Richardson, daughter of Frank W. Richardson. No issue.

William James McGee Jr. Born September 18, 1893, D.C. Died October 21, 1906, D.C. Buried in the Congressional Cemetery in D.C., where his parents would be buried.

Isabel Jarboe McGee. Born February 28, 1895, D.C. Died April 10, 1979, unmarried.

Mildred Jarboe McGee. Born July 13, 1898, D.C. Died April 13, 1982, D.C. Married February 8, 1921, D.C., Leonard Marbury. They had issue.

The *Washington Post* of September 8, 1890, trumpeted "Officer Harbin Dead," and went on to say:

> For years he has been a familiar figure in the Police Court. Officer Philip W. Harbin, one of the oldest and best-known policemen on the Force, died suddenly at his home, at No. 724 Seventh Street southeast, about 5 o'clock yesterday afternoon, from heart failure. Mr. Harbin was in his sixty-fifth year, and has been connected with the police department all his life. For the past twenty-five years he had been stationed at the Police Court. His duties were always faithfully and efficiently performed [part of his job was to convey prisoners from the Court to the jail], and by his death the police force loses one of the best of the veterans, who are now slowly passing away. Mr. Harbin went to the Police Court yesterday

morning, but was soon obliged to give up, and was removed to his home. Many expressions of sincere sorrow on the part of his colleagues were received by his family during last night.

People told stories about Phil all day, such as the one in which, a few years back, on July 23, 1887, some prisoners at the Police Court attempted to play a trick on him. One of them asked for water and it was brought him in a whisky bottle. Officer Harbin inspected it and, finding it all right, passed it on to the prisoner. Then another prisoner became thirsty and the same bottle was sent out by the same friend, but this time it was returned filled with whisky. Officer Harbin, however, suspected the scheme. Instead of allowing the bottle to be passed in without question, as had been expected, he examined it and discovered the fraud (*Washington Post*, July 24, 1887).

Officer Madigan replaced Phil as the policeman detailed to take charge of the prisoners at the Police Court. He reported for duty early on the morning after Harbin died (*Washington Post*, September 9, 1890).

The *Post* of September 10, 1890, said:

> Funeral of Policeman Harbin. Philip W. Harbin, the veteran policeman, who died suddenly on Sunday afternoon from heart failure, was buried yesterday afternoon from his late home, No. 707 E Street, southeast [this address is an error]. The funeral procession left the house at 5:20 o'clock and the interment took place at the Congressional Cemetery. Quite a large number of the dead man's friends on the police force attended the funeral. The floral offerings were simple and appropriate. As Mr. Harbin was an active Odd Fellow, Union Lodge, Maganeau Encampment, and the Grand Encampment, attended the funeral."

It is not absolutely clear what rank Phil attained in the Police Force. He is usually referred to as "Officer Harbin" or "Policeman Harbin." The *Washington Post* of September 27, 1890, tells us that his replacement in the Metro Police was J.E. Gordon, and that the rank was Private Class 2. That would seem right, despite the occasional reference to him as "Sergeant Harbin," and despite the *Post* of September 22, 1889, saying "Captain P.W. Harbin is now anxious to meet with every Odd Fellow he is acquainted with." It may be that Phil suffered promotions and demotions because of his emotions. He was known to beat up the occasional prisoner, especially such an egregious fellow as Jackson, the cop killer. *Washington Post*, October 10, 1884: "A warrant charging Officer P.W. Harbin of the Police Court with assaulting Jackson, the alleged police capper was served on that officer yesterday by Lt. Boteler of the Eighth Precinct. Judge Snell took Harbin's personal bond for his appearance for trial."

On the whole, it does not look as if Phil ever achieved rank beyond ordinary cop. A couple of weeks after his death, his widow, Sarah, was granted a pension of $20 a month by a grateful Metro Police Department.

Sarah and the children would continue to live on at 724 Seventh Street until she died on February 19, 1905. She was buried in the Congressional Cemetery, in Washington, with her husband. Sarah left a will, proved in Washington, D.C. in 1906.

The Harbin children, Samuel P. and Mary Isabelle, continued on at the Seventh Street house for years, Samuel working as a carpenter and Mary Isabelle as a stenographer. They would take in lodgers, the most interesting being Valentina (Bobbie) Poppescu, a Rumanian telegraph operator who, when she wasn't telegraphing, was playing volleyball at the Capitol Athletic Club. Bobbie Poppescu, born on October 22, 1895, stuck around D.C. for decades, never married, and wound up working in the Patent Office, and always playing volleyball. She died in January 1982.

Samuel P. Harbin died on October 16, 1923, in Washington, D.C. His sister, Mary Isabelle, died unmarried on July 27, 1939, aged 87, at home, and was buried with her parents at the Congressional Cemetery in Washington. Officer Philip W. Harbin's line died there.

In 1893 Richard Aloysius O'Brien became the assistant plumbing inspector for the District of Columbia. In 1900 he was promoted to inspector, a position he held until his death sixteen years later. He was also very busy on the military front, working his way up through the officer ranks until he made colonel. He fought in the Spanish—American War with General Michael Emmet Urell.

In 1893, in Clarksville, pretty much everything on Virginia Avenue, from Fourth Street to the river, was wiped out by a huge fire, and Charlie Russell built a new four-story factory on Virginia Avenue, near where the Clarksville Furniture Company is located today. The Russell wagons became famous throughout the East, and the business waxed mighty. In its heyday the company was producing between 3,000 and 4,000 wagons a year.

A big display ad in the *Clarksville Clipper* around this time (January 10, 1889), complete with the picture of a wagon, says: "C.H. Russell and Son, manufacturers of farm and road wagons. At prices which defy competition. Nothing but first class jobs in every respect turned out. Write for prices. Clarksville, Va."

The *Clarksville News* had an even bigger ad, with three wagon pictures (example, November 7, 1890): "C.H. Russell and Son, Clarksville, Va. Manufacturers of square box farm wagons and railroad carts. Situated in the heart of the finest hickory and oak timbered lands in the South, employing skilled labor, and a thorough knowledge of the business, enable us to offer better goods for less than any manufacturer in the world. One-horse thimble skein wagons our specialty for the trade. We are prepared to shade any prices quoted by manufacturers of first-class goods. All we ask is a trial."

In 1899 Charlie Russell's nephew, Charles W. Brooks Jr., a clerk in the

Pensions Office, and a private in the re-formed National Rifles, married Kate Costello, the daughter of wealthy but insane saloon keeper Jeremiah Costello of 624 Sixth Street. Kate's mother, Catherine, who had already been granted custody of her husband in 1894, had died in 1896, worn out with the strain of Jeremiah. Now Jeremiah's children were looking after him, and Charles W. joined the throng.

Charles W.'s brother, Russell Brooks, the plumber, unable to settle down and marry, took to the road, as an intinerant fixer of toilets and a peripatetic unblocker of drains, working in shops wherever he could, from Texarkana, Arkansas, to Lakota City, South Dakota. He died in the 1920s.

In Clarksville, the Russells needed more space, and in 1901 bought a tract of 19.3 acres from Walter D. Blanks and built a huge factory on Musk Island (not really an island), located behind what is today's Clarksville Crossing Shopping Center.

Down in Clarksville they still talk about the mystery lady, the one who, with some regularity, would come to visit Charlie Russell around the turn of the century. A Russell she was, they said, and she would stay on Virginia Avenue (i.e. Main Street), a few short blocks down from Charlie's house. But there never was a mystery, not really. It was only Charlie's sister, Sally Brooks. In those days Sally was spending most of her time living with her other brother John H. Russell in Washington, D.C., and now, as her life drew to a close, she was using more and more of it to visit her only other remaining sibling—Charlie.

Sally Brooks died on July 12, 1902, in her 74th year. All the papers agree on that. However, one paper says she died at her home, 1309 South Carolina Avenue southeast, and another says at the home of her sister, Alice R. Joyce, at 623 East Capitol Street. Either way, she was buried on July 15, 1902, at the Congressional Cemetery, in Washington, D.C., in Lot r16/177.

Charlie Russell's nephew, Charles W. Brooks Jr., died at his home, 416 Second Street northwest, on July 5, 1904, after an illness of two days. His funeral was on January 7, from St. Patrick's Church, and he was buried in the Congressional Cemetery. His widow, Kate, would marry again, to Ray Baker, but she herself died not long afterwards, on September 17, 1914, at her new home, 1411 N Street northwest.

In April 1905 the pox hit Daniel Harbin's family. At first they thought it was chicken pox, when Mamie, the eldest daughter, then 16, came down with it on April 14. The authorities came around to their home, at 1109 N Street southeast, in early May and whisked Mamie and five of the other children off to the smallpox hospital. The parents and the infant, Vergie, were sent to the detention camp where they were heavily quarantined. Mamie had, in fact, been vaccinated, but she was the only one of the children who had been, and the authorities were baffled as to how she could have contracted it. Anyway they all pulled through (*Washington Post*, May 4, 1905).

Charlie Russell's brother, John H., died at home at 10:20 in the morning of July 25, 1905, after an asthmatic fit. He had acute enteritis anyway. His death certificate says he was 90, but he was almost certainly only 88. The funeral was held at St. Joseph's Catholic Church in Washington, at 9 o'clock in the morning of July 27, 1905, the Reverend George B. Harrington of Buckeystown, Maryland, officiating. The Reverend Ignatius Fealy, assistant pastor at the church, said the requiem mass, and the funeral sermon was preached by the Reverend James A. Smyth. John H. was carried to the Congressional Cemetery by pallbearers Alex McKenzie, Charles S. Price, James Hutchinson and John J. Higgins.

Pallbearer Alexander McKenzie was the assistant tax assessor for the District of Columbia. In the 1870s he had been married to Nannie Harbin, the daughter of John H. Russell's stepbrother Officer Phil Harbin.

The *Washington Post* headline of June 14, 1909, yelled, "Killed by Suitor. Mother of seven children falls before bullet. Slayer commits suicide. Jealousy aroused by woman's intention to return to husband. Mrs. Elizabeth Harbin, 41 years old, found dead by the side of Frederick Kramer, aged 23, by her 15-year-old son. Kramer and Harbin business partners until three months ago. Latter left wife then."

Young man, older woman, classic story. The *Post* continues:

On the eve of a reconciliation with her husband, from whom she had been estranged for about three months, Mrs. Elizabeth Harbin, wife of Daniel Harbin, and mother of seven children, was shot and instantly killed last night by Frederick Kramer, who, after firing the fatal shots, turned the revolver on himself and sent a bullet into his brain.

The man and woman were found lying across a bed in the latter's home, 1109 N Street southeast, locked in each other's arms. Mrs. Harbin was shot through the heart, and in the right breast, and the bullet Kramer fired into his own brain crashed through the skull and emerged just below the left ear. The revolver was found on the bed.

The shooting occurred during the absence of Mrs. Harbin's children, and the shots were heard only by Thomas J. Welsh [the *Evening Star* calls him John J. Welsh], who occupied a room on the second floor of the house. The man did not investigate, and when the woman's 15-year-old son Eugene entered the bedroom he found his mother dead, and Kramer in the last throes of death. The latter attempted to speak but died before he could do so.

The shooting is said to have resulted because of jealousy on the part of Kramer, who is said by the police to have been enamored of the woman. When he learned that Mrs. Harbin was about to effect a reconciliation with her husband and that they were to meet today for the first time in three months, he called at the woman's home and told her that he meant to kill her and then himself.

Mrs. Harbin laughed at the threat. On Tuesday Kramer is said to have again threatened the woman and admonished her not to effect a reconciliation with her husband. Mrs. Harbin told him she was tired of the separation, and that she had decided to return to her husband. Kramer left the house in anger, and that night he returned and, it is said, flourished a revolver, at the same declaring that he would kill Mrs. Harbin if she persisted in carrying out her intentions.

About five o'clock yesterday afternoon Mrs. Harbin went to the home of her married daughter, Mrs. Mamie Greggs [should be Griggs], 1333½ Eleventh Street southeast. As she passed out of her house, Kramer, who was regarded almost as a member of the family, entered. He spoke to the woman as she passed, and asked when she would return, saying he would wait for her.

Mrs. Harbin returned from her daughter's about an hour later, and when she entered the house Kramer was sitting in the dining room, reading. The woman then went into the bedroom, was followed by Kramer, and a few minutes later the fatal shots were fired. Coroner Nevitt last night viewed the bodies and gave permission for their removal to undertaking establishments.

About three years ago Mr. Harbin and Kramer entered into a partnership in a wood and coal business, and three months ago the partnership was dissolved. Harbin paid no attention to the frequency of Kramer's visits to his house until then, when he suddenly notified his wife that he would be obtaining lodging elsewhere, but would see that the children were provided for.

Harbin is employed as a machinist at the Washington Navy Yard, and each week he would send a certain sum to his wife for the maintenance of herself and children. Several days ago he called at the house and when he left he told his friends he probably would return to his wife. The news reached Kramer and he went to Mrs. Harbin and demanded an explanation. The woman explained that she was tired of the estrangement and that she meant to adjust their differences.

The revolver with which the shooting was done belonged to Wilmer Harbin, who lent it to Kramer last summer. Kramer carried the weapon with him always, and is said to have threatened to use it on Mrs. Harbin several times. His relatives have taken charge of the body.

Before her marriage Mrs. Harbin was Miss Elizabeth Mammel, of this city, and was regarded as one of the most beautiful women in Southeast Washington. Mrs. Harbin was 41 and Mr. Kramer 23 years old.

The *Evening Star* of January 14, 1909, fills in some holes in the story, such as the fact that immediately prior to the killing Daniel Harbin came to visit his wife at about 3:30 that afternoon. They talked for about half an hour, and they agreed to get back together. Then he left for work at the Navy Yard. Just after that Fred Kramer appeared on the scene.

The *Star* elaborates on the immediate post-murder scene: "Within a few minutes two of the children, Eugene and Ethel, entered the house. Going to their mother's room they found her and Kramer dead, lying across the bed."

This paper carries on:

Eugene pushed his little sister from the room and closed the door. He ran from the house crying. Policeman Wood of the Fifth Precinct learned from him what the boy knew. He called an ambulance and then went to the house. Dr. Moffitt arrived with the ambulance of the Casualty Hospital. The man and woman were already dead.

Mr. Harbin was at work at the Navy Yard when a friend told him of the shooting. He returned to his home to find his wife, whom he had left but a few hours before, cold in death. The weapon, a five-chamber, .32 caliber revolver was found near the bodies. Three discharged shells were in its chambers.

By the time all this happened, Daniel's brother James Samuel and his wife Midie were living at 155 E Street southeast; his other brother, John Henry, and his wife, Mary Ann, were at 747 Eleventh Street southeast; and John Henry's son, James Wilbur, now 24, and married to Susie King, was living at 1427 Potomac Avenue, and also working as a machinist at the Navy Yard.

Daniel W. Harbin didn't last long after his wife's murder. He passed away in Washington, at the Garfield Hospital Annex, of congestive heart failure, aged 47. His occupation was described as "helper." He was buried, in the same burial site as his late wife, at the Congressional Cemetery in Washington, on October 7, 1911. Thomas R. Nalley was the funeral director.

Daniel's daughter Vergie (short for Virginia) died, aged 8, on August 7, 1913. The rest of the children—Mamie, Harry Wilmer ("Skinny"), George, Gene, Ethel and William would lead, if not normal, then relatively news-free lives.

Daisy Isabella Joyce, or Daisy Isabel Joyce as she later called herself, was educated at Notre Dame Convent, in Baltimore, and as a young woman was a soprano, chorus girl, musician, organist and choir director at St. Joseph's Catholic Church; she was even invited to the White House on many occasions. Her organ recitals were part of the annual Christmas services at the Old Convent of the Visitation, at Connecticut Avenue and De Sales Street. She would later become the music and drama critic for the *Washington Times*.

In her twenties she wrote poems regularly for the *Washington Post* and other papers. There are too many to reproduce here, but three—shown in Appendix B—will suffice to show the remarkable style of this truly remarkable lady.

While working as a reporter in Washington, Daisy Joyce met a man who had just come to town from Iowa.

In Illinois, in the village of Lowell, in La Salle County, in the township of Vermillion, lived a farmer named John B. Elliott and his second wife, a Canadian named Minerva. It was a big family, what with John B.'s children by his first wife, Elizabeth, and Minerva's Calwell offspring by her previous husband. One of the children they had together was John S Elliott, born on March 9, 1876. (The S didn't stand for anything.) In the 1890s John S Elliott, now styling himself Jackson (Jack) S Elliott, largely self-educated, left Illinois for Iowa, to stay with his cousins. There, in 1894, he landed a job as a reporter with the *Sioux City Journal*. He would continued at various Iowa journals for eight years until he made the move to Washington. From 1902 to 1903 he was with the *Washington Times*, and then made the move to the Associated Press. He would soon meet Daisy Joyce.

On August 18, 1909, in Philadelphia, they were married by the Reverend Father Cavanaugh, chancellor of the cathedral there. Then they went off on a honeymoon tour of the South. When they returned to the capital they moved to the Granada, an apartment block on Tea Street, in Washington, D.C.

While living at the Granada Jackson S Elliott and Daisy Joyce had a couple of children, the elder of whom, Louise, died as an infant. Jack Jr. lived.

Jack Sr. was chief of staff of the Washington office of the Associated Press from 1911 to 1912, and superintendent of the Eastern Division 1912–15. Then they moved to New York, to 967 East 18th Street, Brooklyn, as Jack's AP career took off, and Daisy Joyce (as she was known professionally) wrote articles for the *New York Herald*. Their third child, Joyce, was born there, in 1914.

In June 1915 Elliott was back in D.C. as director of the Washington Bureau, but he became chief of the news department in New York in 1918; general superintendent in 1920; and assistant general manager of the Associated Press in April 1921.

Joyce, the daughter of Jackson S Elliott and Daisy Joyce, would marry Jules Andrew Morris and, after years living in Wilmington, Delaware, and in Key West, Jules died in 1968 and Joyce moved out to San Diego to be with her brother, Jack Jr. Joyce died in San Diego in 1982.

Jack Jr. went to the University of Pennsylvania, then went into the same business as his father. In 1939 he married Anne Mudgett in New York. He died in 1988, in San Diego. Anna died in 1981.

Curiously, in 1920, at the Granada, lived Lydia Russell, unmarried daughter of John Alexander Russell of Maryland, and cousin of Charlie Russell. Lydia would die in 1928.

On August 23, 1911, Jennie Russell, Daisy's unmarried aunt and Charlie Russell's niece, died of "melancholia" at Laurel, Maryland, and thus the trio of Alice Russell Joyce—Alice O'Connell Joyce—Jennie Russell was broken. Jennie, who, like her step-grandmother Janette, had converted to Episcopalianism, was buried at the Congressional Cemetery in Washington, D.C. The two remaining Joyce ladies rented an apartment in a block at 1811 Wyoming Avenue.

Rather curiously, the sanitarium at Laurel, where Jennie died, was an outgrowth of the Keeley Institute founded by James T. Harbin (the spy's son) twenty years before. Located in midtown Laurel, on the corner of Contee Road and what later became US Route 1, the Keeley Institute had flourished and expanded, so that by 1911 it had become merely the Keeley Building in what was now a large complex called the Laurel Sanitarium. In the 1960s they burned it to the ground to make way for a shopping complex.

Colonel Richard Aloysius O'Brien, the husband of Charlie Russell's niece little orphan Molly, died on April 1, 1916, at 108 Carroll Street southeast, the home of his daughter Mrs. Colliflower. He was 56. The funeral was held at St. Peter's Catholic Church in Washington, D.C., on April 4, 1916, and he was buried at Arlington.

Molly, who had suffered from a softening of the brain for the last three and a half years, died of an embolism on April 26, 1919, at 8:45 P.M., at 157 Randolph Place northwest, the home of her daughter, Mrs. James J. Murray, where Molly had moved after her husband died. Her death certificate says she was 59 years 8 months and 16 days, but she was, in fact, 60. The funeral was at St. Martin's Church, where requiem mass was sung at 9 A.M., and then she was buried at Arlington, with her husband.

C.H. Russell Sr., wagon manufacturer, died of "organic heart" at 4:00 A.M., on December 14, 1919, in Clarksville. His death certificate says he was 86 years 9 months and 24 days, but that would put him born on February 18, 1833. He was actually born on February 22, 1833, which is the date given on the death certificate. The doctor had been attending him since November 1, and last saw him on the day of death. The death certificate also says he was born in Charles County, Maryland, and that his father was William Russell, born in Maryland, and his mother was Mary Cohill [sic], also born in Maryland (Alice, his daughter, was the informant).

Charlie was buried in Oakhurst Cemetery, near Clarksville, with his first wife, Mary Ann. On his grave are the letters "C.S.A." This does mean Confederate States of America, but it also means Confederate States Army. We will never know now which of the two he meant it to signify, but it was a radical thing to put on one's tombstone in 1919, just after the boys had got home from the First World War. He died a fighting Rebel, did Charlie.

His will, drawn up on February 10, 1915, was proved on January 19, 1920. For this will, in toto, see Appendix B.

Charlie's second wife, Jennie, died on November 27, 1920, also in Clarksville, and was buried with him. After her death Alice left Clarksville to live in Washington, D.C., with her sister, Annie McGee. The two girls brought a lawsuit against their brother, Willie, but he died at 11 o'clock in the morning of October 9, 1926, very definitely settling out of court. Some of his descendants are alive today.

Charlie's house on Virginia Avenue was later sold to another Catholic, Peter Cooper. Incidentally, there was no Catholic Church in Clarksville until the 1940s.

John Wesley Stant died on March 23, 1921, in Washington, D.C., and was buried in the Congressional Cemetery. Janie, his widow and the last remaining daughter of William Ignatius Russell, died on September 25, 1928, in Washington, D.C., and was buried in the same place.

The notorious James Wilbur Harbin, son of John Henry Harbin and grandson of James H. Harbin, was in trouble in 1924. *The Washington Post* headline of October 25 of that year screamed: "Spouse struck her, wife says, in filing action for divorce. Navy Yard machinist slashed her wrist, Mrs. Harbin also contends." The article went on to identify James W. Harbin— who besides his work at the Yard was also said to be a chiropractor"—as the man charged with this abuse. The wife, "Susie" (the former Susan Eugene King), whom James Wilbur had married on April 10, 1905, also charged her spouse with the receipt of "letters and post cards from other women." The paper noted that the couple had one child; that would be James Wilbur, Jr., born May 17, 1908.

James Samuel Harbin, son of Charlie Russell's step-brother James H. Harbin, died on July 4, 1928, at 155 E Street southeast, aged 74, his wife, Midie, having predeceased him on February 13, 1922. Lelia, their daughter, died October 31, 1971, in Washington, D.C., unmarried.

After being sick for some time, Alice, Captain Joyce's widow, died of a heart attack on November 7, 1930, at her home, 1627 Lamont Street, Washington, D.C., and was buried on November 10. She was 82.

On March 14, 1934, Daisy Elliott died at their home, 967 East Eighteenth Street, Brooklyn. Four years later Jackson S retired from AP, moving out to Palm Springs, California, where he married again, in 1940, to sculptress Frances Savage. A Congregationalist by religion, Jack died on March 10, 1942, and most of what he had—heirlooms, family bibles, documents—went to Savage Frances who, rumor has it, burned them.

Captain Charles Emmet Joyce's elder daughter, Alice O. Joyce, then of 3348 16th Street northwest, died at Providence hospital on January 30, 1939, aged 67. She had worked all her life as a clerk in the Capitol. Her estate was administered by one Florence Brennan.

On August 14, 1939, John Henry Harbin, the former riverboat skipper, and son of Charlie Russell's stepbrother James H. Harbin, died at his home in Piney Point, Maryland. He was buried at 2:30 the following afternoon, at the Congressional Cemetery, Washington, D.C. His wife, Mary Ann, had died on September 10, 1919, at 1140 North Capitol Street, aged 55. His fellow masons didn't turn out in force. John Henry, a mason since 1916, had been expelled from the Grand Lodge on September 30, 1927, for nonpayment of dues. His son James W. followed him into the masonic order.

Alice Russell, Charlie's spinster daughter, died on February 28, 1946, in Clarksville, and her sister, Annie McGee, on September 18, 1948.

The *Washington Post* of September 19, 1948, reported: Mrs. McGee Dies. Former Clubwoman. Mrs. William J. McGee, 88, wife of the retired Chief of the Mineral Division of the Interior Department, died yesterday at her home, 1810 Lamont Street, NW. She had been bedridden for the past three years. "The obituary described a long life in social and charitable organizations, including the Herbert Chapter of the United Daughters of the Confederacy, and mentioned that in her job as a typist in the Pension Office ca. 1890, she "used one of the first typewriters in Washington." Surviving her were her husband; son Charles; two daughters, Isabel and Mrs. Leonard Marbury; and two granddaughters.

Kate, Willie's widow, also died in 1948, at 6:30 in the evening of Friday, October 11, in Clarksville.

William J. McGee, Annie's husband, died at Georgetown Hospital on April 26, 1952, and is buried in the Congressional Cemetery with his wife and son William Jr. Some of Annie's descendants are alive today, including Mike Herring.

II

The Life and Family of Tom Harbin

Tom Harbin

The Harbins were a long-standing Catholic family in Bryantown, the principal village in upper Trinity Parish, Charles County, Maryland. They were also quite a considerable presence in Piscataway, one of the more populated communities in neighboring PG (Prince George's County). Long-standing and quite considerable but not of any real consequence—not until Tom came along.

The Harbins originated in England. William Harbin and his wife Jane were already ensconced in the village of Charminster, Dorset, across the River Cerne from the more populous and famous Dorchester, in the late 1500s when a peculiar royal order came down to all the churches in the land: records of baptisms, marriages and burials—of everyone—were henceforth to be made and kept, and copies were to be sent to the bishop. This meant that, for the first time, the lives of ordinary folk were to be somewhat documented. It was the beginning of the paper trail.

William and Jane Harbin's son, Erasmus, married Ann Knight on January 15, 1611, and they begat Henry Harbin, who was baptized at Charminster on November 25, 1614. Henry married Joanne and begat William, baptized in the Charminster font at St. Mary's Church on March 30, 1634. It was Francis Harbin son of William, by Sarah Smart—baptized the day after Christmas of 1670—who left the Dorset countryside forever, going to sea as a young fellow. By the age of 25 he was commander and part proprietor of the *Owners' Adventure*, a ship plying the Atlantic. Captain Francis put down roots in Maryland, married, and had, among others, William Harbin.

William started the plantation called "Gleanings," in Prince George's County, and was the progenitor of all the Harbins in Maryland. He died on March 25, 1733, after having begotten several by his first wife and three by Mary Villers, his second; one of the latter three was Edward Villers Harbin, born in PG in 1731. By his wife, Lydia, Edward V. had several children, one of them being Rezin (pronounced "Reason") Harbin, born in PG on August 27, 1757. This Rezin would later be known as Rezin Harbin Sr. He married Mary McNea in PG on November 14, 1778, and had several children, including Rezin Jr. and John Walter (known as Walter) Harbin.

Walter Harbin was born on February 16, 1785, in Bryantown. Like his brother, Rezin Jr., Walter fought in the War of 1812, as a private under Colonel Hawkins—the 1st Regiment of the Maryland Militia. Several of Walter's Harbin relatives would also fight under Hawkins—Roswell, Horace and Samuel P. among them.

During the mass migration out of Maryland after the Revolutionary War, old Edward Villers and his son Rezin Sr. went south, where Rezin Sr. died in South Carolina in 1790, and his father, Edward V., died in Rowan County, North Carolina, in 1815. Walter Harbin stayed in Maryland. On

II. The Life and Family of Tom Harbin

February 6, 1816, at the Catholic Church at Mattawoman in the Charles County village of that name, he married Catherine Langley, who had been born in Charles County on December 4, 1796. One hears it said that Walter was a hotel keeper in Charles County, and that may be. Whether that is true or not, Walter inherited a lot of land from his father, Rezin Harbin Sr.—488 acres in all—and owned at least two plantations in Charles County, near Bryantown—"Three Brothers," in Newport, about nine miles from Bryantown and very close to the village of Allens Fresh, and "Dement's Enlargement," at Centreville, halfway between Bryantown and "Three Brothers."

In the 1700s and 1800s many of the Southern plantations had pretty fancy names, some verging on the bizarre. Dement's Enlargement and Three Brothers were two of the more conservative ones. Three Brothers had at one time been owned by, among several others, Richard Lee and his son Richard Lee Jr., cousins of Robert E. Lee. Walter lived at Dement's Enlargement, which had once been a huge estate started and owned by Walter Dement, and then, over the years, it had been fragmented and sold off, Walter and his family now living on their section. Walter owned a lot of slaves.

Walter and Catherine Harbin had ten children in Charles County, baptized at the Catholic churches of Upper Zachia (which would later be replaced by St. Mary's Church, in the upper part of Trinity Parish) and also at Mattawoman.

Joseph B. Harbin was Tom's eldest brother, born on October 20, 1817, and baptized at Upper Zachia on December 1 of that year. His godmother was Julie Ann Langley. Joseph it was who would make the first family forays into the dry goods business. He had the goods, but couldn't deliver.

After Joseph came Jane, Tom's eldest sister. She was born on July 2, 1819, and baptized on August 4 of that year at Upper Zachia. Her godmother was Mary Langley. Jane would marry notorious Confederate spy Thomas Austin Jones, and would thus enter the history books as a footnote to a footnote.

Julia Ann was the next child, born on June 5, 1821, and baptized on June 21 at Upper Zachia. Elizabeth Langley was her godmother. In 1837 Julia (as she was known) would be godmother to James Augustine Langley in Charles County. Julia would eventually become the leader of the family, and die unmarried.

These first three children were all confirmed together in 1835, at Upper Zachia.

John Walter Harbin Jr. was next, baptized on December 7, 1823, at Mattawoman. Elizabeth Langley was his godmother. John never amounted to much, and never married.

Johanna, the next child, was born on December 7, 1825, and baptized on March 6, 1826, at Mattawoman. She married John H. Howell, and would live until 1909.

Then came James Alexander Harbin, baptized on May 16, 1829, at Mattawoman. He was mentally disabled, and died in his early 20s.

Catherine Cecilia Ann Harbin was next, baptized at Upper Zachia on December 10, 1831. Catherine's multiplicity of names has led some researchers to believe that there were two girls—Catherine and Cecilia—but there was only one. Catherine would die in 1868, unmarried.

The notorious Thomas Henry Harbin was next, born in Bryantown on August 25, 1833, and baptized on November 2, 1833, at Upper Zachia. He would amount to something. He had the goods, and he delivered.

Sarah Priscilla was the youngest daughter, baptized on June 19, 1837, at Mattawoman. She never married, and worked most of her life in her brother George's dry goods store in Washington, D.C. She died in 1905.

Finally, the tenth and last child, George Francis Harbin was born on February 29, 1840, and baptized at Mattawoman on May 7, 1840. George would do time in the Old Capitol Prison; he would also make a fortune in the dry goods racket. Although he never married, this youngest of the sons was the one who became the patriarch, the pillar of stability—a pillar that was only to crumble in the last years of his life.

Those are the ten children of Walter and Catherine Harbin.

By the time of the 1840 census Joseph B., the eldest, had already left home; he is not named in that census, only heads of household. He was probably lodging with someone in Charles County, perhaps someone in the dry goods business. That's a logical deduction because sometime in the 1840s Joseph opened a dry goods store of his own in Allens Fresh District, Charles County, and toward the end of the decade he would have several of his brothers and sisters working for and living with him.

Likewise, we'll never know where Tom's mother Catherine was staying the night of the 1840 census, but, in the scheme of things, it's not that important.

On January 18, 1845, at Mattawoman, Jane Harbin (Tom's sister) married Thomas Austin Jones, and they moved to his place on Pope's Creek, in Charles County, in the community of Tompkinsville in Allens Fresh District, where they would raise a large family and live until the Civil War. By marrying Tom Jones, Jane would, to some extent, avoid the Harbin family tragedy that would unfold in the next decade. However, she let herself in for her own set of tragedies. She herself was too busy having children to contribute anything more than that to history. Like so many women of her day who likewise produced many children, she died young and spent. But, when all is said and done, she achieved a reflected fame, prismatic almost, for being the sister of one famous Confederate agent and the wife of another.

Thomas Austin Jones, destined to become one of the biggest and baddest of all the Confederate agents, had been born on October 2, 1820, in Charles County, the son of Elisha Jones and Mary Stuart. He grew up as an informal foster brother to his neighbor, Samuel Cox, a powerful local landowner and also, later, a major Confederate agent in his own right.

Walter Harbin, Tom's father, was a Whig, and was a delegate to that political party's county convention in August 1845 (*Port Tobacco Times*, August 21, 1845). On February 29, 1848, Bryantown farmer Thomas Carrico, father of young physician Thomas A. Carrico, brought a suit against Walter Harbin and his nine heirs-at-law: John H. Howell (really meaning Johanna Howell, Walter's daughter), Julianne (Julia), Catharine, Joseph B., John W., Thomas H., Thomas A. Jones (meaning Jane), George F., and Priscilla (meaning Sarah Priscilla). James Alexander, being mentally disabled, was not mentioned as an heir-at-law. We don't know what this Carrico suit involved, but it probably had something to do with Joseph B.'s business ventures, something which Walter co-signed.

Tom's sister Johanna had married farmer John H. Howell, who had been born on Christmas Day 1825. Like her sister Jane, by marrying, Johanna, to some extent, also saved herself from the Harbin family tragedy that was about to unfold. She and John H. Howell would have several children, all born in Charles County.

1850 Census
Bryantown District
Charles County
Maryland

Walter Harben, 65, farmer, born in Maryland
Catherine Harben, 52, born in Maryland
Walter Harben, 26, born in Maryland [this is John Walter, who went by John]
Sarah P. Harben, 13, born in Maryland
George F. Harben, 10, born in Maryland
1 female slave aged 23
1 male slave aged 3

These are Tom's parents, with the children who were still at home. In this census the name is spelled Harben, which is simply an alternative. One will also see the name spelled Harbine, Herbin, Harven, even, on rare occasions, Hardin, but the normal rendering is, and always has been, Harbin.

This household was next door to the Adams Family, which was next door to.

William Oliver, 22, farmer, born in Maryland
Susan Oliver, 18, born in Maryland
Lucinda Jenkins, 37, born in Maryland
Catherine Jenkins, 18, born in Maryland

It is just curious to note that Jenkins was Mary Surratt's maiden name, and Mary Surratt was the lady who was hanged for her role in the Lincoln assassination.

This household was next door to.

Joseph Jenkins, 35, farmer, born in Maryland
Evelina Jenkins, 51, born in Maryland
William Howell, 17, laborer, born in Maryland
Gustavius Howell, 15, born in Maryland
Catherine E. Jenkins, 11, born in Maryland

And this family was next door to Tom Harbin's sister:

John H. Howell, 25 farmer, born in Maryland
Joanna Howell, 25, born in Maryland
Joseph Howell, 1, born in Maryland

The Howells would leave many descendants.

1850 Census
Bryantown
Charles County
Maryland

Richard Harben, 36, farmer, born in Maryland
Margaret Harben, 38, born in Maryland
Sally Harben, 41, born in Maryland

We do not know who these people are, but they were living next to.

Henry Langley, 45, farmer, born in Maryland
Sarah Langley, 30, born in Maryland
Ann Wallace, 70, born in Maryland
John J. Langley, 6, born in Maryland
Mary A. Langley, 3, born in Maryland
William H. Langley, 2, born in Maryland

And this family, at Langley's Farm, are next door to.

Rizen Harbin, 65, farmer, born in Maryland
Elizabeth Harbin, 10, born in Maryland
Jesse Harbin, 45, farmer, born in Maryland
Zephaniah Queen, 1, born in Maryland
Mary Steward, 15, born in Maryland
15 slaves

This Rizen Harbin is Rezin Harbin Jr. (born in 1785), the brother of Walter Harbin, and uncle of Tom Harbin the spy. The Mary Steward, aged 15, is really Mary Elizabeth Stewart, the daughter of Thomas Stewart and Mary Harbin, Mary Harbin being Rezin Jr.'s daughter. So, this young Mary Elizabeth was the first cousin once removed of Tom Harbin, and in 1855 would become his first wife.

1850 Census
Allens Fresh District
Charles County
Maryland

Joseph B. Harbin, 32, merchant, born in Maryland
Julia Harbin, 21, born in Maryland
James Harbin, 22, laborer, born in Maryland
Thomas H. Harbin 17, clerk, born in Maryland
1 female slave aged 55

This little satellite band of brothers and sisters had broken away from home and were all living at the store, which was the first incarnation of Harbin's Dry Goods.

This 1850 census is the one that has caused so much confusion for Harbin genealogists. Joseph's name on this census really does look like Jonas B. Harbin. However, because of a "dot" over the name some interpret it as Josias, and some as Louis—but it is none of these, it is Joseph. There is no such person as Jonas B. Harbin, or Josias, or Louis. A genealogical trail is littered with "codes," that must be broken in order to discover the truth beneath. Some codes are very, very difficult to crack, but this Jonas / Joseph conundrum is one of the easy ones.

Julia is helping out at the store. Brother James is merely a laborer at the store. Tom, the future spy, is clerking there.

Not long after the 1850 census was taken Joseph B. Harbin, with his band of brothers and sisters, up and moved back to Bryantown, opening up a new store there. Joseph B. Harbin had mail waiting for him there that year, according to the *Port Tobacco Times* of April 10 and July 3, 1850, and Joseph B. Harbin is listed in the 1851—52 *Mercantile Directory* of Bryantown, Charles County, as having a store.

The *Port Tobacco Times* of January 22, 1851, has this: "John A. Farrell, deceased. Orphans Court. Joseph B. Harbin, ad." This John A. Ferrell (as he really was) was born in 1841 in Maryland, son of William and Mary Ferrell. We can't determine what this all implies, except that Joseph B. Harbin was the administrator of something. This is a genealogical fact, as opposed to a code, and therefore would need clarifying, rather than breaking. But one has to be selective in what to spend one's time on. Will it be productive? Will it lead to something else, something that will further the story significantly?

Unfortunately, one of the little band of Harbin siblings didn't make it. James Alexander passed on in 1852, aged 23, and was buried at St. Mary's Catholic Church in Bryantown.

Joseph B. couldn't make a go of the Bryantown store either, so he took his surviving brothers and sisters from the little satellite band and moved to

Benedict, where he opened up yet another dry goods store. Benedict was and still is a tiny village, part of Bryantown District, tucked away in the little eastern panhandle of Charles County, right on the Patuxent River looking out over Calvert County. Ferries would ply the Patuxent from Benedict to Calvert and back on a regular basis, so the town offered opportunities.

In early January 1853 Joseph B. became postmaster of Benedict, keeping the post office in his store. It was a one-year appointment.

The children's mother, Catherine, died on June 26, 1853, and was buried at St. Mary's Catholic Church in Bryantown. Walter, the father, died a month later, on July 28, 1853, and was buried with her and their dead son, James Alexander.

There was no will, so Walter's land all went to Joseph B. While he filled out his term as postmaster in Benedict, someone had to man the family plantations. The little band of brothers and sisters, at least those surviving, went back to Dement's Enlargement. At that point, George, the youngest, was still only 13. Julia, his eldest sister, really a mother figure, was 32, and Tom was 19.

There was a preliminary sale of Walter Harbin's estate near Bryantown (*Port Tobacco Times*, November 11, 1853). A man named John A. Burch was one of those who attended this event, and he lost a young hound while he was there. We know that because he subsequently advertised for it in the papers.

Meanwhile, back in Benedict Joseph B.'s term as postmaster was up, and the *Port Tobacco Times* let the public know in its January 12, 1854, edition that Thomas Johnson had taken over as postmaster from Joseph B. Harbin.

Joseph B. had been accumulating a larger and larger debt to his suppliers—Byrd, Smith & Tiffany out of Baltimore, jobbers and importers of foreign dry goods. They now refused to supply him any longer. He tried other suppliers, but the word was out. Joseph B. had to move fast, as the jobbers were pressing for their money. And now that Joseph was owner of his late father's plantations, they could sue for the land. He got an idea.

The village of Benedict sported, among not much else, a tavern and hotel run by young Henry A. Canter. Canter was unsuccessful, so Joseph B. Harbin formed a company and bought the hostelry, taking out a big loan using Dement's Enlargement and Three Brothers as collateral. Amid such a welter of failure, it's gratifying to be able to report that young Canter got married, stayed in the area, went into farming, and did well for himself.

The June 15, 1854, *Port Tobacco Times* wrote, "Joseph B. Harbin & Co announced to the public that they have fitted up the Old Tavern in Benedict as a house of entertainment." The paper went on to say that Joseph B.

"has fitted up rooms for ladies where they can remain until the departure of the boat."

The same paper of October 26, 1854, reported: "Commissioners will meet on the premises of the late Walter Harbin to value and divide his estate." The jobbers were closing in.

In 1854 Julia, now the matriarch, had had enough of her brother Joseph B., and moved to Washington with John, Catherine, Tom, Sarah Priscilla, and young George, where they all set up house at 462 L Street south, between Seventh and Eighth streets east. The girls did tailoring and the boys did whatever they could. Within a year George, the youngest, became a salesman, clerk and apprentice at James W. Sears' dry goods store, at 48 Market Space, between Seventh and Eighth streets. When Sears' gave way to S. & W. Meyenberg, also dry goods, at the same address, George stayed with Meyenberg's, where he would work until the Civil War interrupted his meteoric rise within the capital's business society.

On October 2, 1855, Thomas Henry Harbin took out a license in Washington, D.C. to marry his cousin Mary Stewart. They were married that very day, a day of some of the heaviest rain within living memory. The *Port Tobacco Times* reported, "Thomas H. Harbin of Washington married Mary E. Stewart of Bryantown, 2nd of Oct." The wedding ceremony took place at St. Peter's Church. "This is to certify that Thomas H. Harbin and Mary Elizabeth Stewart were lawfully married on October 2, 1855, according to the rite of the Roman Catholic Church in conformity with the laws of the District of Columbia, the Rev. E.A. Knight officiating in the presence of Christopher C. McKenny and Catherine A. Harbin, witnesses."

The Reverend E.A. Knight was the very same priest who would marry Charlie Russell and Mary Ann Jarboe two years later, at the very same church, St. Peter's. Catherine A. Harbin was Tom's sister, and Christopher Columbus McKenney (sic) was a 19-year-old patternmaker at the Navy Yard, like his father Benson McKenney, who was also a blacksmith there. Less than two years after Tom Harbin's marriage, on April 14, 1857, Christopher would marry Marion E. Kirbey. At the age of 53, suffering mental illness, Christopher entered St. Elizabeth's Hospital, where he died in 1902; he was buried at the Congressional Cemetery.

Tom and Mary Harbin moved back to Bryantown at the beginning of their marriage, to try to do their part in solving the family crisis on the farm, and Tom became postmaster of Bryantown in 1856. Like his brother Joseph's job at Benedict this was a one-year appointment, but during Tom's term, with Dement's Enlargement and Three Brothers—and thus his financial safety net—collapsing all around him, and with Joseph's death, Tom and Mary moved a few miles away, to the little village of Piscataway, in Prince George's

County, the county to the immediate north of Charles County, where Tom opened up a hotel.

The hotel was right downtown Piscataway, on the south side of the street. Directly across the road was Tom's house, next to Martha Holt on one side and Dr. George Harris on the other. The Catholic church was just up the road, past Mrs. Holt's, to the corner, where well-to-do physician Philip Edelin lived; then it was the first building on the left as you go up the Surrattsville Road. Piscataway was Tom's home for four years.

On September 22, 1856, they had their first child, James Thomas Harbin, in Piscataway.

Meanwhile, brother Joseph B., was getting into more and more crushing financial trouble. The Old Tavern was not working, creditors were pressing in on all sides, and his land was being devoured by the jobbers. Subsequent details we do not know, but the story's unhappy ending is reported laconically in the *Port Tobacco Times*, June 18, 1857: "Joseph B. Harbin deceased."

Dement's Enlargement and part of Three Brothers were sold at auction to satisfy the suits of Isaac J. Pollard, James C. Smith and Edward Tiffany (the jobbers). One hundred thirteen acres were sold.

Tom and Mary had their second son, Joseph, in 1860, but he died as an infant on May 4, 1860 (*Planter's Advocate*, Upper Marlboro, May 16, 1860). Mary suffered from complications during this pregnancy, and these led to consumption, from which she died on Sunday morning, May 27, 1860, in Piscataway, in her 24th year (*Planter's Advocate*, May 30, 1860).

1860 Census
Piscataway
5th Election District
Prince George's County
Maryland

Thomas H. Harbin, 26, hotel keeper, born in Maryland, no real estate, no personal estate
James T. Harbin, 3, born in Maryland
John E. Thompson, 21, barkeeper, born in Maryland
John B. Harris, 35, born in Maryland
Benjamin Bench, 36, carpenter, born in Maryland
1 slave house
1 female mulatto slave aged 75
1 male mulatto slave, aged 24, a fugitive from the state

Incidentally, or coincidentally, only a few minute's brisk walk up the road, in Surrattsville, also in Prince George's County, was another hotel of sorts, more a roadside tavern that put up guests, owned by John Harrison Surratt and his wife Mary.

II. The Life and Family of Tom Harbin

In the other direction from Mary Surratt's tavern, Tom's hotel was just a couple of miles from Dr. Samuel Mudd's place in Bryantown. Harbin knew Sam well. Both the Mudds and the Harbins had been in the area for ages, and, besides, Tom knew everyone, partly because he was well-connected, partly because he had been postmaster at Bryantown; on top of that, he was the assistant marshal responsible for the 1860 census of Prince George's County. As a matter of pure coincidence, his youngest brother, George Francis Harbin (born in 1840), was the 1860 assistant marshal responsible for the census in the 6th Ward of Washington, D.C., a very young marshal indeed, being only 20 at the time.

Tom's hotel in Piscataway was still standing in 1991, although about to fall down.

1860 Census
462 L Street south, between Seventh & Eighth Streets east
Washington, D.C.

Julia A. Harbin, 37, tailoress, born in Maryland, no real estate, $600 personal estate
John W. Harbin, 35, clerk, born in Maryland
Catharine A. Harbin, 28, born in Maryland
Sarah P. Harbin, 22, born in Maryland
Geo. F. Harbin, 20, clerk, born in Maryland

None of these Harbin siblings, including John, ever married. Tom, Jane and Johanna were the only three to embrace espousal, and Tom did so twice. Catherine died in 1868. There is no record of her burial in Mount Olivet cemetery, in Washington, which is odd, as all the others are buried there.

The Julia Phenomenon (i.e. the same person being captured twice, in different places, on the same census), occurs here as well, with Tom's brother John Harbin. In this D.C. census, taken on the night of June 11, 1860, he is living with his siblings. Yet, two weeks later, in the census of Piscataway, Prince George's County, Maryland, taken on June 25, we find him again:

1860 Census
Piscataway
Prince George's County
Maryland

Peter L. Hutton, 35, steamboat captain, born in Maryland, $9,000 of real estate, $3,000 of personal estate
Velinda P. Hutton, 24, born in Maryland
Dent Hutton, 1, born in Maryland
John A. Millett, 14, born in Maryland
John W. Harbin, 33, born in Maryland, no occupation listed

John W. is staying just down the road from his brother, Tom, probably visiting and lodging with the Huttons. So, in effect, he was captured on census by both of his census-taking assistant marshal brothers—George in D.C. and Tom in Prince George's Country. This might well be unique in the annals of census-taking.

As war broke out Tom Harbin placed his son James T., then only four, with his (Tom's) brother George Francis Harbin in D.C., and embarked on a career as the most important and notorious of all the Rebel agents, an agent of such high standing that he reported personally to Jefferson Davis, the president of the Confederate States of America. At least, that's the story he told later in life, when the danger was past.

Tom wasn't just an agent. He was also a courier and a smuggler of contraband. Most important, though, he was entrusted by the Confederate government to open up a mail route from Richmond to Baltimore and thence to Canada. Tom was a spy and a spymaster, running a string of agents in, among other places, Charles County, Maryland, and King George County, Virginia—agents such as his brother-in-law Thomas Austin Jones, the merry widow Quesenberry, Dr. Samuel Alexander Mudd, William L. Bryant, Ben Grymes, Dr. Richard Henry Stuart, Dr. William Queen, Sam Cox, and who knows how many more.

Tom Harbin needed to be alone, with no family encumbrances. His was a dangerous job.

He took the alias Thomas A. Wilson and used it frequently during the war, and even afterwards. In the wake of the Lincoln assassination word came to the Federal detectives that "Thomas A. Wilson" had played a major part in the coup, and a big manhunt ensued. Twelve decades later, 1980s researchers James O. Hall, Bill Tidwell and Dave Gaddy also went in search of this Wilson, and found that Tom Harbin had used this alias when he secured a pass to travel from Richmond to King George County, Virginia, on October 21, 1864.

On July 8, 1861, George F. Harbin, Tom's youngest brother, also a rabid Secessionist, and still living with his sisters in the capital and working at Meyenberg's, wrote a letter to his brother-in-law Tom Jones: "I hope and sincerely believe that the day is not far distant when the people of the North will condemn Abe's cruel acts and hurl him from power." Given what was to come, this was an indiscreet letter.

One equally incautious was written to Jones on August 8: "I am well and in fine spirits since the great victory at Manassas and expect from rumors to soon be living under another president. I think that Lincoln is pretty nearly played out and that one more victory in favor of the South will knock down his house."

For a man living in Washington at this time, to be writing seditious letters like this was an incredible miscalculation. George F. would pay for it.

In September 1861 a Federal party led by Lieutenant Wilson raided

Tom Jones's house in Pope's Creek and found the Harbin letters. They didn't waste much time. George was arrested in D.C. by Major E.J. Allen (a pseudonym of the famous detective Allen Pinkerton), under orders from Brigadier General Andrew Porter, the provost marshal of the District of Columbia. On September 23, 1861, George was thrown into the Old Capitol Prison in Washington, as a suspected or disloyal person. He was charged with having written letters denouncing the Federal government and invoking the success of the Rebel arms, and for being in earnest sympathy with the success of the insurrectionists. In short, George was in big trouble.

That same day Rudolph Watkins and George S. Watkins were also captured in Georgetown and, along with George F. Harbin, inserted against their will into the Old Capitol Prison. They found languishing there Frank Renehan and William J. Walker, both suspects rounded up with Rebel Rose O'Neale Greenhow, the spy mistress, on August 23 (Mrs. Greenhow was under house arrest at her home). James A. Donnelly was there too, also arrested in August, in Georgetown.

There were only a few prisoners then in the Old Capitol Prison a former schoolhouse, and they were all politicals. The year 1861 being of a still gentlemanly time, the prisoners were treated quite magnificently. The Old Capitol functioned more like a low-end country club. Each prisoner had his (or her) own room, and within that room was a cot, a good mattress, blankets, sheets and a bed-cover, all as clean as those in any modest hotel. There were two large bathing rooms, both supplied with hot and cold running water, which could be used freely by the inmates, and this made for clean, healthy prisoners in generally good spirits. The kitchen was well equipped, and the prisoners provided with good food—fresh meat, rice, peas, beans, coffee, sugar, tea, and fresh bread. The dining room had tables, seats, plates, knives and forks, and drinking cups. There was a well-outfitted dispensary and a top-notch exercise yard. The Old Capitol Prison was the place to be.

On September 24, 1861, Thomas Austin Jones was arrested and thrown into a detention camp for alleged Confederate activity, i.e., for rowing people across the Potomac.

William F. Getty was caught in Washington on October 1, 1861, and was a most welcome addition to the Old Capitol. On October 4 Thomas Austin Jones himself was transferred there from his detention camp, and glad about it. Samuel G. Acton was brought in on the same day as Jones, and more and more filed through the big door—not on a daily basis, but regularly. On November 14, 1861, arrived the Dent boys—George and George, from Pope's Creek, Maryland, the same little community that Thomas A. Jones lived in. By November 26 there were 33 political prisoners confined within the walls of the Old Capitol.

There is a letter of October 18, 1861, indicating that George F. Harbin was in the Thirteenth Street Prison. This was a house on the southeast corner of Pennsylvania Avenue and Thirteenth Street, at one time the Prescott House hotel, and now, in 1861, leased by the government. During this early part of the war the hotel did house political prisoners, but later it mostly confined persons charged with military infractions.

For all of those imprisoned at the Old Capitol the petitions began immediately, family and friends frantically visiting the authorities, pulling strings wherever they could, struggling to fabricate immaculate references to present to the secretary of state so that he might find it within himself to offer release. Those interned were simply being held, without trial, as persons gauged to be a threat to the Union; there was no punishment in mind for them at this stage, beyond the confinement they already suffered. However, it would be nice to be out, hence all the activity on their behalf, and hence their own letters to the Hon. Mr. Seward.

Doctors, lawyers, businessmen, the great and the good—anyone and everyone who could be found to risk their reputations for the (very guilty, to a man) Rebel agents—were brought into play like the big guns on a battleship in a mad and desperate game to free the prisoners (who all claimed to be very innocent, to a man).

Jones, who was a shade or perhaps several shades cleverer than all of them combined, admitted, quite boldly, that he had rowed people across the river, but only for profit. To think that he would have a Secessionist cell in his brain was unthinkable, an unspeakable calumny. He was in it for the money. Being Americans, the government lads could understand that, surely.

George F. Harbin was one of those who simply said, "Moi?"

Sixth Ward physician and city councilman Sam McKim, himself originally a Boston Yankee, was found to testify to the sterling qualities of George F. Harbin, in a plea letter to the government on October 24, 1861:

> I have known Mr. George F. Harbin, who is now held as a political prisoner, for several years. I have, during this time, been the medical attendant of the family. He is very young and may have been indiscreet but I should be loath to think he had done any disloyal act willfully. His sisters are most excellent ladies and, while I have never exchanged a word on the political questions of the day with the young man, I have with his sisters, and that too early in the spring, and I have never heard a disloyal sentiment or word from them. S.A.H. McKim.

This doesn't seem to have done much good for George, at least not in the short term. However, McKim would be prevailed upon to try his luck again in 1865 with another unlucky captive, Dave Herold, a fellow parishioner of Christ Church Episcopalian on G Street. Again McKim would fail in his oratory, despite telling the court that he felt Dave's mental age was only eleven. The judge didn't buy it, and Davey wound up dancing a jig at the end of a rope.

II. The Life and Family of Tom Harbin

On December 20, 1861, Frederick W. Seward, the assistant secretary of state and son of the secretary of state, William H. Seward, wrote to Brigadier General Andrew Porter, the provost-marshal, "General, you will please transfer George S. Watkins, Thomas A. Jones, Rudolph Watkins, Samuel G. Acton, George Dent Sr., George Dent Jr., and George F. Harbin to Fort Lafayette, New York Harbor. I am, general, etc., F.W. Seward, assistant secretary."

This removal to New York didn't happen. On December 22, 1861, George fired off a letter (not his first, by any means) from the Old Capitol Prison to the secretary of state:

> Hon. W.H. Seward. Sir, I beg leave to call your attention to my case again. I have been confined in prison three months without knowing what the charges against me are. I have a family of sisters depending upon my labor for a support, and as I have never violated any law that I am aware of in any manner whatever I do think it very hard that I am kept in prison when I have always been willing to take the oath of allegiance. I am ready to prove my innocence if you will grant me a trial, or even an interview with you or General Porter. I reside in this city and have never visited or corresponded with anyone in the States in rebellion against the Government. I have never aided the enemies of the Government in any way whatever. I have been pursuing my business in this city for six years and the records will show that I have been a law-abiding citizen. All this I can prove if I am allowed a trial. My friends will call on you in a day or two I hope and give you sufficient evidence of my innocence. I hope my petition may meet your early consideration and that I may be permitted to return to my home to comfort my family. Yours, Geo. F. Harbin.

Nothing happened. So George wrote Seward again on December 30:

> Hon. William H. Seward, Secretary of State, Washington. Sir, I was arrested on the 23rd day of September and have been confined in prison since my arrest without knowing what the charges against me are. I was informed at General Porter's office at the time of my arrest that I was charged with treason, but no act was specified. If I had been informed of any charges of having committed any act of hostility against the Government, I could have given you sufficient evidence of my innocence long before this time, but as it is, I am entirely ignorant of what I am charged with. I have never corresponded with anyone in the States in rebellion. I have never aided the enemies of the Government in any manner whatever that I am aware of. I have never been in any of the States in rebellion nor ever did I intend to go. I have been pursuing my business in this city for the last six years and my numerous friends are ready to give you ample assurances of my integrity. I am ready and willing to take the oath of allegiance. This I have been willing to do at any time. I have a large family of sisters who are without protection or support during my absence. I trust, Sir, that this, my appeal, may meet your favorable consideration. All I ask is a trial, for I feel sure that I can satisfy you of my innocence. Yours respectfully, Geo. F. Harbin.

The constant bombardment, as effective as that at Fort Sumter, finally convinced Secretary Seward, and he wrote to General Porter on January 9, 1862:

Sir, let George Dent Sr., George Dent Jr., Thomas A. Jones, Rudolph Watkins, George S. Watkins, and George F. Harbin, prisoners confined in the Old Capitol Prison, be released on taking the oath of allegiance to the Government of the United States stipulating that they will neither leave the state of Maryland nor enter any of the states in insurrection against the authority of the Government of the United States, nor hold any correspondence whatever with persons residing in those states during the present hostilities without permission from the Secretary of State, and also that they will not do anything hostile to the United States during the present insurrection. I am, Sir, etc., William H. Seward.

Things looked very promising at this moment for George (and the others, including, of course, Tom Jones). Two days later, on January 11, 1862, Seward's son, F.W., sent a letter to General Porter, saying, "General, I inclose herewith a letter from George F. Harbin, a prisoner confined in the prison in this city. Will you please examine the case and return to this Department with your report this inclosure. I am, Sir, etc, F.W. Seward, assistant secretary."

However, Porter was not a man easily fooled by facile protestations of innocence. That same day, he replied to the secretary of state himself:

To Hon. William H. Seward, Secretary of State. Sir, I have the honor to acknowledge the receipt of an order from you directing the release of George Dent Sr., George Dent Jr., Thomas A. Jones, Rudolph Watkins, George S. Watkins, and George F. Harbin, prisoners confined in the Old Capitol. I would respectfully represent that the above named prisoners are of the most dangerous character and have been actively engaged in furnishing information to the rebels and in transporting men to Virginia for the purpose of joining the rebel army, as also in the nightly transportation of contraband goods to the enemy; that the prisoners Dent and Jones were duly accredited agents of the rebel government for the purposes above set forth, and in the house of Dent was found a copy of the signals arranged for signaling between the Maryland and Virginia shores as appointed by the officer commanding the rebel forces at that time at Mathias Point; that the two Watkinses were unceasing in their endeavors to acquire information of the numbers, arms, positions, etc, of our army in Virginia, and forwarding the same to Dent to be transmitted to the rebels. They (the Watkinses) were also engaged in sending forward to Dent contraband goods and persons for transportation to Virginia. Knowing the extremely dangerous character of these men and the probability that untruthful representations connected with these cases had been made to you I submitted the subject of their release to Major-General McClellan who directs that it is a military necessity that these persons should be held in custody, and I have the honor to herewith inclose to you the order for the release of the within-named parties with the endorsement thereon of Major-General McClellan for such further action as may be deemed necessary thereon. Very respectfully, your obedient servant, A. Porter, Brigadier-General and Provost Marshal.

In other words Porter nixed the idea. McClellan's endorsement was only a final nail in the coffin of George's freedom, but it read, "Headquarters, Army of the Potomac, January 10, 1862. I am instructed from Major-General McClellan to say that considering the character of the within-named parties (Harbin and others) as shown at the time of their arrest, it is deemed a matter of military necessity that they should, for the present, be retained in custody. Respectfully, S. Williams, Assistant Adjutant-General."

Rose O'Neale Greenhow created a stir when she was transferred from her 398 Sixteenth Street home (known recently as "Fort Greenhow" and the subject of curious stares from an increasing number of passers by) to the Old Capitol Prison, but aside from that life there continued as normal, prisoners coming in, prisoners going out.

The said George F. Harbin remained in custody at the Old Capitol Prison until February 15, 1862, when, in conformity with the order of the War Department of the preceding day, he was transferred to the charge of that department.

On March 15, 1862, Major E.J. Allen (i.e., Allen Pinkerton), the officer with the provost general's office, who had arrested many of these persons, wrote of Thomas A. Jones in a letter to secretary of war Edwin Stanton that "Jones is a most dangerous man to be at large even for the shortest length of time." Yet, a mere six days later, on March 21, Jones took the oath of allegiance, along with George S. Watkins and the Dents, and was let go. The letter ordering the release of Rudolph Watkins, subject to taking the oath, was written on April 1, 1862.

Although we can't find a release order for George F. Harbin, he was released, and about this time. On May 30, 1862, he freed his only slave, Annie E. Taylor, aged 35, and applied for reimbursement from the Federal government. Ditto June 16, 1862, with Julia's slave Harriet A. Mills (worth $800, according to George's application, which he made in his sister's behalf).

On April 16, 1862 Abraham Lincoln had signed an Act of Congress freeing Negro slaves in the District of Columbia. A commission was formed—the Emancipation Commission—one of whose missions was to receive from D.C. slaveholders petitions filed for reimbursement. The holders listed the names and numbers of slaves held, and value of each slave. However, the commission had the final say on how much was to be paid out for each slave. It has been oft stated, with ironic justification only, that at that point in time, with all these purchases, the District of Columbia became the largest slaveholder in the history of mankind.

George F. Harbin, on October 10, 1862, was elected one of the trustees of the Young Catholics' Friend Association for the ensuing year. This was an organization that held their monthly meetings on Sundays, at 5 o'clock, at St. Peter's Church on Capitol Hill, and was a group that George had long belonged to, in fact since it was formed in 1857. So, in short, he wasted no time in getting back into the swing of things in Washington.

When Tom Jones got out of the Old Capitol Prison after several months he found his place had gone to seed, and so had his wife. At this point

William Norris, new head of the Confederate Secret Service, and his top agent Tom Harbin approached Jones with the idea of his becoming a full-time, full-fledged Confederate agent himself, to which Jones agreed. Tom Harbin it was who helped Jones keep afloat the ferry across the Potomac, the one that carried the Rebel mail. Jane, Tom Harbin's sister and Tom Jones's wife, died on January 29, 1863, a used-up woman.

George Alfred Townsend, ace war reporter, says this about the Confederate mail service:

> The Rebel mail service which Jones conducted was almost as efficient as the United States mail at the present time. Washington, Baltimore and New York papers were subscribed for by different Rebel individuals in the vicinity of Allens Fresh, the subscription price being paid by the Confederacy, and one person would go and call for the mail of all the neighbors. These papers would be deposited in the stump under Jones' Bluff, and then the boat would come over, as described in the gray of the evening, and take the papers out, and the next morning they would be in Richmond, going by way of Port Conway, Port Royal and Bowling Green. This became the great route for blockade-runners and go-betweens, and finally Booth's route.

It's curious to note that John and Roberta Wearmouth, the biographers of Tom Jones, afforded Jane Harbin Jones about one line, and saw fit to give no lines at all (!) to Tom Harbin. In fact, there is no information on the Harbin family in the Wearmouth book. Considering that they were Tom Jones's in-laws, and that Tom Harbin was so important to the Jones story, this omission is more than a trifle mystifying.

In 1863 Tom Harbin approached a newly-widowed lady in King George County, Virginia. Given that she was a pretty widow, aged 39, with secessionist sympathies as rabid as Tom's, it's easy to see why Tom approached her.

Two of the mighty families in the Georgetown area before the creation of the District of Columbia were the Rousbys and the Platers. George Plater III, for example, was the sixth governor of Maryland. His second wife was Elizabeth Ann Rousby, of the estate known as Sotterley. One of their daughters, Rebecca, married General Uriah Forrest on October 11, 1789. These were the grandparents of the widow Quesenberry.

Uriah Forrest, born in St. Mary's County, Maryland, in 1746, had been a captain in the Revolutionary War. In fact, Charlie Russell's grandfather Cahoe had served under him. Forrest and his wife lived at Rosedale, their magnificent house between Georgetown and Tenallytown, which was then in Montgomery County, Maryland, but which later became part of the D.C. area, with the address 3501 Newark Street, NW. Later still it became known as the Forrest—Marbury home, and in 1992 it became the Ukrainian Embassy.

One of General Forrest's daughters, Ann, known as Nancy, was the widow Quesenberry's mother. Born in 1790, she married, on July 21, 1814, at Rosedale, John Green, Esq., a Georgetown man twelve years older than her. High up in the Navy Department was John Green, the son of old Ralph Green, the privateer captain who had gone down with his ship during the Revolution.

Another Forrest daughter, Maria (the widow Quesenberry's aunt), was born in 1799; she married, in 1817, John Tayloe IV, from the very important Tayloe family. They had John Tayloe V, in 1818, who would wind up marrying, as his second wife, his first cousin, Mary W. Green (the widow Quesenberry's sister), and living in King George County. They all lived at Rosedale at one time or another, for varying periods of time.

In September 1843 Rebecca Plater Forrest (the widow Quesenberry's grandmother) died, aged 80, and Rosedale passed to her daughter, Mrs. Nancy Green.

John Green and Nancy had several children, all born at Rosedale. Elizabeth Rousby Green, known her whole life as Rose, or, later, as the widow Quesenberry, was one of them, born on October 25, 1823.

On May 15, 1849, at Rosedale, in Georgetown, a year before her father died, Rose Green was married by the Reverend Len Branch to a King George County, Virginia, planter named Nicholas Austin Quesenberry, ten years older than her, and son of George Quesenberry. They moved out to Nick's farm, "the Cottage," at Edge Hill, in the district of Hampstead, where their neighbors included the very well-off Dr. Richard Stuart. They spent about half their time there and half in Georgetown, at Rosedale.

Another Green daughter, Alice, married a Mexican prince on June 9, 1855, at Rosedale. Don Angel de Yturbide, now the Widow Quesenberry's brother-in-law, had been born in 1816, in Queretaro, Mexico, second son of the first native emperor of Mexico. One of his children by Alice, Don Agustin de Yturbide, was adopted by the subsequent (French puppet) emperor Maximilian, and later became a professor of languages at Georgetown.

Yet another Green daughter, Imogene, married Fielding Lewis, and went to live with him at "Marmion," also in King George County, Virginia.

There are various spellings of the name. Quesenberry is the spelling preferred in Virginia. As for the pronunciation of the name, the widow herself pronounced it "Quee-zen-berry," but the locals in King George County called her "Mrs. Cue-zen-berry." In some parts of the country it's pronounced "Cushion-berry."

The Quesenberrys had been in Virginia since 1624, when the first of the family arrived in Jamestown from England. Before England they had been in Germany, and known as Quesenberg. By the time Nick married Rose Green they owned a lot of land in Westmoreland County. In 1835 Nick had moved to neighboring King George County and bought 625 acres, at about 10 dollars an acre, from Henry D. Storke and his wife. In 1860, Nick's estate alone was worth $20,000, and Nick himself was worth $22,740 that year.

Nick Quesenberry had been married before, in 1841, to Mary Louisa Grymes, daughter of George Nicholas Grymes of the estate known as Mont Chene (Mount Chinn), in King George County. By Mary Louisa he had a son, George Nicholas, in 1841 and a daughter, Mary Louisa, in 1843. With this second child Nicholas's wife died in childbirth. The wife was taken back to Mont Chene to be buried in a little chapel on her family's land. Young Mary Louisa, a baby, was raised with her grandparents at Mont Chene, while Nick worked the land back at the Cottage.

Nick remarried six years later, to Rose Green, bringing his two children into the marriage. However, young George Nicholas died at the age of 10, in 1851.

It wasn't long before Nick and Rose had their first child: Lucy, born at Rosedale in 1850. John Rousby Quesenberry was next out, in 1852, but he died on August 13 of that year. Child number three was George Forrest Quesenberry, born in 1854, but he died that year. Then came Nicholas Jr., also born at Rosedale, in 1856. In 1857 Austin Quesenberry was born, but died the following year, and in January 1858, Alice Yturbide Quesenberry was born. The last child was Rousby Plater Quesenberry, born on April 13, 1862, at the Cottage.

The Cottage was a beautiful house, trellised and manicured, with a front lawn reaching to the wide Machodoc Creek about fifty yards away. On this lawn, among other cabins, was a small schoolhouse, fitted up for the education of the children. The educator was a governess named Miss Duncanson.

They weren't starving, the Quesenberrys, but the war cut heavily into their fortune. On February 6, 1863 Nick died, without leaving a will, and he was buried by the side of his first wife. There is no grave marker. Nick's estate was inventoried in King George County on October 12, 1864.

Thus in 1863 Rose became the widow Quesenberry, with a baby, a young son and a hostile teenage stepdaughter.

Tom Harbin asked her if she would contemplate using her house as a safe haven for Confederate agents and couriers. Upon her agreement, the plan developed and the property became a permanent Confederate signal station used to communicate with other Rebels in Maryland and hold open their mail route to the North and Canada. The signal officers, as a rule, were genteel men and they all thought highly of their hostess. They occupied the schoolhouse, at least two of them did: Tom Harbin and Joseph Baden.

The widow became one of Tom's trusted agents, and perhaps more than that. He certainly spent a lot of time at the widow's house. It was a natural. Tom was a representative-looking Maryland gentleman, tall, almost gaunt, yet supple (to quote George Alfred Townsend, who knew him well), "with a smile ever on his countenance, dark brown hair, high cheek bones, with somewhat sunken cheeks, but cautious and thoughtful, and tender to women." Tom was a bold, swashbuckling type, a widower himself, only 29, and she was a pretty widow of 39. There is no proof of anything more than friendship between them—in fact, Townsend (in his article in the *Cincinnati Enquirer* of August 1, 1884) claims Tom "had as much respect for Mrs. Quesenberry as if she had been the wife of Jefferson Davis"—yet one can read Townsend's his unwritten words. The reporter says "she would have been a superior woman anywhere."

No one knows for sure when John Wilkes Booth came up with the idea of kidnapping Abe Lincoln, but it was sometime during the war, probably early on. There are reports of him talking about such a plot in 1863. By late 1864 Booth was making a frantic tour of the likely places—The Navy Yard, the National Hotel, Southern (Catholic) Maryland, notably Charles County—seeking the usual suspects to enlist as conspirators in his cause. He experienced no difficulty.

This from John Wilkes Booth's diary, dated November 10, 1864: "Met with planters Bowman, John Thompson, Samuel Cox, and Thomas Jones. They have all pledged their assistance. A Thomas Harbin can be enlisted but he has a family to support and would require $100 a month. Brother-in-law to Jones. Survey tedious."

Bowman was well-to-do farmer Andrew Bowman, then in his mid–30s, or possibly his brother Tom, a constable. They were next-door neighbors of old Thomas Carrico, the physician's father who had sued old Walter Harbin back in 1848.

This statement about Harbin needing a hundred dollars is odd. Tom didn't have a family to support. He was a widower, leading a fugitive life, and his only child, James T., then eight, was well ensconced with Tom's brother George in D.C. This is too specific a detail for Booth to have invented, or to have gotten wrong.

The famous meeting between Booth and Harbin took place at Montgomery's Tavern in Bryantown, on December 20, 1864 (or December 18, depending on which researcher's version you believe). Sam Mudd, who had already met Booth at St. Mary's Church, in Bryantown, back on November 13, arranged this tavern meeting. He met Booth there, and when Tom Harbin showed, Mudd introduced Harbin to the actor. For this meeting Tom had come over the Potomac from King George County, where he was spending a lot of his time working with the widow Quesenberry. Tom described this meeting with Booth in the famous "Harbin Interview" with Townsend in 1885. Remembering that Harbin was short of cash, Booth told him, "There's not only glory, but profits in the undertaking." Tom agreed to help in the plot to kidnap Lincoln. His role would be to help get the abducted president across the Potomac and down to Richmond.

On December 23, 1864, Sam Mudd met Booth again, at the National Hotel in Washington, where the two spent some time in Booth's room talking with John Surratt.

In January 1865 "Thomas A. Wilson" (i.e. Tom Harbin) introduced Booth to George Atzerodt. Harbin, who knew both men, of course, felt that Atzerodt would be a good man to join the conspiracy. This rather unfortunate German, known by the nickname "Port Tobacco" (from the Charles County, Maryland town he operated out of as a repairer of carriages) had been, for some time, a ferryman of Confederate messages across the Potomac. This was a meeting Atzerodt would swing for.

By early 1865 Booth had mutated his kidnapping idea into one of assassination. The war was pretty much over, and the South had lost. It didn't take a great brain to figure out the probable consequences of such an assassination, and previous conspirators fell off like dead flies. The few dedicated ones who remained were, of course, rabid, but there were others who stayed the course who weren't so committed. They felt they were too far into the plot to back out now and lacked the courage to say "no" to the very determined and persuasive Booth. It's hard to believe Tom Harbin lacked courage in any field of endeavor, so he was probably one of the first group; yet one senses, from his demand for $100, that he was trying, in a lukewarm way, to wriggle free.

According to Tom, the day of the assassination he arranged for a horse to be waiting for Johnny Booth outside the stage door of Ford's Theatre in Washington, just in case Booth succeeded in killing Abraham Lincoln at the showing of *Our American Cousin* that night. Then Tom took off, with his buddy, Joseph Baden, and the two made their way to the town of Newport, in Charles County, where they went to ground in a room at Austin Adams's hotel. That's where they spent the night, waiting for Booth, waiting to play their part in getting the assassin across the Potomac to Virginia. But Booth was delayed...

After Booth jumped to the stage and broke his leg, he wasn't sure he could press on. As the assassin told Tom later, in Virginia, if he (Booth) "had not been a very courageous man [he] would have given up and have been taken right there, as [he] was, for an instant, about to faint."

Immediately after the assassination Booth and his now willing, now unwilling accomplice Dave Herold escaped to Charles County, Maryland, thundering along the southern road to Surrattsville in the dead of night. At the Surratt tavern they picked up from John Lloyd, the drunk tavern tenant, a gun and some provisions, and then a few minutes later were on their way again to Dr. Sam Mudd's house, near Bryantown, where they arrived at about four in the morning of the 15th, the day after the assassination. The good (bad) doctor set Booth's shin bone, which had been broken during his theatrical plunge to the stage.

One who witnessed firsthand Booth's mad and crippled sprint from the stage to the back door of the Ford's Theatre was stage hand John Matthews, who also had a small part in the play. Matthews was an old friend of Booth's, and the killer had recently entrusted him with a letter, which Matthews now hurried to read. It was a letter for the *National Intelligencer*, justifying the assassination. Matthews felt that he could never explain his possession of this letter, so he burned it, and then, in a panic, and not knowing what to do, made a beeline for the one man who could advise him, another old friend, an old school chum from St. Mary's College in Baltimore: Father Francis E. Boyle, pastor of St. Peter's Church on Capitol Hill.

Father Boyle, noted scholar and philanthropist, born in Baltimore in September 1827, had attended St. Mary's College and St. Mary's Seminary and was ordained in 1851. After a few Maryland postings, during which time he had come to know Mary Surratt, he had arrived in Washington as assistant to Father T.J. O'Toole of St. Patrick's in 1860, the year Father Jacob Ambrose Walter—Mary Surratt's staunchest defender and apologist—took over as pastor. In 1862 he transferred to St. Peter's, to help the ailing Father Knight, and in September of that year he took over that church when the good pastor died. He was also the Catholic chaplain to the prisoners in the Old Capitol Prison.

"Frank, what do I do? What do I do?," cried Matthews to his friend.

"Sit down, and tell me everything," demanded Father Boyle, taking control. And Matthews sat down, and told the priest all about the letter. Boyle assured the distraught man that he had done the right thing, and then slipped him a small, folded piece of paper.

"What's this?" asked Matthews through his confusion.

"That's an address in Canada. I advise you to go there as soon as possible."

"I will, Frank, I will." Matthews stuttered his thanks and walked out, not literally, but virtually into the hands of the police. They interrogated him, but he said nothing, and then he fled to the address on the missive.

This giving of the address in Canada is a supposition. The meeting of Matthews and Boyle under these very circumstances is a fact (*Lincoln's Assassins*, by Roy Z. Chamlee). However, would Matthews have gone to his old pal just to hear the words "Go to Canada"? Anyone could have given those pearls of wisdom, including Matthews. No, Matthews was bent on acquiring practical help from Boyle. Could Boyle have been the Washington end of the D.C.-to-Canada pipeline?

Meanwhile, in Charles County, Maryland, Booth and Herold stayed at

Sam Mudd's farm for 12 hours. After he set Booth's leg, Sam sent the fugitives on their way, to Sam Cox's place. Colonel Samuel Cox was a very successful planter. His foster brother was none other than Thomas Austin Jones, to whom the fugitives were next sent. Jones it was who guided them through the marshes to the river and who gave them a boat in which they finally made it to King George County on the Virginia side of the Potomac.

Their first port of call in King George County was Rose Quesenberry's house.

On that day Tom Harbin and Joseph Baden were at the widow's place (surprise, surprise!). The widow had gone out on her horse to visit neighbors. Someone was sick in the Quesenberry household, so Harbin and Baden set out across the Machodoc Creek to Colonel Baker's house to get some medicine. On the way back a storm blew up off the Potomac and they almost drowned. Making it back to the Quesenberry property, they found Miss Duncanson, the governess, waiting for them.

"Mr. Harbin," she said, "there is a strange man here who has come to buy horses."

Baden went to the house with Miss Duncanson and found that the strange man was Dave Herold. Dave was a mess and looked awful, covered in dirt and grime. Baden went back to Tom Harbin and told him who the visitor was. Tom's heart sank a little (as he later said) on hearing that the boys had arrived. Saying nothing to anyone, he went to the house and saw Herold.

"Herold," he said, "where's Booth?"

"He's over here, at the next farm, and you must go and see him," replied Dave.

Years later Tom Harbin claimed he hadn't heard of the assassination until the Wednesday five days after the event. Certainly, though, when the fugitives arrived at the widow Quesenberry's, Tom knew exactly what the score was.

Harbin and Baden took Dave Herold down to the schoolhouse and got him cleaned up. At that point the widow Quesenberry returned from her visiting, and was tempted to sell the horses to Herold owing to the fact that the war had reduced her nearly to poverty.

Tom took her aside and said, "You mustn't sell this man a horse. There are circumstances connected with him which make it my duty to tell you to give him nothing more than something to eat."

The widow followed Tom's advice, and refused to sell Herold the horses. She also refused to put up the fugitives, but she did provide food for them, which Tom took to Booth at the next farm. Then they moved on. From the Quesenberry house Tom Harbin took Booth and Herold a mile or two down the road to the farm of another of his agents, William L. Bryant.

Bryant, not a King George County native, was then 64 and impoverished like everyone else as a result of the war, and now only had a little hut and no slaves. No room to put up two fugitives. But Bryant did take them to Richard Stuart's.

Dr. Stuart was then 57. The war was over, he had a family and a lot of money to protect, he'd already been jailed twice for his sympathies, and he knew which way the wind would blow if he aided Booth. He turned Booth away.

Booth finally died at Garrett's barn. "Useless, useless," were Booth's last words. That was the early morning, April 26, that Dave Herold was captured.

On April 15, 1865, the day after the assassination, the police had found out that Tom Harbin had been and still was using the alias Thomas A. Wilson. The top cop Lafayette Baker got on his trail immediately, sending his men out to scour the countryside looking for Tom Harbin, alias Tom Wilson. Tom decided to stay right at the widow's house, rather than run. Safer in the armpit of the tortoise. Many times these officers ran into Tom, or, as Townsend says, "the scent came very close to him, but he was so gentlemanly and obliging that the very officers of the law became rather confidential with him." He was so affable, so charming that they didn't realize it was him, didn't think to question him, never considered that he might be Harbin.

Townsend again:

> After Booth had been killed Lieutenant Baker and a detective and some soldiers came to the place to make enquiries for Wilson (Harbin's assumed name). Harbin kept out of sight as much as possible. The officers said it was necessary that some one person should go up to Washington to testify before the Judge Advocate. Harbin rather pressed that he should go, though the contrary was his design. Mrs. Quisenberry [sic] said that she couldn't go on account of her children. Baden quietly dropped the remark that he had an old mother in Washington whom he had not seen for four years, and the humane officers took him along instead of Harbin. Baden's reward, however, was to be sent to prison for about six weeks. A steamboat came up Machodoc Creek not long afterwards and Mrs. Quisenberry was informed that she would have to go to Washington.

"The boat in which Booth had crossed the river was seized by the Government at Mrs. Quisenberry's," says Townsend, "and it is not known what became of it. Mr. Harbin says that Booth, in his belief, was never in Richmond during the War."

There have been different versions of this story told, but Nick Quesenberry Jr. assured Townsend that Tom Harbin's story was accurate, except that Herold, when he came to the house, was almost in a state of physical collapse, through fright, and blurted out his whole story to those of the family who were at home, even in the presence of the colored servants. When Harbin and Herold went to rejoin Booth in the wood, Nick, who was then quite a young boy, went along with them; and they carried an old-fashioned carpet-sack which his mother, out of humanity, had filled with food for the fugitives. "Mr. Quisenberry [sic] said that they found Booth sitting under a walnut tree in the woods—the wildest looking maniac I ever saw. Booth gave the boat in which he and Herold crossed the river to young Nicholas. It was afterwards seized by the Government detectives, who paid him for it. It was taken to Washington and deposited at the Navy Yard, but for some years past has been one of the attractions at the National Museum."

In the wake of John Wilkes Booth's death the widow Quesenberry was brought to Washington for interrogation. She was allowed to bring her children with her, and to stay at Rosedale while the process went on. She gave her statement to the Federal investigators on May 20, 1865, and she was let go.

There has been much speculation as to why she wasn't punished in some way. There were three main reasons. The first is that the authorities had their prisoners, and it wouldn't look good to keep getting more. Second, they were already due to hang a woman—Mary Surratt—and that shook the very foundation of the United States. To arrest another woman would be unforgivable. And third, she was pretty.

Things were really hotting up for Tom Harbin after Booth's death, and just as soon as he could, just as soon as he had fulfilled his obligations to Booth and the widow, he went on the lam, preparing his own safe exit. He snaffled a Maryland Cavalry uniform and headed down to Ashland, Virginia, a place where the Feds were issuing paroles to Confederate soldiers willing to take the oath of fidelity.

In Ashland, on April 28, 1865, he secured his parole as a member of the Company B, 1st Maryland Cavalry (records of this regiment do not show his name, which is not surprising). He then disappeared—almost.

Apparently Tom somehow got into the prison that was holding Dave Herold and talked to him. Dave told him what happened in the Garrett barn that morning of the 26th.

This from Townsend:

> When Booth and Herold were cornered in a barn at Mr. Garrett's, in Caroline County, Herold proposed to surrender after the barn was fired, and Booth cursed him for a coward, and asked permission to shoot him. This Herold declined; and Booth then pushed him to the opening, saying, 'Quarter for this man, he surrenders,' at the same time shooting himself and dying by his own hand. This story is somewhat different from the accepted version, but Nicholas Quisenberry [sic] had it from Mr. Harbin, who had it from Herold himself, during his imprisonment previous to his execution."

This all sounds very third hand, indeed it is very third hand, and must not be trusted, yet...

General John Hartranft made a very detailed log of all persons visiting the prisoners at the Washington Arsenal between April 30 and July 7,

II. The Life and Family of Tom Harbin

1865, this last date being when the hangings took place. And Davey Herold had been arrested on April 26. This log can be inspected today. It is a meticulous account not only of the visitors but of events connected with the prisoners, on a daily basis. If a mouse got in, Hartranft noted it. You had to have proof of who you were before Hartranft would even speak to you.

According to the log, David Herold received only his sister, his lawyers, and the Episcopalian pastor of his de facto place of worship, Christ Church. However, right at the end, came an unidentified priest. One might imagine the following scene:

The humble turnkey sat at his desk outside the cells, paring his left little fingernail with his grubby right thumbnail. It had been a quiet day, the occasional prisoner banging his head against the wall trying to off himself, Mary Surratt bleeding all over the floor, the odd rat nibbling at the leg of one of the chained assassins, causing squeals that the turnkey felt were inappropriate given the big scream about to come on the gallows.

The jailer stood to attention as the priest came in, a very tall, slim, Catholic priest in his thirties, with gaunt face, dark hair, beard, and sunken cheeks. But it was the eyes the man remembered better than anything, the intense, piercing eyes of the priest. That and the walk. The jailer would always remember thinking at the time how gracefully the priest moved, especially for a big man. Like a mountain cat.

"Bless you, my son," said the priest, as he laid a hand on the jailer's shoulder. There was something very comforting in the Limerick brogue, but it was the tone of voice, at the same time commanding and friendly. To a man of the jailer's humble origins, the priest was quite clearly a superior fellow human being, one used to getting his own way. The jailer, like all fellows of his class in those days, was acutely sensitive to the strata of society, and would respond to someone like the priest in one of two different ways. He would either resent him or he would do anything for him. That was up to the priest. And this priest knew how to do that, all right.

"You're here to see one of the prisoners, Father?"

"I am, my son," replied the priest. "Young Herold, bless his immortal soul."

"I can't let anyone in to see the prisoners without the proper authority, you understand, Father," apologized the jailer.

"I do understand, my son," said the priest. "You're Irish, I see."

It wasn't that much of a gamble. Most people in Washington had Irish blood in them somewhere, the priest knew that. And he could recognize the features. He himself might also have had some Irish blood running in his veins. Almost certainly.

The jailer beamed. "Mother was Irish," he said, almost joyfully.

"I knew it," replied the tall priest. "Terence Aloysius O'Hanrahan, of St. Peter's Church. You've seen me there, I'm sure."

"I think I have, Father. Yes, I have. Father Boyle buried my mother's sister two years back."

"You see him here a lot, my son." It was a statement, rather than a question, but the turnkey answered anyway. He was glad to talk—to someone, anyone, especially a fellow Irishman, and a priest at that.

"I do that, Father. He's the chaplain here. I've seen him work wonders with some of the demons."

"Frank Boyle. A very good man," reflected the priest, and his admiration for the Catholic pastor seemed genuine .

A moment's silence, during which the tall priest reflected on what he knew of Father Francis E. Boyle.

"There has to be a soldier in there with you, I'm afraid, Father," said the turnkey, suddenly, breaking the quietude.

"That's all right, my son, that's quite all right. I have to try to make young Herold's passage to the next world as easy for him as I can. That's my job. The soldier is most welcome to stay."

"I thought Herold was Piscopalian, Father," said the turnkey, a look of very mild perplexity crossing his brow, for he himself had admitted the Reverend Olds from Christ Church only yesterday.

"He doesn't know what he is, my son. It's up to us Irish, ain't it?."

Whatever that meant, it made some sort of sense to the jailer, and his face creased in a smile, a knowing smile.

"Well, if that's all there is, Father, we don't have to worry about it, eh? A guard, I mean."

"I suppose not. You know me anyway, my son."

"Come this way, Father."

This would have made a great story for Tom to tell Townsend and his other Washington cronies in later years. But he never did. All he said was that he got in to the prison to see Herold. And that according to Nicholas Quesenberry. If Tom had told Townsend this story, without the above elaboration, or an elaboration like it, then it would seem just like hot air—but Tom never told Townsend, despite the fact that it's a great story, and that it would have brought in some cash for Tom. In fact, the story wasn't even revealed until after Tom's death, so maybe, just maybe, Tom didn't tell all to the press, and that mysterious priest who visited Davey Herold at the end....

In interviews conducted in the 1880s, near the end of his life, Tom claimed that immediately after the assassination he fled to Cuba, then to England, returning after four of five years. He may have gone to Cuba and England, but he was not away four or five years. Not at all. He's not listed in the 1865 or 1866 city directories for Washington, D.C., which is disappointing although not surprising, but he certainly is listed for 1867 through

1879 inclusive—living and working at the National Hotel, as a clerk. And, as these city directories were published in the January of each year, the information for the 1867 directory, for example, was gathered in the summer and fall of 1866. So, we know he was back in D.C. by then, by mid to late 1866, at the very latest. His exclusion from the 1866 directory (compiled in late 1865) doesn't necessarily mean he wasn't in the city in late 1865—a person could be missed, or request to be excluded—but it's unlikely that he was in the capital in 1865. Things would have been just too hot for him then.

His Washington, D.C. death certificate (# 49547) of Nov. 1885 says he spent the last twenty years in D.C. Now that information is only as good as the informant, in this case his second wife. But she must have known. And twenty years from 1885 is 1865. Nineteen, twenty; it's close enough.

Maybe, just maybe, Tom was telling part of the truth about England. You never know, with a fellow like Tom. It's worth noting that when John Surratt fled to Canada, then from Quebec took ship to England—posing as Mr. McCarty, a man who had compromised himself during the Late Unpleasantness—he was accompanied by a shadowy man who has never been identified. Perhaps this was Tom Harbin. It's a long shot, but worth throwing in as a possibility. Surratt arrived in Liverpool on September 25, 1865, and hid out there at the Oratory of the Roman Catholic Church. Well-financed, from there he made his way to Italy, where, using the nom de guerre John Watson, he enlisted in the Papal Zouaves, the Vatican equivalent of the Foreign Legion. When the U.S. authorities found him the Zouaves happily gave him up (something the Foreign Legion would never have done), but John escaped to Egypt, where he was finally taken. On the way back to the U.S.A. he claimed that the assassination plot had been arranged by several men, some of whom were now living in New York and others in London. He didn't name names, but one of them may have been Harbin.

The National Hotel, a fashionable and famous place to stay, was where John Wilkes Booth had resided whenever he stayed in Washington. It's the same hotel where Tom Harbin worked the last part of his life, as a desk clerk.

The hotel, the largest in the city, at the corner of Pennsylvania Avenue and Sixth Street, was well placed geographically, and plied trade from the early 1830s until 1942.

In 1826 the Calverts began buying up land in the block that would be the hotel, and finally got a majority interest in the lots concerned. In 1830 an agreement was reached by George Calvert (who was descended from the Lords Baltimore), Roger C. Weightman, William A. Bradley, John Gadsby and Henry T. Weightman, whereby they would open a hotel, 200 by 250 feet. It cost $157,500, with George Calvert putting up $102,500. Gadsby and Augustine Newton became the first landlords of the five-story brick hotel.

Although always officially called the National Hotel, it was more commonly referred to as Gadsby's, then Coleman's. In 1849 the entire ownership passed to Calvert & Co., which was now headed by Charles Calvert (the son of George) and Dr. Richard Henry Stuart (George's son-in-law, and himself descended from the Royal Stuarts). Henry Clay died at the hotel in 1852. By this time, gone were the names Gadsby's and Coleman's, and everyone knew it as the National.

In 1857 Colonel Franklin Tenney, a Yankee, bought it. In 1873 William H. Crosby came in as co-owner. A lot of things happened at the National Hotel during the time Tom was a clerk there. Everyone stayed there. Tom knew everyone.

Not far away lived his son James T., who had spent all his meaningful life with his Uncle George. One doesn't quite know what the dynamics were between father and son, uncle and nephew, but one gets glimpses.

Tom continued on at the National Hotel for the rest of his life. Throughout such a long career at such a famous hostelry, and given his background, naturally he became part of the fiber, not only of the National, but, to some extent, of "society" life in Washington. Tom was far from invisible the last eighteen years of his life. His name often appeared in the newspapers in connection with some event happening at the National—some congressman committing suicide, someone famous coming to town.

One such happening was the Curtis-Tydings rape case (reported in the April 19, 1879 *Washington Post*). E.H. Curtis, alias Ray, was on trial for violating Miss Ella Tydings. "Mr. Thos. H. Harbin, clerk at the National Hotel, gave closing testimony for the prosecution, as to the registration of the name 'Maj. E.H. Curtis and Lady' on the hotel register of March 23, 1876."

By 1878 Tom was chief clerk. He finally married again, in early 1879, to Ella A. Cread. It had to have been the first two months of 1879 because the 1879 city directory still lists him as living at the National Hotel, and that directory reflected the summer and fall of the year before. And in the 1900 census Ella says she had been married 21 years (21 years ago is what she meant), and finally their daughter Blanche was born in November of 1879, so it had to be before, say, March 1879.

Some say Ella's last name was Langley, but that's wrong. Ella A., as she was always known, was—to put it kindly—casual about age, but she seems to have first seen the light of day in September 1846. Certainly by 1870 she was living in Washington, as Ella A. Cread, by herself, in a room at painter John C. Callahan's boarding house in the Second Ward. In the census of that year she was 24, a clerk at the Treasury, and born in Virginia (the part of Virginia that in 1863 became West Virginia). Both of her parents were born overseas, which bears out the family legend that she was an Irish girl.

We cannot find Ella in the 1850 census, or in the 1860. It is rare, very rare, that one is unable to find a person in two successive censuses. One maybe, but two! Who was she, really? There may be a mystery connected to this woman. It wouldn't be surprising in a girl who eight years later would become Tom Harbin's second wife. She had probably been in Washington since the war ended. She did not get married to Tom until 1878. Why did it take her all that time to get married?

Anyway, she and Tom set up house together at 718 First Street northwest, and had a daughter, Mary Blanche (known as Blanche) Harbin, on November 26, 1879, and a son, George Francis Harbin, on November 24, 1881. In the 1880s they would make their last move, to Number 11 Seventh Street southeast, a row house that Tom and his son James T. built in 1882.

After the war Thomas Austin Jones, Tom Harbin's widowed brother-in-law, moved to Baltimore with his children, and became an officer within the Baltimore correctional system (i.e. a jailer). He married again, to a woman forty years younger than him, Maggie, and they had a child. Tom Jones wrote a book about his life, especially about the good old days, a vainglorious book in humble sheep's clothing, in which he subtly maximizes himself and his role as Top Dog Confederate Agent, and barely mentions Tom Harbin, his own brother-in-law and probably his boss. In 1895, a year or two after the book came out, Tom A. Jones died.

Tom's sister, Johanna Howell, stayed on in Piscataway, in Prince George's County, Maryland.

Tom's other siblings remained together, as they always had (except when George was in jail, of course), and moved from their L Street house to 223 Eighth Street, between B and C streets. This would be George F. Harbin's address for a very long time.

Tom Harbin's elder surviving son, James T., spent the war years with his aunts and his Uncle George. George became young James T.'s bachelor father, in effect, and would remain so until he became an adult.

After the war, the widow's stepdaughter, Mary Louisa, filed suit against her for her share of the Nicholas Quesenberry estate. The case dragged on, the court ordered that the estate be auctioned off and Mary Louisa be given her share. The widow had a brother named Osceola Green (Zola, for short), who bid in and bought it for $4,035, and made an agreement with the widow that he would return the property to her if she would divide it between her children, which is what happened.

The estate was divided into three parts. The first, the home place (this would later become Jack's Marina), was 114.88 acres of open land, and 34.19 acres of wooded land. This went to Alice Yturbide Quesenberry. The second parcel, to the north of Alice's, comprised 237.74 acres, and this went to Nick Jr. Rousby Plater got the third section, 203 acres more or less of open land and 34.17 acres of wooded land to the east of Alice's lot. Mary Louisa, the stepdaughter who started all this dismemberment, got, of course, the money from the auction. Only Uncle Zola was out of pocket—four grand out of pocket—but he must have felt warm.

While this was all going on the widow continued on in Edge Hill, living with Tom Massey and his family. In her fifties the widow was farming in Potomac, King George's County, with young Nick, Alice and Rousby.

Young Nicholas Austin Quesenberry married Emma Coakley on November 23, 1887, and died in 1894. He and Emma had three daughters, only one of whom, Elizabeth Rose, survived childhood. That daughter married and had eight children, dying at 78.

The widow's daughter, Alice Yturbide Quesenberry, married Edwin Bruce. She sold her inheritance in the "Cottage" and moved to Texas to raise her three children. The widow, in her later years, would join Alice for a while in Texas.

Rousby Plater Quesenberry married Caroline Belle Price on Nov. 16, 1887, and died on Jan. 3, 1938, leaving descendants.

The famous widow Quesenberry died in Maryland on Sept. 13, 1896 and was buried the following day in Lot 204, Section 19, in Holy Rood Cemetery, in Washington, D.C.

In 1872 George F. Harbin opened up his dry goods store at 319 Pennsylvania Avenue, at the corner of Fourth Street southeast. This store, and more importantly, its successor in the same location (built, as new, out of brick in 1879 for $3,000), would become a well-known landmark in Washington, D.C., and George would become a respected and very active citizen of East Washington.

The 1894 book *Washington, D.C.*, says:

> Those residing on Capitol Hill find that there is no necessity for them to go downtown, for at Mr. Harbin's they can find a large and varied stock of fancy and staple dry goods at low prices. There are dress goods of every kind of fabric; then there are linens and underwear, stockings, and the thousand and one articles that ladies need for themselves and their children. The store is 28 × 75, and the stock is attractively displayed. Mr. Harbin is a native of Maryland but established his business in this city in 1872, his success being due to his own energy and constant attention to his customers. Ladies found that they could always be promptly waited upon and that they could be sure to find the prices as reasonable as elsewhere. Under such conditions success was the natural result.

George sold white goods, lawn, percales, summer merino underwear, parasols, sun umbrellas, oil cloths and mattings, Indian linens, striped and checked nainsooks, ginghams, seersuckers, black and colored cashmere, and last, but not least, gauze underwear for ladies, gents and children. If it was dry, George stocked it.

James T. Harbin, Tom's son, was a talented mimic and actor, and as soon as he was able to, he went on the stage. At first he played in every kind of role, but finally, by the late 1870s, he was specializing in comic readings. But acting wasn't going to pull in the money, so he clerked in his uncle's dry goods store to support his habit—one of a few habits, actually, and not all as benign as thespianism.

On January 15, 1878, according to the *Washington Post*, James T. was elected vice-president of St. Peter's Library Association. This group, also known as the St. Peter's Reading Room Association, was located on Capitol Hill. James T.'s uncle George F. Harbin was elected one of the directors. The society was young and aggressive, competing for the attention of Washingtonians with every other similar and dissimilar organization. But they were successful, at least for a time. There was talent, and so the people came.

They would do a lot, charity-wise, for St. Peter's, for both the church and the parochial school. The school had been built in 1867 by Father Boyle. On the evening of March 5, 1878 they packed the house for a musical and dramatic "entertainment," of which the *Washington Post* opined that "the comic reading of Mr. James T. Harbin was excellent." The group also performed the play *The Idiot Witness*, in which James T. had a part.

On the night of May 24, 1878, they put on James Pilgrim's play *Shandy Maguire, or the Bould Boy of the Mountain* at St. Peter's Schoolhouse, and it was a hit with the big crowd. They would always open with a variety performance, in which James T. would do his comic readings or some other humorous turn.

His little performing group, at that stage known as the Washington Octette Club, but which would soon become the Olivette Club due to a misprint in one of the papers (the little band liked the new name better), comprised Benson Kelly, Messrs Muller & Mawdsley, Katie De Barry, Nellie Darr, Charles Lenman, and Messrs Pic, Foley, Murphy, Kelly and Shea.

He was a joiner, was James T., trying to get a leg up in the Masonic world of postwar D.C., like everybody else. He belonged to everything, every club he could lay his hands on. For example, the Y.B.A.—the Young Bachelors Association. On May 8, 1878 the *Post* reported the Y.B.A.'s "hop" of the night before, dancing going on until 3 in the morning at McCauley's Hall.

Julia Harbin, Tom's eldest sister, died unmarried, aged 58, in 1879, and is buried in Mount Olivet Cemetery, in Washington, D.C. The *Washington Post* and the *Evening Star* both carried the same death notice: "On May 30, 1879, at 3 o'clock P.M., Julia A. Harbin. Funeral on Sunday, June 1, at 2:30 P.M., from 223 Eighth Street southeast, and proceed to St. Peter's Church. Relatives and friends of the family invited."

For a couple of years a serial rapist had been at large, and most Washington women (and some men) were scared to death come nightfall, although there were always some who perambulated nocturnally, propelled by the need for physical, if not emotional, closeness. These lonely souls provided cannon fodder. In February 1880 the villain struck again, but they got him just after he had violated Miss Lena Leins. The violator was a fearsome-looking black joker named Tom Smothers, and following his capture the capital was in a lynching mood. The outraged citizens of East Washington, to name but one section of the city, assembled together at McCauley's Hall on the evening of March 1 (*Washington Post* of March 2, 1880) and proceeded to work themselves into not only a committee but a frenzy. Hempen ropes came out, in the shape of nooses, and guns too, in the shape of guns. "Shoot the brute!" some said. "String him up," yelled others. George F. Harbin and Charles E. Joyce were leading members of the group that night, a group that got heated, but finally, when faced with clear mental images of the reality of the deed they were proposing, extinguished themselves of their own volition, and the law took its course. Tom Smothers never made another crack.

1880 Census
318 Pennsylvania Avenue, SE
Washington, D.C.

John W. Harbin, 56 [?—50 something], clerk in dry goods store, single, born Maryland, as were his parents

He was living virtually next door to (at 323)

James Coleman, 47, guard at jail, born in D.C., father born in Ireland, mother born in Scotland
Virginia Coleman, wife, 43, born in D.C., parents born in Maryland
Francis Coleman, son, 15, at school, born in D.C.
Charles Coleman, son, 13, at school, born in D.C.
Edwin Coleman, son, 11, at school, born in D.C.
Harrison Coleman, son, 7, born in D.C.
Maggie Coleman, daughter, 5, born in D.C.

And they lived next door but one to George F. Harbin's famous dry goods store at 319.

To have Tom Harbin's brother living next door to Charlie Russell's eldest daughter's godmother is more than a coincidence. It leads to the question "What was Thomas H. Harbin's connection to the Russells?"

Well, Charlie Russell's stepmother Janette was a Harbin, not by birth probably, but certainly by marriage. It's a fair bet that Thomas H. Harbin was her first husband's cousin—either first, second or third cousin—once removed. No more distant than that. Given the closeness of the Maryland community of the 1830s and 1840s, and of that of Washington during and after the Civil War, they must have known each other well. On top of that you have Tom Harbin's brother living next to Ann Virginia Smoot.

When you add to all this the fact that in the 1890 and 1891 city directories George F. Harbin, dry goods, has his business address at 318 Pennsylvania Avenue southeast, then things begin to take shape.

John Walter Harbin died in 1888 and was buried in Mount Olivet Cemetery in D.C. The *Washington Post* of May 18 of that year said: "On Thursday, May 17, 1888, John Walter Harbin, aged 63 years. Funeral from the residence of his brother, 223 Eighth Street southeast, Saturday morning at 8.30. Mass at St. Peter's Church at 11 o'clock." The *Evening Star* ran the same death notice, except it said that Mass would be at 9 o'clock.

Ann Virginia Smoot Coleman died on January 3, 1934, at Providence Hospital, in D.C.

Tom Harbin was an avid Democrat, which is not surprising (Abe Lincoln had been a Republican). In 1880 he belonged to the Jackson Democratic Association (now called the Jack Dem Ass, the old Dem Jack Ass), 16th District, and then, later that year, when the Democrats nominated Winfield Scott Hancock and William Hayden English to run for president and vice president against Garfield and Chet Arthur groups were formed around the country called "Hancock and English Clubs" (there were also, of course, "Garfield and Arthur Clubs"). South Washington formed their Young Men's National Hancock and English Club, and on the evening of July 20, 1880, at the Cosmopolitan Hotel in Washington, Tom Harbin was enrolled as a new member (*Washington Post*, July 21, 1880). This group would meet frequently at places such as Beeker's Hall, on the corner of Seventh Street and Virginia Avenue southwest. Tom's son, James T., was also a member.

Then there were major events, such as presidents coming to town for their inaugurations. Tom saw Grant in 1869 and 1873, Hayes in 1877, Garfield in 1881, and Cleveland in 1885.

It would have been distressing to Tom that Garfield won in 1880. On March 1, 1881, the president-elect arrived in Washington, D.C., for his inauguration, and to take up residence. A couple of months later another man moved to Washington, and also took up residence in the nation's capital, albeit not in as handsome a residence as the new Garfield home.

That most notorious and despicable of "disgruntled office seekers," Charles J. Guiteau, had had a vision from God. God had given the young Michigander a mission—to assassinate Mr. Garfield. Guiteau duly carried out this mission, at the Washington Train station on July 2, 1881. That Tom Harbin was working at the National Hotel, and was known for his political views, and already having experience in the presidential assassination field, leads to some interesting, but totally unprovable, speculations.

Tom's life had changed drastically since the old days of the Civil War. Now, like his brother George, a respected citizen, he attracted some considerable attention because of who he was, but this was all to his good and to the hotel's. He became a staple, a fixture, a member of carnival committees and fireworks committees. He was also a married man, the last person in the world one would want to associate with an assassination, yet...

At the time of the presidential inauguration of Grover Cleveland in D.C. Tom was on the Committee of Public Comfort, one of the dozen or so heavily-stocked committees that would make sure the event went off without a hitch. It was a rare moment for Tom—a Democrat in the White House, a moment he hadn't seen since before the Civil War.

As for Tom's son, James T., on April 20, 1881, he and the Olivette Club gave a soirée at the Washington Hall, corner of Third Street and Pennsylvania Avenue southeast. Those present included Jennie Mitchell. James T. would run into Jennie again at the most memorable strawberry festival he ever worked the shooting gallery for, the one held on June 8, 1881, for the benefit of St. Peter's Church.

Jennie was really Jane Adele Mitchell, daughter and one of ten children of 928 K Street, D.C. blacksmith Joseph T. Mitchell by his wife Margaret Ann Martin.

With marriage plans afoot, James T. needed something more stable than acting and social events, more financially rewarding than the Catholic Knights of America.

The Catholic Knights were a lot less sinister than they sound. They were a fraternal life-insurance company organized in Nashville in 1877 and who by 1882 had several branches throughout the country. Carroll Branch #224 was formed in Washington on April 10 of that year. One of the founding officers was James T. Harbin, trustee. Another was Andrew P. McKenna, sentinel. James T. Harbin it was who got his father to join the Knights.

Being always conscious of, and willing to take advantage of, his Uncle George's deep pockets, James T. was able to be a plunger. He knew that in the event of failure (which was always a threat, lurking on his shoulder in the form of a booze-ridden specter), George F. would forgive him, smile tolerantly, and hand out some more bread for the next venture. This is not to imply in any way that James T. was anything but a very, very bright lad. It's just that his level of responsibility, whatever it might have been originally, had been considerably lowered by John Barleycorn, and that level was getting lower every day. But, now he had a wife.

So, his next trick was to invent an electroplating process, of all things—the Harbin Process. This is just another example of James T.'s remarkably versatile brain and his boundless energy, his desire to coin, a desire restricted only by his desire to lose. He and his partner, Tap Young, patented the process, and then called in Uncle George F. Harbin to arrange the next step, which was to hold a meeting of local bigwigs at the National Hotel.

George F. and his brother Tom arranged for the use of a room there, and on the evening of July 17, 1882 the Washington Electro-Plating Company was launched. Thirty thousand dollars was subscribed that night, with stock going from $50 to $250, and with stockholders that included George F. and Tom Harbin, and great Harbin friend Joseph Waltemyer, the hatter who would not long in the future be one of the pallbearers at Tom Harbin's funeral.

James T. and Tap incorporated the company under the laws of West Virginia, but headquartered it in Washington. On August 1, 1882, Clement W. Howard was elected president of the company, and by early September they had their plant, in a building they leased opposite the Norfolk Steamer's wharf at the foot of Sixth Street southwest. Steam facilities were included in the lease. The company began operations on September 9, 1882.

On September 25, 1882, James T. Harbin, the spy's son, married Jennie Mitchell, the blacksmith's daughter, at St. Peter's Catholic Church, Washington, D.C. Father Edward F. Ryan performed the ceremony; witnesses were Jennie's sister Nannie V. Mitchell and George De Neal.

Father Boyle was 55 when he developed bladder stones. They rushed him into the operating ward where Dr. McKim, Dr. Bayne, and a team of specialists smashed the stones, and in a jubilant and triumphant mood began to remove them. At that moment something went horribly wrong and Father Boyle's head snapped back, veins bulged on his temples, his face turned color, and he died—March 13, 1882. The funeral was impressive. One of his pallbearers, representing the St. Peter's phase of his life, was George F. Harbin. Father Boyle was laid to rest in Mount Olivet.

Head clerk Tom Harbin of the National Hotel handled crises. The *Washington Post* of September 13, 1883, tells a most fascinating story about "a slick swindler":

> Several days ago an individual calling himself Greenwood arrived in this city and took up his abode at the National Hotel. There was nothing in the man's attire or the language he used that would indicate him to be anything but a gentleman. With a tall, commanding figure and an easy flow of good English, he readily created a favorable impression among those around him. He represented himself as the publisher of a journal or book called *Outings*, and received from Mr. Ed Sterns, of Scheller & Sterns, druggists, a card for which he was paid two dollars in advance. Next he introduced himself to the furnishing house of Perkins & Stevens, and ordered $10 worth of shirts, etc., "sent up to No. 62." The goods were delivered and payment was to be made in the morning. French Queen at the cigar stand permitted him to indulge to the tune of $4.80 without the cash. During the several days he was here he employed a horse and buggy from Price & Son, livery men, which he kept until the bill reached $30, and the same was found Tuesday night late near the Baltimore and Potomac depot lot, where it had been deserted. The horse was nearly dead and it is thought that is what saved it and the buggy for its owner. The hotel he beat to the extent of $20, and because the chief clerk, Mr. Harbin, refused to loan him cash from the drawer he denounced him and reported that he would have him discharged from the house's

employ. These are the facts so far as they have come to light. How many persons he victimized during his stay in the city is unknown, but he certainly proved himself "very smooth." Price, the livery man, is out in the wilds gunning for the impostor.

The *Washington Post* of September 30, 1883, noted that "the show windows of George Harbin's store were a beautiful sight last night," but that edition of the *Post* is more memorable for the bizarre story, totally unrelated, but worth telling again down the centuries:

> Two weeks ago a family named Maginnis moved in one of the houses near the Congressional Cemetery. One of their children, a boy of eleven years, has been acting very strangely ever since they moved. For several days back he felt a strange feeling arising in his throat and yesterday was taken with vomiting, which resulted in his throwing up a full-size frog. The boy, on seeing the frog, fell into a fit.

The *Washington Post* of July 30, 1884 says:

> Seeking speedy death. Congressman Culbertson of Kentucky attempts to commit suicide. Hon. William Wirt Culbertson, the Republican representative from the Ninth Kentucky District, shot himself three times in the head with a revolver commonly known as the Swamp Angel, caliber .38, at the National Hotel, about 11 o'clock yesterday morning, and at 1 o'clock P.M. was removed to Providence Hospital in a serious if not dangerous condition.
>
> The circumstances preceding the shooting as detailed to a *Post* reporter by Mr. Harbin, the well-known clerk of the National Hotel, are interesting as throwing a flood of light on the desperate act of the would-be suicide.
>
> "He came here last Saturday from Cape May," said Mr. Harbin, "looking as though he had been indulging too much. In fact, he told me he had been drinking very heavily and was easing off on lager. He looked nervous and unwell. I don't believe he has drank [sic] anything strong here since Saturday. All day yesterday nothing to drink except soda cocktails was sent to his room."
>
> "Did you see him this morning?," inquired the Post reporter.
>
> "Yes," replied Mr. Harbin, "He came down to the office at 6 o'clock this morning looking very nervous and wanting his room changed. He said the people in the next room had been fighting and raising the devil all night, and that he had sent for the proprietor, who had seemed to side with the disorderly persons. Knowing that there was no one on either side of his room, I said, 'Mr. Culbertson, you are not well. Why don't you send for a doctor? I will change your room, but you need medical attention.' He said if he didn't feel better he would take my advice. I had his baggage moved to 27, one flight up, and at 9:50 o'clock, feeling anxious about him, I took a servant and went to his room, telling the servant to go in, and if Mr. Culbertson was asleep to come out, and if he was awake, to ask him if he wanted anything. The servant had scarcely touched the knob of the door when Culbertson cried out in a startled voice, "Who's there?.' The servant then went in and Culbertson ordered him to bring him a pitcher of ice water, which he did. This is the last I saw of him until I heard the report of the shots."
>
> At about 11 o'clock five shots in rapid succession startled the guests and loungers in the hotel and the Irish porter ran to Culbertson's room, but hearing the fusillade inside beat a rapid retreat, nearly knocking over in his flight Policemen Farrar and Lamb, who were coming up stairs and who were the first to enter the room. On opening the door the would-be suicide stood before them, clutch-

ing the pistol, his head dripping with blood and his eyes distended in terror. "My God, man, what have you done?," ejaculated Officer Farrar.

"I was tired of life," was the reply. "I have fired five shots and fear I haven't finished the job yet. Isn't there another load in the pistol?"

By this time the officers had disarmed him and were pushing him back upon the bed upon which he was disinclined to go, saying, "Let me lie on the oil cloth. There's no use soiling the bed."

Anyway, the upshot was the doctors came, the congressman got better even while he was in the room, and his wife was sent for, something he didn't want at all. Examination revealed that, while he didn't miss with all the bullets, he suffered only scalp wounds.

Tom Harbin became something of a celebrity during his last years at the National Hotel. So did his brother-in-law, Thomas Austin Jones. This was largely because these two remarkable men began to talk, and also because they made the acquaintance of George Alfred Townsend.

Townsend was seven years younger than Tom. He had been the youngest war correspondent during the Civil War and by the 1880s was famous as a reporter and novelist. He used the pen name "Gath." In the 1880s he got to know the two Toms well. They would have long talks, and although politically at opposite ends of the spectrum to the reporter, Harbin and Jones were able, by their frankness and the fidelity of their character (to quote Townsend again), to soften his "feelings on the subject of Mr. Lincoln's abduction." Townsend doesn't say what he thought about the assassination.

There is another article, dated 1883 and, probably from a Philadelphia paper, on the subject of the National Hotel. Titled "A Splendid Hotel," it gives a brief history of the hotel and extols its virtues and rates for Pennsylvanians, and then affably boasts, "The proprietors Messrs [Colonel Franklin] Tenney and [William H.] Crosby, take pleasure in looking after the comfort of their guests, and are ably assisted by a corps of gentlemanly and obliging clerks headed by Col. Harbin and Mr. Joyce."

This Mr. Joyce was James F. Joyce, an Irishman 29 years old at the time (1883). Jim Joyce was very well known, as was Tom Harbin, and was famous for, among others things, using hickory nut crème on his paté. This newspaper clipping, unfortunately minus the title of the publication but with (only) an 1883 date, comes from the "Tenney Family Scrapbook" made up by Franklin Tenney's daughter Georgette A. Chamberlin, which now resides in the Perkins Library at Duke University in North Carolina. Colonel Tenney died on November 22, 1896, aged 89, and his daughter Georgette Chamberlin died at 90, on February 23, 1922.

Then there was Tom's private life. He and Ella had two children, but Tom also had, living close by, his first son, James T., with whom relations were necessarily complex because young James T. had been raised by Tom's brother George. Yet, by and large, he and his son got along well, Tom helping James T. in any way he could, James T. playing on Tom's guilt, Tom subscribing financially to James T.'s ventures, James T. playing on Tom's guilt. They even went into business together, James T. playing on Tom's guilt. On May 17, 1882, they were given a building permit for some construction on Seventh Street. This was Number 11, where Tom would live for the rest of his life.

Thomas Henry Harbin, former Confederate agent, was forced, through illness, to quit his post at the National Hotel, and drew up his last will and testament on December 16, 1884. After 23 days of his last illness, he died of cirrhosis of the liver and stomach on November 18, 1885. For some peculiar reason—but very fitting for that—his death date has been surrounded with mystery, as was his life. Some sources erroneously give November 19, 1886, and his death certificate, unbelievably, is also wrong—it claims November 15, 1885.

The Washington newspapers are the source to go to for accurate details regarding Tom's last moments. The *Post* of November 16, 1885, warned its readers: "Mr. Thomas Harbin, for a number of years connected with the National Hotel, is lying dangerously ill at his residence, No. 11 7th St., southeast." The *Evening Star* of the same day said: "Mr. Thomas Harbin, formerly clerk at the National Hotel, is lying dangerously ill at his residence, No. 11 7th Street southeast."

The *Post* of November 19, 1885 tells us, quite definitely, "Mr. Thomas F. Harbin [sic], formerly a clerk at the National Hotel and a well-known resident of this city, died yesterday at his residence, No. 11 7th St., southeast, after an illness of several weeks' duration." The *Evening Star* tells us that he drew his last breath at 8:10 A.M. His death certificate says he was 52 years 2 months and 24 days when he died.

The *Post* of November 21, 1885, relates, in its section "Bits of Local News," that "A large number of leading citizens and members of the Catholic Knights of America yesterday attended the funeral of Thomas H. Harbin, for many years one of the clerks at the National Hotel and a well-known resident of East Washington. The remains were taken to St. Peter's Church, where services were conducted by Rev. Father Sullivan. The casket was covered with floral tributes. It was borne to the hearse by Messrs Crosby and Britton of the National, Joseph Waltemyer, Shaw [sic], F.X. Dooley, and M.I. Weller."

Dr. Francis Xavier Dooley (died in 1913), a pharmacist and druggist and neighbor of hatter Joseph Waltemyer, was a pioneering physician in D.C., and, not unincidentally, a peddler of tonics with the most alluring of Arabian, Persian and other Eastern names. Britton was a fellow clerk, Lloyd L. Britton; and Crosby was William H. Crosby, co-owner with Franklin

Tenney of the National Hotel. Immediately after the funeral Crosby took his first trip in seven years, to New Hampshire.

Tom's funeral procession left St. Peter's Church in Washington, bound for Lot 154, Section 27, in Mount Olivet, the biggest Catholic Cemetery in Washington, where Tom was buried with his brothers and sisters. There is a big marker there for the Harbins as a family and small surface markers for the individuals. Tom has a surface marker.

Tom's will left everything to his wife Ella and to the two youngest children. James T. was excluded, because he was doing so well. Tom's will, in its entirety, is given Appendix B.

Just before Tom died on November 18, 1885, correspondent George Alfred Townsend, who had known Harbin for some time, and who had, indeed, written at least one previous article on him (*Cincinnati Enquirer*, August 1, 1884), did another interview with him as part of a 20th-anniversary series he was doing on the Lincoln assassination. This interview was published in the *Daily National Hotel Reporter*, despite its name a semi-weekly out of Chicago. Unfortunately there are in existence in the United States no copies anywhere of any edition close to 1885 of the *Hotel Reporter*, not at any recognized repositories, anyway. Champaign—Urbana has a later run, 1920s and 1930s; the Chicago Historical Society has only a few editions; and the Chicago Public Library has nothing at all. This is a disaster in itself, but for collectors of Harbin material it is a deathwatch beetle.

However, all is not lost. We can get a flavor of this interview. A few days after Tom died Townsend wrote an obituary on him in a Washington newspaper (unknown paper—masthead lopped off, but it is not the *Star* or the *Post*; we have only a typed copy of the clipping).

This obituary was titled "A Hotel Clerk with a History." Its sub-headline was "Thomas Harbin, who was a rebel spy, and who furnished Wilkes Booth his horse at the time of Lincoln's assassination."

Then it goes on to say.

> The *Chicago Hotel Reporter* contained a few weeks since a brief sketch of the life of Thomas Harbin, for over fifteen years a clerk at the old National Hotel in Washington. Harbin died a few days ago, and, although during life a very quiet, reserved man, and singularly reticent as to himself, since his death one or two of his most intimate friends have unconsciously told little scraps of history concerning the deceased, which show him to have been a man with a history, and do much toward clearing up one of the mysteries connected with the assassination of Mr. Lincoln. It appears that Harbin, during the Rebellion, was in the secret employ of Jefferson Davis, who used him to carry dispatches between Richmond and Baltimore. Many instances of the hardships and dangers encountered by Harbin are related. On one occasion, while disguised as a farmer, he was carrying an important message from Mr. Davis to an employee of the Confederacy, in Baltimore. Harbin was surrounded by twenty or thirty Federal cavalrymen, who demanded his immediate surrender. He realized the fact that his capture meant

death and, grasping a revolver in each hand, fired at his would-be captors. The audacity of the man probably saved his life, for the soldiers were amazed at his pluck, and before the fire could be returned Harbin had put spurs to his horse and made his escape. It will be remembered that J. Wilkes Booth, after the shooting of the President at Ford's Theatre, made his escape on horseback from the city. The horse ridden by Booth was traced by Colonel [Lafayette] Baker's detectives to the possession of a man named Wilson who caused the beast to be properly bridled and saddled and taken to the stage door of the theatre. Baker's detectives hunted all over the world for a clew to the identity of the man Wilson, and, at one time, a reward of $5,000 or $10,000 was offered by the War Department for his apprehension. It is now said that Harbin was Wilson. Harbin was in Washington just before the assassination occurred, and at Booth's request provided him with a horse. Harbin recently told his friends that he did not understand the reason why Booth desired the horse or he would not have been a party to the scheme. He said Booth deceived him, and he did not realize the fact until after the shooting. Harbin made his escape from Washington the same night. He went South, thence to Cuba and England, returning to Washington after a lapse of four or five years, and has been at the National Hotel ever since.

So, that's the unidentified obituary, written by Townsend, and based on the article he'd written not long before in the *Hotel Reporter*. This obituary is also the source of much of the Harbin lore that is repeated as the unvarnished truth. However, who knows how much of what Tom told Townsend is true? Tom sang, indeed, but he had a chronic tendency to warble off-key.

Anyway, at the bottom of the typescript copy of this obituary it says "From Elizabeth E. Atwater's Scrapbook at the Chicago Historical Society, paper date 11/1885."

Seven years later Townsend's byline appeared on a front page item of the April 18, 1892, *Cincinnati Enquirer*. This wasn't an article at all, merely a filler, something the paper thought would be useful to fill space and to gain a bit of attention. It was a series of notes badly cobbled together, and it is very doubtful if Townsend even knew it had gone in.

This *Enquirer* "article" focuses on Booth's escape after the assassination, and very definitely gives the impression of being a summary of the Townsend story, or a combination of Townsend stories, but it is certainly not the Harbin interview itself. It tells very little that we don't already know. Primarily it discusses the meeting in the Bryantown tavern in 1864 between Mudd, the Marylander Harbin (the principal signal officer or spy, as he is described) and Booth, and not much of that. It says that Booth and Harbin went up to a room on the second floor of the tavern and that Booth paced around theatrically looking for enemy ears, and outlined his plan to kidnap Lincoln. The piece describes Harbin as a cool man, who had seen many spies and liars. It says he thought Booth was a crazy fellow, but that he (Harbin) decided to go in with the kidnap plot. That's it.

Many years later, in the 1980s, when the new breed of scholars began to penetrate remaining assassination mysteries with new tools and devices, they went looking for what they'd heard was the famous Harbin interview, and found what they thought was it—on the front page of the *Cincinnati Enquirer* of 1892. They didn't realize that there were at least four pieces that could be termed "The Harbin Interview"—the 1884 *Enquirer*, the 1892 *Enquirer*, the *Hotel Reporter* article written just before Tom's death, and the November 1885 obituary (in newspaper unknown), also written by Townsend.

This 1892 *Enquirer* piece entered the assassination canon as the famous "Harbin Interview," as written by Townsend in 1885. This, despite a problem that no one seemed able to address, let alone answer: Why did it take seven years between the time Harbin gave the interview and the time it appeared in the *Enquirer*? The answer is, because this is not the "Harbin Interview." The Harbin interview, at least the 1885 interview, along with the paper that contained it—the *Hotel Reporter*—was lost.

Then it came to the attention of someone, probably James O. Hall, that the Chicago Historical Society had a collection of correspondence of a woman named Elizabeth E. Atwater. Somehow this collection had come to contain a clipping from an unidentified newspaper of an article entitled "A Hotel Clerk with a History." This was the obituary, written by Townsend just after Tom died.

Elizabeth Emerson Atwater herself has been described as mysterious. She was the wife of Samuel T. Atwater, an official of the U.S. government during Lincoln's administration. Mrs. Atwater, best remembered as a herbologist and botanist, was born in Greenport, Long Island, NY, and educated at Madame Emma Willard's Seminary in Troy, N.Y. She died on April 11, 1878, in Buffalo, a full seven years before Harbin died. In 1867 Mrs. Lincoln, the President's widow, had given her an album, which today resides in the Peggy Noedebart Library in Chicago. Aside from it being Mrs. Atwater's, this album is not connected in any way with her correspondence, which is held in the Chicago Historical Society's library.

Mrs. Atwater did not collect the Harbin Interview, because she died seven years before it was written. But someone did. And whoever did put it in with her correspondence. That's all there is to it.

There is another obituary of Tom, a much shorter one, in the *National Republican Newspaper*, printed in Washington, D.C.

On May 22, 1886, the *Washington Post* announced that Ella A. Harbin had been appointed guardian to the children of Thomas H. Harbin, on a $1,000 bond. This was standard procedure, to make sure she was a fit mother. She and the two children—Blanche and George—would continue to live at the Seventh Street house until Ella died in 1918, and even then the children would continue to live there until Blanche died.

Tom's youngest brother, George F. Harbin, the dry goods man, outlived them all. In the period following Tom's death, George was constantly on the go—not just with his dry goods business, and not just with buying and selling real estate, renting out his properties, and placing ads for his business and rentals, but also with the civic responsibilities that came with his position in the community. He was a member for years of the East Washington Association. His name appears all over the newspapers as a member of this or that committee, this or that posse comitatus that went to see the commissioners for some hearing to do with improving his Capitol Hill neck of Washington, D.C. If there was trouble in his community, George was in there.

Washington, D.C. [1894], says, "Mr. Harbin has been associated with the growth and development of the Eastern section of the city and … is considered one of the solid citizens of Capitol Hill, and is quite popular in all circles."

He was a director of the National Capital Bank of Washington (which in 1889—to cite but one year—had a capital of $200,000); he would be one of the founding members and a director of the East Washington Savings Bank.

This latter was quite a venture, begun by principals of the National Capital Bank. It was started in the first week of May, 1905, in a building on the north side of Pennsylvania Avenue southeast, between Third and Fourth streets, very close to George's store, Capitol Hill being one of the best business areas in Washington at that time. It was capitalized without any problem at $100,000, divided into 10,000 shares of $10 each. John E. Herrell was elected president, and George F. Harbin was one of the first directors.

All the newspapers ran a display ad which really maximized the use of space: "The East Washington Savings Bank opens for business this morning, at 9 A.M., in the directors' room of the National Capital Bank. Open an account." Big letters for this last, but not so big as to be gaudy. A nice ad.

George was a very popular pick for juries, notably the one in November 1884 that decided on the trial of George Hough, accused of murdering William McMahon on September 26. He was rejected for as many juries as he sat on, however, both by defense counsel and the prosecution. This was nothing unusual. Everyone was rejected sooner or later. George was bounced off the Soltedo Murder Case of 1882, as well as the trial of Langster, the police capper (cop-killer), which was probably just as well, as "Langster grinned and scowled by turns" at his trial (*Washington Post*, October 28, 1884), and that might have been more than George could bear, firebrand enemy of crime that he was, former jailbird and rabid Secesh.

Pallbearing duties often called him, the older he got, usually at his own place of worship—St. Peter's Catholic Church, on Capitol Hill. Father Boyle, on March 13, 1882; Andrew Leonard, on March 14, 1884; Mrs. Ann Dooley, Michael Dooley's widow, on Oct. 1, 1890. Many more, as they all died off.

Any worthy cause that was going, George was there. He collected contributions (and made them) for the victims of the Johnstown Flood in 1889 (he gave $15), and for the Destitute in Ireland (in 1880 he was on the executive committee of 25 for this fund).

He would also take on limitless responsibilities. Having no wife helped. In 1886 George F. Harbin won custody, in Case # 1147 in the D.C. courts, of a family of orphaned minors, the children of Washington carpenter turned cop, major St. Peter's parishioner and Catholic Knight Andrew P. McKenna. The McKennas were next door neighbors of chemist Francis X. Dooley, a friend of Tom Harbin's, and also lived a few doors down from hatter Joseph Waltemyer, another Harbin friend, and more to the point, were also immediate neighbors of Ann Virginia Coleman, nee Smoot, Charlie Russell's daughter's godmother.

This good McKenna deed was similar to one George pulled off on March 19, 1884, when he was made trustee of the will of the late Mary L. Brawner, so he could pay her debts and distribute the balance between her children and grandchildren. George would spend the next several months doing this, and auctioning off her property. George was the one trusted. Another time the widow Brooke's son Andrew got drunk one night in July 1894, flexed his egregiousness, and was sentenced to three months. George interceded on the widow's behalf, and the boy was pardoned.

George F. Harbin was a member of the Catholic Club, and on October 4, 1891 was elected its president. He was also very active in getting funds together for a new St. Peter's Church (the old church, built in 1820, had been only the second Catholic church in D.C.—St. Patrick's had been the sole place of Papist worship in the capital until then).

Just like George was the Eastern Dispensary and Casualty Hospital. It had all started in 1888 when it became apparent to the thinking citizens of East Washington, and more importantly to the sick and damaged persons who had no money, that a dispensary was needed in their part of town to provide free medical help to the indigent. The great and the good got together and enlisted the help of more big wheels, and articles of incorporation for the "Eastern Dispensary of the District of Columbia" were filed on April 14, 1888, the corporation being good for ten years. George F. Harbin was one of the signatories, and would be treasurer for years.

They rented a building just across the road from George's store, on Pennsylvania Avenue southeast, between Third and Fourth streets, and bought all the necessary equipment and personnel to run such an institution. But it was tough going. Money was always needed, and the expenses were fantastic. An "Eastern Dispensary Association" was formed, mostly by concerned ladies, and fund drives were endless—events such as lawn parties, steamer excursions, musical soirées, even jousting and traveling bands of musical Eskimos. All this kept the money trickling in, but it was not enough, not in those early days, anyway. As an example, the period between July 1, 1888, and April 30, 1889, saw 883 patients treated. During this span the dispensary received only $506.03 from voluntary contributions, and $150 from the District of Columbia.

The National Hotel did more than its fair share to help. With George Harbin's connections there through his late brother Tom, W.H. Crosby and Georgette Chamberlin came through in spades, giving free space to events and becoming board directors of the corporation. Miss Chamberlin was vice-president of the Eastern Dispensary Association. George's sister, Sarah Priscilla Harbin, was a "lady patroness."

It was dangerous to belong to the Eastern Dispensary. The *Washington Post* of August 23, 1888, reports: "Dr. Carraher [Dr. John Victor Carraher, a young Irishman born in Scotland, who came over with his parents in 1860, and who was recently of Montgomery County, Maryland], of the Eastern Dispensary, while standing at one of the windows of that institution, about two o'clock last Tuesday afternoon, narrowly escaped being injured. A bullet struck the sash, splintering and breaking the glass in his face. Fortunately he only received a few scratches."

On May 10, 1895, the subject of adding an emergency department to the dispensary came up, and they commenced construction, adding on, and in 1896 finally bought the building for $10,000. Still it was difficult financially; they were always running at a loss, and the stream of fund-raising events never ceased. At one, on December 17, 1899, the extraordinary Daisy Joyce provided accompaniments. In 1897 the name of the venture changed to the Eastern Dispensary and Emergency Hospital, which would eventually mutate into the Eastern Dispensary and Casualty Hospital, the name it is best remembered by. The institution re-incorporated on April 1, 1898, for twenty years.

George F. Harbin also had to put up with the seamier side of life firsthand, like everyone else. In 1893 a gang was going around robbing houses in East Washington. The modus operandi was the same each time: daring entries through windows, silent, stealthy, taking all sorts of stuff—heavy stuff like cabinets, tables, chairs, you name it—even while the inhabitants of the house slept, and slashing with a knife anything and everything that couldn't be carried away. It was an awfully disturbing time for the citizens of East Washington. Then George's house got hit.

His niece Margaret's husband, Adam Weschler, was staying with him on the night the gang cut the slats on his guest window, the room Adam Weschler was sleeping in. He didn't hear a thing (*Washington Post*, November 13, 1893). In March of the following year they finally nabbed the gang, which turned out to be a gang of one—"Jack the Slasher," as they called him, a very strong man, actually a normal man made strong by sheer madness, who, it seems, could often be discerned at two o'clock in the morning carrying tables and armoires on his back through the streets of Washington. Anyone who bothered to ponder such an unusual sight would have figured he was a one-man removals outfit. And besides, who, including the police, is going to question the motives of a man strong enough to carry a fully-loaded armoire on his shoulders?

Jack the Slasher, upon being caught, made the classic understatement: "I have done wrong and I know it."

On another occasion George was bilked by a very respectable looking man who bought some dry goods (gauze underwear for his wife) to the tune of $12, gave George a check, and then left. They never caught the bilker with the gauze underwear.

With all this frenetic activity George sometimes forgot the more mundane things of life, such as his taxes. He appeared several times in the delinquent list. One would think, surely it's not as if he didn't have the money. It's just that he forgot. Well, did he…? The warning bells were clearly tolling, for those who could hear them.

Tom's eldest son, James T. Harbin, had a couple of daughters by his wife Jennie Mitchell—Marie Anna on September 17, 1883, and Margaret on January 21, 1891. But despite these cuddly additions to his life, early on the booze problem began to rear its ugly head.

James T.'s drinking problem was the undoing of the marriage, short term and long term. By 1890 he was living at a hotel at 1458 Corcoran Street northwest, still heading the Electro-Plating Company. Jennie was staying with her family at 919 New York Avenue northwest, with the children. Then they got back together, and then it happened again.

Those time-worn words "You'd better do something or I'm leaving you" had an effect on James T., such that it propelled him northward to the Illinois town of Dwight.

Alcoholism has always been rampant in the U.S.A., and no period of American history can be said to be more sotted than any other, but the last twenty years of the 19th century certainly had its fair share of alcoholics. In 1879, in the little town of Dwight, Illinois, Dr. Leslie E. Keeley, New York–born son of an Irish immigrant, attempted to address this problem (and at the same time, but purely as a secondary intention, to make money) by opening the doors to his huge mansion-style headquarters of the first Keeley Institute. Keeley had invented a radical and what became a controversial cure for the "liquor, opium, chloral and cocaine habits." Other nasty habits, such as tobacco, were also included in his catalogue.

The Keeley Cure consisted of substantial injections of bichloride of gold (despite the fact that there is no such thing!), alcohol and strychnine, hence its alternate name "The Gold Cure," which certainly had a ring to it, an aura that attracted thousands and thousands. Group therapy and community service also played a large part in the treatment, and it was all very successful, both for the patients and for Keeley. They got cured, local governments provided interest-free loans to patients because of the Cure's evident efficacy, and Dr. Keeley became rich.

"Graduates" of the Keeley Cure were encouraged to go public and take their triumph on the road as franchise-holders. These franchises, called either the Keeley Institute or, more elaborately the "Bichloride of Gold Club," would soon spring up all over the world, and, of course, all of this made Dr. Keeley even richer. One of his star pupils, one of his big success stories, was James T. Harbin. James T. had seen the light at Dwight.

Each franchise had a medical director, a physician in charge, who lived on the premises. There was also a business manager, who might or might not live in, depending on how he was otherwise set up (i.e. was a certain propinquity desirable?). The nurses and other key staff also lived on the premises, so they could all get to a frothing patient if need be—and there were frothing patients.

In 1891 James T. made the first moves toward opening up a franchise in Washington, D.C. He would be the business manager, which was a natural because he had access to a lot of old Uncle George Harbin's money.

The *Washington Post* of January 28, 1892, reported: "The initial steps toward the formation of a Washington branch of the Bichloride of Gold Club were taken last evening. A small company of former patients of the Keeley Institute met at the residence of Mr. J.T. Harbin, 207 C Street southeast, and discussed the project most enthusiastically." James T. was secretary and general manager, and his uncle George was treasurer. (Maybe George F. went to Dwight too; we do not know what George's drinking habits were). None other than Franklin P. Tenney, owner of the National Hotel, was one of the directors.

On the night of February 4, 1892, the club met again at James T.'s house and the franchise was officially initiated. James T. was elected temporary chairman and W.F.M. Bolies temporary secretary.

Dr. Keeley came down from Dwight, proud of his protégé, and they all threw a big party for the big man at the Arlington Hotel on the night of February 8, 1892.

This franchise officially opened at 1008 F Street northwest, under the guidance of J.R. Ragan.

In 1892 James T. opened his own franchise, on Virginia Avenue, in Hagerstown, Maryland, and planned yet another one, to open at Oak Crest, Maryland. However, instead, he finally opened his second franchise at Laurel, Maryland, in Prince George's County, in September 1892. Again, this was organized under the laws of West Virginia, with a capital stock of $100,000. He called this one "the Leslie," after his rich mentor. Dr. A.D. Leech was physician in charge. "The Leslie" was a three-story house, with forty well-ventilated, modern rooms, heated by the Bolton hot water system, and powered by electricity from its own plant. The house was under the personal charge of Mr. Harry S. Benson, a well-known hotel man, who was, for a number of years, connected with the National Hotel in Washington. James T. and his company ran the Hagerstown and Laurel franchises simultaneously.

As the book *Washington, D.C.* (1894) says, "Mr. James T. Harbin, the general manager of this institute [Laurel] and one at Hagerstown, Md., is a well and prominently known and connected businessman. He is a native of Prince George's County, Maryland, but for a number of years resided in Washington where he followed his profession of stenographer."

His partner in the Hagerstown franchise was Dr. Frank Percival, with whom he became very close. James T. even named one of his children after the good doctor. However, there was a dispute over the city water supply to the institute and James T. sued the City of Hagerstown. The water issue left a bad taste.

At 4 o'clock in the afternoon on Friday, September 29, 1893, a stenographer named Frank Doyle was admitted to the Laurel clinic, shaking badly with delirium tremens. The staff wrestled him onto the bed, stuck a needle into him, and he fell asleep. However, at midnight, he woke up raving and frothing. They knocked him out again, but when they went to check on him at seven o'clock the next morning, the trembling stenographer was dead, stiff as a board. The Keeley Institute was exonerated (*Washington Post*, October 21, 1893).

James T. and Jennie had a third and last child, a son, Francis Percival Harbin—"Frank," as he became known—on January 3, 1895, but unfortunately the old devil came back and James T. fell off the wagon. The franchises all failed, and he and his family moved back in with old Uncle George. James T. was fulfilling his destiny.

Then came the Spanish—American War, and James T. thought he'd try that. He left Jennie and the children with Uncle George and went off to Jacksonville, Florida, to enlist as a volunteer hospital steward on June 20, 1898. It has always been assumed that he went to Cuba to serve, but the fact that in the early 1900s, after the war was over, he was living in Manila, in the Philippines, by himself, seems to indicate that he served there during the Spanish—American War, and not in Cuba.

Regardless, he was discharged in Savannah on November 30, 1898, only five months after enlisting. He then came back to Washington, D.C., and they all lived for a few years with Old Uncle George again at 223 Eighth

Street. It was a roller coaster of a marriage for Jennie Mitchell—and for James T. The death of Jennie's youngest sister, Mary, at only 24 on August 19, 1900, didn't help, and neither did her father's death on September 19, 1903. Incidentally, Dr. Keeley died in 1900, aged 65, his cure then in the early stages of being discredited. He didn't even give James T. his money back for a failed cure. Unbelievably, it wasn't until 1966 that the Keeley Cure and cures like it were finally and irrevocably exposed as a hoax.

Something had to give with James T. and Jennie, and it did. James T. moved to the Philippines, and Jennie moved in with her family. This was a very strained situation for everyone, especially their son Frank, who was then still very young. Frank never remembered his father very well, and what he did recall he had hauntingly bad memories of. He basically only ever knew a man who went off to the Spanish war and never came back. The name James would be anathema to Frank for the rest of his life.

Tom's younger son, George F. Harbin, went to local D.C. schools, such as St. Cecelia's Academy, where he excelled and won prizes, and St. John's College, where he excelled, and, in 1894, won a prize for elocution. In 1898 he started at Georgetown University, where he excelled and where he received his bachelor's degree in 1902. George excelled.

In 1905 Catholic University in Georgetown awarded young George F. Harbin a degree in electrical engineering, and he got a job with Westinghouse at its Washington terminal. He subsequently got a post teaching at the Georgetown University Preparatory School, that is, when he was not discovering dead bodies floating in the sewage. This from the *Washington Post* of September 5, 1911: "The body of Richard Smith, 50 years old, an employee of the District sewer department, was found floating in the Eastern Branch near the Pennsylvania Avenue Bridge yesterday morning by George Harbin, 635 L Street southeast, and Allen Lloyd, 1248 Pennsylvania Avenue southeast. No marks of violence were found and Coroner Nevitt gave a certificate of suicide."

Back to the older generation. Tom and George F.'s sister, Sarah Priscilla Harbin, also a busy bee at social events over the years, died on December 16, 1905, at George F.'s house, 223 Eighth Street southeast. The funeral was at St. Peter's Church on December 18, and she was buried in Mount Olivet Cemetery. Her will was drawn up November 4, 1905, and petitioned through her attorney, F. Edward Mitchell, on January 6, 1906, and letters of administration were granted in Washington, D.C. on April 24, 1906, to her brother, George F. Harbin. However, as late as October 1909 the will was still in the probate court, new letters of administration having been petitioned by a new attorney, W.R. Andrews.

The last of Tom Harbin's sisters left alive, Johanna Howell, died on September 23, 1909, at the home of her daughter, Mrs. Adam Weschler, at New

Glatz, Prince George's County, Maryland. She was 84. The funeral took place from there on September 27, and was held at St. Mary's Church, Piscataway, at 9 A.M. Requiem mass was at 10 A.M.

George F. Harbin was now the last of the Harbins of that generation, and his final decade of life would be fraught.

James T.'s estranged wife, Jennie Harbin, bought land from the Braddock Building and Development Company on February 22, 1907, at Braddock Heights, a tiny mountain resort community just outside Frederick, Maryland, where she built a boarding house called "Nibrah House" [Harbin backwards] at what is now 6724 Jefferson Boulevard, just opposite White's Horse Farm.

In those days what was hers was his too, so Jennie and James T. transferred the property to F. Edward Mitchell (Jennie's younger attorney brother in D.C.) and his wife Annie, of D.C., and on August 28 of that year they transferred it to Jennie, "for the sole and separate use of Jennie A. Harbin for and during the term of her natural life, etc.," and "free from the control of the present or any future husband."

This large house had an open air dance pavilion, and Jennie occasionally lived there with her children and two black servants, Vergie and Sam. The rest of the time she lived in an apartment that she had acquired at 1138 Twelfth Street northwest, in Washington, D.C., with her son Frank and daughter Margaret.

At 9:30 in the morning of June 8, 1907, at St. Patrick's Church in D.C., James T.'s daughter Marie married Thomas Francis Maguire, an engineer, trained at MIT, working for the government. He was 32, and she was 23. The Rev. Thomas E. McGuigan officiated. Marie's sister Margaret was maid of honor, and carried ferns. Joseph Travers Maguire, brother of the groom, was best man. The couple left for Norfolk and the Jamestown Exposition, then on to Providence and Boston, and finally reached their new home, Indianapolis, on July 1. The Maguires would move several more times: from Indianapolis back to Washington, D.C., and ultimately they would be transferred to the West Coast, having several children along the way.

Tom Harbin's granddaughter, Margaret, the daughter of James T. and Jennie, went to school at the Visitation Academy, at Frederick, an institution of which she would, later in life, in the 1930s, become alumni president. As a young adult she launched into the social world of Washington, becoming one of the big Democratic women of that town. Every move she made was reported.

As for Tom's grandson, Francis Percival "Frank" Harbin, despite his hatred for his father James T., he did inherit many of the good traits. He acted on the stage as a young man, he was a joiner of associations, he went into business, he was always out there pushing, and, to cap it off, he volunteered for the Army.

On April 27, 1918, Francis P. Harbin qualified as a second lieutenant in the Field Artillery after successfully completing an officers training course at Fort McClellan, Alabama. When he got out of the Army he moved in again with his mother, who had relocated down the street to 217 Twelfth Street.

On November 14, 1916, old George F. Harbin, the survivor, sold off the rear of 321 Pennsylvania Avenue, the lot (Lot 3, square 790) next door to his store, for $10, to Ann Virginia Coleman (nee Smoot), his neighbor on the other side of 321. George knew what was coming. And it did, four months later.

It's a real shame to have to report that George F. Harbin, for so many years a pillar of society in East Washington, a successful wheeler dealer, went bankrupt in 1917. His earlier tax delinquencies should have given a clue. The *Washington Post* of March 20, 1917 said:

> Bankrupt after 50 years. George F. Harbin, long a merchant, files voluntary petition. George F. Harbin, more than half a century a dry goods merchant at 319 Pennsylvania Avenue southeast, at his own request was adjudicated a bankrupt yesterday by Justice Hitz in the District Supreme Court, and James J. Hayes was appointed receiver under $2,000 bond. Harbin's petition stated that a proposition of 25 cents on the dollar had been made to creditors. Ill health was the cause of his business troubles. His debts are placed at $22,411.51 and his assets at $16,917.

Some say George married and went west after the bankruptcy. False rumor. He stayed in the area, probably with relatives.

George F. Harbin died, a broken man, at Mount Hope, Maryland, on August 20, 1919. The *Washington Post* of August 22, 1919, didn't give him the big obituary he deserved, just a death notice: "Suddenly, on Wednesday, August 20, 1919, at Mount Hope, Md., George F. Harbin, in the seventy-ninth year of his age. Funeral from his niece's residence, Mrs. McGuire [sic], 641 E Street northeast, on Saturday, August 23, at 8.30 A.M., thence to St. Peter's Church, Second and C Streets southeast, where mass will be said at 9 A.M. Interment at Mount Olivet cemetery. Relatives and friends invited to attend."

He was, indeed, buried on August 23, in Section 15, Lot 21, of Mount Olivet Cemetery, in Washington, D.C.

This Mount Hope, Maryland: The logical conclusion to jump to is that it was Mount Hope Retreat for the Insane, in Baltimore County, Maryland, or Mount Hope Asylum, as it was more popularly called, under the administration of Dr. Charles B. Hill. This institution had been incorporated in 1872 to care for the insane, sick and inebriate, and was run by the Catholic Sisters of Charity. However, there is not record of George Harbin in their records, so he probably died at the community of Mount Hope, in Prince George's County, near Camp Springs, hard by where Andrews Air Force

Base is today. He was probably visiting or staying with his Weschler relatives in nearby New Glatz.

James J. Hayes, who had worked in George's store since 1890 when he was 14, became the new owner of the store in October 1921, and carried it on until he himself died in 1936. He inherited from old George Harbin all the civic responsibilities that went with being the owner of Harbin's Dry Goods Store—a directorship of the National Capitol Bank, membership of the Holy Name Society and of the St. Vincent de Paul Society, things like that.

Ella, Tom's widow, lived on in D.C. until March 26, 1918. The March 27, 1918, *Washington Post* reported the death of Ella A. Harbin, aged 62 (sic), at 11 Seventh Street southeast. She was buried in the same lot at Mount Olivet as her husband had been and as her two children, George and Blanche, would eventually be. The children continued to live at the Seventh Street house.

James T. Harbin, back from the Philippines, lived in old soldiers' homes for the rest of his life, the last few years being spent at the National Soldiers Home in Elizabeth City, Virginia. He died on February 14, 1933, at the Veterans Administration Hospital, in Hampton Roads, Virginia. He was buried on February 17, 1933, at Arlington Cemetery.

Jennie Mitchell Harbin continued to live at Twelfth Street. On April 30, 1930, she, along with the Farmers and Mechanics National Bank of Frederick, Maryland sold Nibrah House in Braddock Heights to Harry L. Ebert, the ice cream king, and it became Ebert House, at least until 1944, when it was sold again. Today, after another 12 transfers of ownership, it is Braddock Apartments. Jennie died on November 26, 1938, at the Sacred Heart Home, Hyattsville, Maryland, and was buried at Mount Olivet Cemetery, Washington, D.C.

Again, also like his father, Frank P. Harbin was 25 when he got married, on October 27, 1920, to Corrine Marie Lothrop. Corrine was born on September 9, 1897. They would have five children. Frank was with the Automatic Heating Corporation, of 1719 Connecticut Avenue northwest, and in 1926 was a pioneer in selling the Nokol silent heating system for homes. He died on March 28, 1963, and was buried in Arlington Cemetery. This must be unique—the son and grandson of a Confederate agent both being buried in Arlington. Frank's widow, Corrine, died in June 1983, in Cardiff, Maryland.

Margaret Catherine Agnes Adele Harbin, James T.'s daughter and Tom's younger granddaughter, married Robert Brooks Dawkins Jr. on Jan. 24, 1921, in Baltimore.

Robert Brooks Dawkins Jr. was born in 1896, the son of Robert Brooks Dawkins Sr. and his wife Louella. Senior was a judge in the Louisiana Court of Appeals, and in 1914, when the time came to find his son some work, he pulled in a political favor and got the boy a job as stenographer and secretary to the newly elected Louisiana congressman Riley J. Wilson. When Rep. Wilson moved to Washington to assume his congressional seat, young Dawkins went with him, and thus began a brilliant career.

In 1917 he interrupted his shorthand for a year or so to go off and fight the Hun, in an airplane, what's more, equipped with a leather helmet.

On his return to D.C. he resumed his secretarial activities, and then met Margaret Harbin, socialite. At the same time, 1920, his father, the old judge, died down in Lincoln Parish, Louisiana, and his widowed mother and bereaved sister Edith both relocated to D.C., where Robert Jr. got them a house at 1464 Spring Road.

Robert and Margaret got a place on 15th Street northwest. They had a daughter, Margaret Louella (Peggy Lou) on September 16, 1922, in D.C., named for her mother and paternal grandmother.

By the early '20s Robert Brooks Dawkins was studying law at Georgetown University, and clerking for the Chief Justice of the Supreme Court of Washington, D.C.

The marriage was already on the rocks, in fact had been for some time. Who knows why. Some say it was because he was several years younger than her, and that may be, but there was only five years' difference. Maybe her dedication to the social scene outgunned her feelings for him. Maybe.

They got a place in Brooklyn, on East 10th Street, and one would stay there and the other in D.C. Meanwhile Peggy Lou was sent to a whole mass of schools, beginning with, in 1929, her mother's alma mater, the Visitation Academy in Frederick, Maryland, followed a year later by the Sacred Heart Academy in Washington. That was the year her parents moved from 15th Street northwest to 3701 Sixteenth Street, in yet another last ditch effort to save the marriage.

Also in 1929, Robert Brooks Dawkins went to work as an attorney at the Federal Trade Commission. They were back and forth between Washington and Brooklyn, New York, trying to escape from each other, perhaps from themselves.

Dawkins was on the rise as an FTC lawyer—he would become something of a wheel over the years, arguing cases before the Supreme Court in the 1940s. Margaret worked as Admiral "Bull" Halsey's social secretary during World War II—at least, so they say.

Also working at the Navy Department was one Marguerite Plummer. Robert Brooks Dawkins knew, as soon as he saw her, that this was the real thing.

Marguerite had started off life in Chatham County, North Carolina, the daughter of Gustavius Adolphus Brooks. She'd come to Washington and married famous 1920s *New York Times* reporter Nixon Plummer, who covered the Hoover White House. They had a daughter in 1920, Marguerite (Peggy) Plummer.

Nixon went insane, and they put him away. So here was Marguerite: single, yet married; available, yet tied by law to a marriage that didn't really exist. This situation couldn't last, not with someone like Robert Brooks Dawkins. And it didn't.

Dawkins and Marguerite flew to Reno. Both got quick divorces, and they returned, married to each other. Nixon Plummer died in Greensboro, in North Carolina, in the 1950s.

Young Peggy Plummer married J. Fred Stamps, an Arkansas lad living in Falls Church, Virginia, and young Peggy Lou Dawkins married Illinois soldier Robert Kenneth (Bob) Jensen (born April 14, 1919, Oak Park, Illinois, son of Peter and Mary Jensen) at St. Matthews Church, D.C., on December 19, 1945. She was given away by her great uncle, Professor George F. Harbin of Georgetown University. Both Peggys had children.

Robert Brooks Dawkins Jr. retired from the FTC legal business in 1957 and died of a heart attack on June 14, 1959, in McLean, Virginia, aged 62, leaving a wife, Marguerite Brooks Plummer Dawkins; an ex-wife, Margaret Harbin Dawkins; a daughter, Peggy Lou Jensen Pliscou; and a stepdaughter, Peggy Plummer Stamps.

Margaret Harbin Dawkins, Tom's granddaughter, and the first wife of Robert Brooks Dawkins, died in January 1978, in D.C. Marguerite Brooks Plummer Dawkins, the second wife of the FTC lawyer, died in 1984, leaving descendants. But, more to the point of our story, his first wife left Mrs. Peggy Lou Jensen Pliscou, and Peggy Lou has descendants.

Washington Post, March 25, 1928: "Mary Blanche Harbin died March 24 at Providence Hospital. Beloved daughter of the late Ella A. and Thomas H. Harbin and sister of George F. Harbin. Funeral from her late residence, 11 7th St., southeast, on Monday, March 26, then to St. Peter's Church. Interment at Mt Olivet."

In 1929 George F. became a math professor—algebra and geometry—at Georgetown University. He remained there until he died. He never married and gave a lot of money to the University during his lifetime. He was an active Catholic layman in D.C. and was a member of the Society of Saint Vincent de Paul, the Holy Name Society, and chairman of the Washington Catholic Bowling League. He was also a member of the district National Guard.

In 1949 George F. Harbin was awarded the university's Vicennial Medal, given to professors who had served 20 years, and at the 1952 commencement at Georgetown University he was awarded the honorary degree of Doctor of Science. That year's graduates dedicated their yearbook to him.

He died on June 29, 1952, of cancer, at Georgetown Hospital. His funeral service was at St. Peter's on July 1, 1952, and he was buried at Mount Olivet Cemetery, in D.C.

Professor George F. Harbin's will was probated in D.C. on July 23, 1952. He bequeathed $77,000 to the university, including $10,000 to be designated for the education of young men to the priesthood. He also left $5,000 to the Little Sisters of the Poor; $5,000 to the pastor of St. Peter's Catholic Church in D.C., for masses; another $5,000 to the St. Peter's Conference of St. Vincent de Paul Society of St. Peter's Church; $10,000 to the Particular Council of the St. Vincent de Paul Society; $5,000 to the Carmelite Fathers; $5,000 to the Capuchin College; and $10,000 to the pastor of St. Mary's Catholic Church, Upper Marlboro, Maryland. He also left $1,000 apiece to his step-nephew Frank and step-nieces Marie and Margaret. That's a total of $125,000—not bad for a math professor. A million of today's money.

In 1965 Harbin Hall was finished at Georgetown University, and named after George Francis Harbin, son of the Confederate spy at large.

Appendix A: Graves in the Historic Congressional Cemetery, Washington, D.C.

Plot Number	Name	Date of Death
r5/84	Joanna W. Silcott	Aug. 1874
r6/22	child of John W. Stant	June 16, 1872
r8/238	Agnes Russell	Dec. 8, 1895
r8/238	Margaret R. Russell	May 19, 1885
r8/238	dau. of John W. Stant	July 22, 1918
r13/106	Forrest E. Stansbury	Nov. 5, 1910
r16/177	Sarah A. Brooks	July 11, 1902
r16/178	Charles W. Brooks Jr.	Jan. 5, 1904
r16/178	Charles Brooks	Feb. 17, 1884
r37/93	Philip Russell	June 5, 1847
r37/93	William Ignatius Russell	Sept. 4, 1878
r41/61	Joseph Franklin Snyder	Aug. 11, 1850
r41/61	Catherine E. Snyder	Sept. 26, 1849
r41/62	Mrs. Nicholas Snyder	July 17, 1845
r41/63	Nicholas Snyder	Oct. 10, 1862
r41/63	Caroline Snyder	June 24, 1880
r43/231	John H. Russell	July 25, 1905
r43/232	Janette Russell	Feb. 8, 1876
r43/232	Mary Russell	Dec. 13, 1854
r43/233	Catharine Oakley	March 10, 1869
r43/234	Jennie A. Russell	Aug. 23, 1911
r43/234	child of c.e. Joyce	Aug. 19, 1872
r43/234	child of Wm Russell	April 17, 1856
r43/235	child Russell	Oct. 21, 1850
r43/235	Martha Russell	Dec. 19, 1881
r49/280	Vergie Harbin	Aug. 7, 1913
r54/242	Charles W. Stant	Oct. 21, 1967

r54/242	Laura M. Stant	Sept. 7, 1952
r63/273	William J. McGee Sr.	April 26 1952
r63/274	Annie R. McGee	Sept. 18, 1948
r63/275	William J. McGee Jr.	Oct. 21, 1906
r65/328	Sarah Harbin	Feb. 19, 1905
r65/329	Philip W. Harbin	Sept. 9, 1890
r65/329	Mitchell Harbin	Aug. 19, 1865
r65/330	Mary Isabelle Harbin	July 27, 1939
r65/331	Samuel P. Harbin	Oct. 16, 1923
r72/328	Charles E. Joyce	Dec. 17, 1884
r72/328	Alice R. Joyce	Nov. 10, 1930
r72/329	Alice O. Joyce	June 30, 1939
r79/328	Alexander McKenzie	Feb. 29, 1896
r79/329	Grace McKenzie	May 30, 1969
r79/330	child of Jn S. McKenzie	Sept. 28, 1898
r80/328	Nannie McKenzie	July 11, 1877
r80/329	Alexander McKenzie	Nov. 3, 1929
r80/330	Alice E. McKenzie	Feb. 4, 1914
r96/282	James H. Harbin	Nov. 13, 1893
r96/282	Jane E. Harbin	Aug. 5, 1878
r96/282	Lula Steiner	Oct. 28, 1911
r112/233	John M.J. Stant	March 23, 1921
r112/233	Jane Elizabeth Stant	Sept. 25, 1928
r116/230	George F. Stant	Nov. 11, 1954
r122/258	John W. Stant	Feb. 2, 1955
r122/258	Sarah E. Stant	Sept. 7, 1940
r122/258	William Stant	April 25, 1919
r122/258	William H. Stant	Nov. 5, 1918
r134/178	Ethel May Stansbury	April 3, 1898
r134/178	Fred Owen Stansbury	April 4, 1900
r134/178	Clarence E. Stansbury	Jan. 8, 1899
r134/179	Forrest E. Stansbury	May 25, 1940
r134/179	Maggie M. Stansbury	March 11, 1962
r136/178	Mary S. Stansbury	March 3, 1900
r136/178	William W. Stansbury	June 9, 1901
r136/206	Horace Jarboe	Dec. 12, 1892
r136/227	Julia Russell	Dec. 19, 1893
r148/210	Adelaide C. Snyder	Oct. 25, 1908
r148/211	William N. Snyder	Sept. 13, 1907
r148/211	Thomas A. Snyder	June 25, 1908
r148/211	Francis W. Snyder	Nov. 5, 1919
r148/211	Charles A. Snyder	June 1, 1911
r151/205	Daniel Harbin	Oct. 4, 1911
r151/205	Elizabeth Harbin	Jan. 13, 1909
r153/209	Susanna Snyder	Sept. 13, 1907
r153/210	William H. Snyder	Dec. 27, 1916
r153/210	George O. Snyder III	July 20, 1945

Appendix B: More Census Information and Related Documents

1830 Census
Bryantown
Charles County
Maryland

Walter Harbin
1 white male under 5 [James Alexander Harbin, Tom's brother]
1 white male 5—10 [John Harbin, Tom's brother]
1 white male 10—15 [Joseph B. Harbin, Tom's brother]
1 white male 40—50 [Walter Harbin himself, Tom's father]
1 white female under 5 [Catherine Harbin, Tom's sister]
2 white females 5—10 [Johanna and Juliana Harbin, Tom's sisters]
1 white female 10—15 [Jane Harbin, Tom's sister]
1 white female 30—40 [Walter Harbin's wife, Catherine, Tom's mother]

1840 Census
Charles County
Maryland

Walter Harbin [this is Tom Harbin's father]
1 white male under 5 [George F. Harbin, Tom's brother]
1 white male 5—10 [Tom himself]
1 white male 10—15 [James Alexander Harbin, Tom's brother]
1 white male 15—20 [John Harbin, Tom's brother]
1 white male 50—60 [Walter Harbin himself, Tom's father]
1 white female under 5 [Sarah Priscilla Harbin, Tom's sister]
1 white female 10—15 [Catherine Cecilia Ann Harbin, Tom's sister]

2 white females 15—20 [Julia and Johanna Harbin, Tom's sisters]
1 white female 20—30 [Jane Harbin, Tom's sister]

1850 Census
Election District No. 4
St. Mary's County
Maryland

Philip H. Burroughs, 34, manager, born in Charles County [this is Charlie Russell's brother-in-law]
Mary Burroughs, 29, born in Charles County [this is Mary Eliza, Charlie Russell's sister]
Sally Burroughs, 6, born in St. Mary's County [this is Phil Burroughs' daughter by his previous marriage]
William Burroughs, 1 month, born in St. Mary's County [this is Charlie Russell's nephew]

1850 Census
Second Ward
Washington, D.C.

O.J. Preston, 31, born in New York
Rebecca Preston, 29, born in New Jersey
Danyell Preston, 5, born in D.C.
Clementina Preston, 1, born in D.C.
Eliza Harbin, 40, born in D.C.
Margaret Hughes, 18, born in D.C.
Sarah Russell, 12, born in Maryland [this is Charlie Russell's sister, and her age should be 22]

1850 Census
Second Ward
Washington, D.C.

Nicholas Snyder, 41, blacksmith, born in Germany
Sarah A. Snyder, 23, born in Maryland
Caroline Snyder, 11, born in D.C.
W.H. Snyder, 9, born in D.C.
M.E. Snyder, 3, born in D.C.
Joseph F. Snyder, 1, born in D.C.
Chas Russell, 17, blacksmith, born in D.C. [this is Charlie Russell]
Wm Speiden, 24, blacksmith, born in D.C.

1850 Census
Sixth Ward
Washington, D.C.

James H. Harbin, 29, [brass] finisher, born in Maryland [this is Charlie Russell's stepbrother]
Jane E. Harbin, 27, born in Virginia [this is Charlie Russell's step-sister-in-law]

Joanna C. Harbin, 4, born in D.C. [this is Joanna W. "Annie" Harbin, Charlie Russell's step-niece]
Martha V. Harbin, 2, born in D.C. [this is Charlie Russell's step-niece]

They were three doors down from....

William S. Venable, 33, tin and copper smith, born D.C. [this is the man who witnessed Janette Russell's bounty land claim in the 1850s]
Ellen Venable, 29, born D.C.
Thomas E. Venable, 8, born D.C.
Mary E. Venable, 6, born D.C.
William J. Venable, 4, born D.C.
Laura Venable, 6 months, born D.C.
James Venable, 24, waterman, born D.C.
Joseph Venable, 22, blacksmith, born D.C.
Sarah Venable, 19, born D.C.
Mary Venable, 12, born D.C.
George Venable, 10, born D.C.
Ralph Carroll, 19, born D.C.

1850 Census
Allens Fresh District
Charles County
Maryland

Thomas A. Jones, 30, collector, born in Maryland [this is Tom Harbin's brother-in-law]
Jane Jones, 30, born in Maryland [this is Tom Harbin's sister]
Jane Jones, 4, born in Maryland [this is Tom Harbin's niece]
Alace Jones, 2, born in Maryland [this is Tom Harbin's niece, Alice Jones]
Asa Jones, 7, born in Maryland [this is not one of their children]

Janette Russell's bounty land claims of 1852 and 1855:

On this 20th day of December eighteen hundred and fifty two, personally appeared before me, a Justice of the Peace within and for the county and district aforesaid [District of Columbia and Washington County], Julia Stansbury, aged 33 years, a resident of the City of Washington, D.C., who, being duly sworn according to law, declares that she was present at the marriage of William Russell and Jane Harbin and that they lived together until his decease, which occurred about the 29th of Augt. 1839 [legal term meaning on the 29th of August, 1839]. And at the same time appears also before me Mary J. Russell [Janette's daughter, for the last seven years wife of John H. Russell], aged 25 years, a resident of Washington, D.C., and after being duly qualified deposeth that she was present when the marriage between William Russell and Jane Harbin was celebrated and that they lived together as husband and wife till his decease which was on the 29th Augt., A.D. 1839. And they swear they are disinterested witnesses. [signed] Julia Stansbury and Mary J. Russell. Sworn to and subscribed before me the day and year above written, and I hereby certify that Julia Stansbury and Mary J. Russell are credible witnesses. [signed] Jas. Crandell, JP.

In the "Form of Declaration for Widow of a deceased Officer or Soldier," filled out on that same day in that same James Crandell's office, we learn that Jane Russell was 47, and that she was a resident of D.C. William Russell, her late husband, was a private "in the company of Capt. Samuel Maddox in the regiment of Maryland Militia commanded by (blank) in the War with Great Britain declared by the United States the 18th day of June, A.D. 1812." We learn that William Russell "was enrolled at (blank) on or about the 17th day of July, A.D. 1813," for term of "indefinite," and "continued in actual service in said war for the term of about 50 days and was honorably (blank) at (blank) on the Tenth day of August, A.D. 1814, as will appear by the muster rolls, no written discharge being found." Janette went on state that

> she was married to the said William Russell in Washington City, D.C., on the 28th day of March, A.D. 1836, by one Vanhorsighe [sic], a Catholic priest and that her name before her said marriage was Jane Harbin, that her said husband died at Charles County, Maryland, on the 29th day of August, A.D. 1839, and that she is still a widow. She makes this declaration for the purpose of obtaining the bounty land to which she may be entitled under the Act passed September 28th, 1850, she not having received under any former act of Congress, nor knowing that she is entitled. [signed] Jane Russell. Sworn to and subscribed before me the day and the year above written [Dec. 20, 1852], and that she cannot procure either public or private record proof. [signed] Jas Crandell, JP.

Evening Star, Saturday, Oct. 31, 1857, page 3: "On the 29th instant, by the Rev. Mr. Knight, William T. McNeir to Sarah A. Heffernan, both of this city (Annapolis, Md. papers please copy). On the 29th instant, by the Rev. Mr. Knight, Charles H. Russell of this city, to Mary Ann, daughter of the late George and Ann Jarboe of Alexandria, Va."

1860 Census
523 Eighth Street east
Sixth Ward
Washington, D.C.

Geanett Russell, 54, boarding house, born in Maryland, $150 personal estate [this is Charlie Russell's step-mother]

John Russell, 45, carpenter, born in Maryland [this is Charlie Russell's eldest brother]

Mary A. Russell, 12, born in D.C. [this is Charlie Russell's niece, Mary Alice (Alice) Russell, later Mrs. Alice Joyce]

Geanett A. Russell, 8, born in D.C. [this is Charlie Russell's niece, Janette Alice (Jennie) Russell]

Marcelano Pariz, 46, musician, born in Spain [this is the lodger]

They are living next to James Harbin, Janette's eldest son.

1860 Census
Fifth Ward
Washington, D.C.

Mary Burrows, 43, seamstress, born in Maryland [this is Charlie Russell's sister, Mary Eliza Burroughs]
Mary E. Burrows, 2, born in D.C. [this is Charlie Russell's niece, Molly Burroughs]
Sarah Russell, 26, born in Maryland [this is Charlie Russell's sister, "Sally," and her age should say 32]

1860 City Directory
First Street east near M Street south
Washington, D.C.

Mary Burroughs, widow of Philip [this is Charlie Russell's sister, Mary Eliza]

1860 City Directory
525 I Street south
Washington, D.C.

William Russell, watchman [this is Charlie Russell's brother]

1860 Census
Fifth Ward
Washington, D.C.

William Russell, 36, watchman, NY [Navy Yard], born in Maryland, no real estate; $100 personal estate [this is Charlie Russell's brother]
Margaret Russell, 37, born in D.C. [this is Charlie Russell's sister-in-law]
Julia Russell, 9, born in Virginia [this is Charlie Russell's niece]
Jane Russell, 6, born in Washington
Martha Russell, 2, born in Washington [this is Charlie Russell's niece]

1860 Census
527 E Street South
Sixth Ward
Washington, D.C.

Charles H. Russell, 27, blacksmith, born in Maryland, no real estate, personal estate of $150
Mary A. Russell, 22, born in Virginia [this is Charlie Russell's first wife, Mary Ann Jarboe]
Wm H. Russell, 1, born in D.C. [this is Charlie Russell's son, Willie]
Elizabeth Jarboe, 17, born in Virginia [this is Charlie Russell's sister-in-law]

1860 Census
525 Eighth Street East
Sixth Ward
Washington, D.C.

James H. Harbin, 38, brass finisher, born in Maryland [this is Charlie Russell's stepbrother]

Jane Harbin, 35, born in Virginia [this is Charlie Russell's step-sister-in-law]
Johanna Harbin, 14, born in D.C. [this is Charlie Russell's step-niece]
Eliza G. Harbin, 10, born in D.C. [this is Lula, Charlie Russell's step-niece]
Kate M. Harbin, 8, born in D.C. [this is Charlie Russell's step-niece]
James S. Harbin, 6, born in D.C. [this is Charlie Russell's step-nephew]
John H. Harbin, 6 months, born in D.C. [this is Charlie Russell's step-nephew]

1860 City Directory
393 G Street south
Washington, D.C.

Philip W. Harbin, shoemaker (home) [this is Charlie Russell's step-brother]

1860 City Directory
543 Eighth Street
Washington, D.C.

Philip W. Harbin (shop) [this is Charlie Russell's stepbrother]

1860 Census
Beltsville
Prince George's County
Maryland

Philip W. Harbin, 36, shoemaker, born in Maryland [this is Charlie Russell's stepbrother]
Sarah Harbin, 34, born in D.C. [this is Charlie Russell's step-sister-in-law]
Mary E. Harbin, 9, born in D.C. [this is Charlie Russell's step-niece, Mary Isabelle Harbin, although her name varies from census to census]
Sarah A. Harbin, 7, born in D.C. [this is Charlie Russell's step-niece, Nannie]
Samuel P. Harbin, 5, born in D.C. [this is Charlie Russell's step-nephew, Samuel Philip Harbin]
Sarah A. Nesmith, 68, born in England [this is Philip's mother-in-law]

1860 Census
Tompkinsville
Allens Fresh District
Charles County
Maryland

Thomas A. Jones, 39, farmer, born in Maryland, $9,000 in real estate, $7,000 in personal estate [this is Tom Harbin's brother-in-law]
Jane Jones, 39, born in Maryland [this is Tom Harbin's sister]
Jane Jones, 13, born in Maryland [this is Tom Harbin's niece]
Alice Jones, 12, born in Maryland [this is Tom Harbin's niece]

Richard Jones, 8, born in Maryland [this is Tom Harbin's nephew]
Sarah Jones, 10, born in Maryland [this is Tom Harbin's niece]
John J. Jones, 7, born in Maryland [this is Tom Harbin's nephew]
Ann C. Jones, 3, born in Maryland [this is Tom Harbin's niece]
Henry C. Jones, 2, born in Maryland [this is Tom Harbin's nephew]
Julia Jones, 3 months [born in March 1860], born in Maryland [this is distinctly Julia, despite the fact that the Jones child born in March 1860 is Mary E., Tom Harbin's niece]

1860 Census
Piscataway
5th Election District
Prince George's County
Maryland

John H. Howell, 34, farmer, born in Maryland, personal estate of $200 [this is Tom Harbin's brother-in-law]
Joanna Howell, 34, born in Maryland [this is Tom Harbin's sister]
Joseph H. Howell, 10, born in Maryland [this is Tom Harbin's nephew]
Margaret I. Howell, 9, born in Maryland [this is Tom Harbin's niece]
Catherine M. Howell, 7, born in Maryland [this is Tom Harbin's niece]
John H. Howell, 4, born in Maryland [this is Tom Harbin's nephew]
James W. Howell, 2, born in Maryland [this is Tom Harbin's nephew]
George S. Howell, 7 months, born in Maryland [born Dec. 1859; this is Tom Harbin's nephew]

Oct. 18, 1861, letter from Assistant Secretary of State F.W. Seward to Brigadier-General Andrew Porter, Provost Marshal, Washington, D.C. "General: will you have the kindness to report to this Department the proofs in the case of George F. Harbin, a prisoner confined at the Thirteenth Street Prison [sic]. I am, General, very respectfully, your obedient servant, F.W. Seward, assistant secretary."

National Intelligencer, March 31, 1862: "On Sunday morning, March 30, Miss Eliza Harbin, at the age of 70 years. Funeral April 1, at 10 o'clock, from her late residence at Mrs. Downer's, on D Street between 13th and 13½ Streets."

Cork Examiner, Oct. 31, 1864: "October 12, at his residence, near the Chain-bridge, Washington, D.C., Michael Joyce, Esq., formerly of Fermoy, county Cork, Ireland, father of the late Captain Joyce of the 88th Regiment, NYV, Irish Brigade."

1865 City Directory
138 East Capitol Street between 5th & 6th Streets north
Washington, D.C.

John H. Russell (Russell & Davis) home [this is Charlie Russell's eldest brother]

1865 City Directory
Sixth Street west, south of Pennsylvania Avenue
Washington, D.C.

Russell & Davis Metropolitan Livery stable

1865 City Directory
First Street east near M Street south
Washington, D.C.

William I. Russell, boilermaker [this is Charlie Russell's brother]

1865 City Directory
529 E Street south, between 7th & 8th Streets east
Washington, D.C.

Philip W. Harbin, policeman [this is Charlie Russell's stepbrother]

Irish Times, Aug. 3, 1867: "Emigration of Fenians. Charles E. Joyce and Patrick Connolly, lately released from Mountjoy Prison, where they had been confined for Fenianism, on the condition of their quitting the British dominions, left Queenstown by the outward bound steamer on Wednesday."

1868 City Directory
529 E Street south, between 7th & 8th Streets east
Washington, D.C.

Philip W. Harbin, policeman [this is Charlie Russell's step-brother]

1869 City Directory
Boarding House
324 G Street
Washington, D.C.

Chas E. Joyce, clerk at the Adj.-Gen.'s office

Evening Star, March 11, 1869: "On Wednesday, the 10th inst., after a long and painful illness, which she bore with Christian fortitude, Catharine A. Oakley, in the [?] year of her age. May she rest in peace. Her funeral will take place on Friday, the 12th inst., at 3 P.M., from the residence of her sister, Mrs. J.E. Russell, No. 523 8th Street east, and removed to Christ Church. Her friends and acquaintances are respectfully invited to attend."

The Roanoke Valley (Clarksville, Va.), Aug. 19, 1869: "Died: on Saturday, 7th inst., at the residence of her husband, in this place, Mrs. Mary Ann, wife of Chas. H. Russell, formerly of Washington, D.C."

1870 Census
Sixth Ward
Washington, D.C.

J.H. Russel, 52, carpenter, born in Maryland. No real estate. Personal estate $700 [this is Charlie Russell's eldest brother]

More Census Information and Related Documents

Jennet Russel, 65, born in Maryland [this is Charlie Russell's stepmother]
Allice Russel, 21, clerk Patent Office, born in D.C. [this is Charlie Russell's niece, Mary Alice (Alice), later Mrs. Joyce]
Jenny Russel, 18, born in D.C. [this is Charlie Russell's niece, Janette Alice (Jennie)]
Joseph Eaton, 12, black, domestic servant, born in Maryland

1870 Census
Fifth Ward
Washington, D.C.

Charles Brooks, 45, laborer, born in Ireland [this is Charlie Russell's brother-in-law]
Sarah Brooks, 35, born in Maryland [this is Charlie Russell's sister, "Sally"]
John Brooks, 7, born in D.C. [this is Charlie Russell's nephew, John Russell (Russell) Brooks]
Charles Brooks, 4, born in D.C. [this is Charlie Russell's nephew, Charles W. Brooks Jr.]

1870 Census
Christiansville Post Office
Clarksville
Mecklenburg County
Virginia

Chas H. Russell, 35, blacksmith, born in Maryland, $500 personal estate [Charlie was now a widow]
William H. Russell, aged 11, born in D.C. [this is Charlie Russell's son, Willie]
Annie A. Russell, 9, born in D.C. [this is Charlie Russell's daughter]
Alice L. Russell, 5, born in Virginia [this is Charlie Russell's daughter]

1870 City Directory
521 Eighth Street, southeast
Washington, D.C.

James Harbin, machinist [this is Charlie Russell's stepbrother]

1870 Census
Sixth Ward
Washington, D.C.

James Harbin, 45, brass finisher, born in Maryland, $200 of personal estate [this is Charlie Russell's stepbrother]
Jane Harbin, 42, born in Virginia [this is Charlie Russell's step-sister-in-law]
Johanna Harbin, 18, born in D.C. [this is Charlie Russell's step-niece]
Jennet Harbin, 16, born in D.C. [this is Charlie Russell's step-niece, Janette Eliza (Lula)]

Caty Harbin, 14, at school [this is Charlie Russell's step-niece, Katherine M. (Kate)]

James Harbin, 12, born in D.C. [this is Charlie Russell's step-nephew, James Samuel Harbin]

John Harbin, 10, at school, born in D.C. [this is Charlie Russell's step-nephew, John Henry Harbin]

Daniel Harbin, 7, born in D.C. [this is Charlie Russell's stepnephew]

1870 Census
Sixth Ward
Washington, D.C.

P.W. Harbin, 46, Met. Police, born in Maryland [this is Charlie Russell's stepbrother, Philip Harbin]

Sarah Harbin, 48, born in D.C. [this is Charlie Russell's step-sister-in-law]

Mary E. Harbin, 18, born in D.C. [this is Charlie Russell's step-niece, Mary Isabelle Harbin]

Sarah A. Harbin, 17, born in D.C. [this is Charlie Russell's step-niece, Nannie]

Samuel P. Harbin, 14, born in D.C. [this is Charlie Russell's step-nephew]

H.R. Ivins, 15, female, born in D.C., at school [we do not know who this is]

1870 City Directory
Seventh Street, between B and C Streets, southeast
Washington, D.C.

Chas E. Joyce, clerk

1870 Census
Sixth Ward
Washington, D.C.

Charles Joyce, 23, clerk, born in Ireland, parents born overseas

1870 Census
National Hotel
Fourth Ward
Washington, D.C.

Thos H. Harbin, 36, clerk hotel, born in Maryland

1870 Census
Second Ward
Washington, D.C.

Ella A. Cread, 24, clerk Treasury, born in Virginia, parents born overseas [this is Tom Harbin's future second wife]

1870 Census
Seventh Ward
Baltimore
Baltimore County
Maryland

Thomas A. Jones, 49, Asst. Insp. of [?], born in Maryland, no real estate, $150 in personal estate [this is Tom Harbin's brother-in-law]

Jane A. Jones, 23, at home, born in Maryland [this is Tom Harbin's niece]

Alice C. Jones, 21, at home, born in Maryland [this is Tom Harbin's niece]

Richard T. Jones, 18, servant boy, born in Maryland [this is Tom Harbin's nephew]

Anne C. Jones, 14, at home, born in Maryland [this is Tom Harbin's niece]

Henry C. Jones, 12, at home, born in Maryland [this is Tom Harbin's nephew]

William E. Jones, 8, at home, born in Maryland [this is Tom Harbin's nephew]

1870 Census
Piscataway
Prince George's County
Maryland

Joanna How, 44, born in Maryland, $100 of personal estate [this is Tom Harbin's sister, Johanna Howell]

Joseph How, 21, fisherman, born in Maryland [this is Tom Harbin's nephew, Joseph Howell]

Catherin How, 18, no employment, born in Maryland [this is Tom Harbin's niece, Catherine Howell]

John How, 15, at home, born in Maryland [this is Tom Harbin's nephew, John Howell]

James N. How, 14, at home, born in Maryland [this is Tom Harbin's nephew, James Howell]

George S. How, 12, at home, born in Maryland [this is Tom Harbin's nephew, George Howell]

1870 City Directory
Eighth Street, between B and C Streets, southeast
Washington, D.C.

Geo. F. Harbin, clerk [this is Tom Harbin's youngest brother]

1870 Census
Sixth Ward
Washington, D.C.

George Harbin, 30, clerk dry g store, $3,500 in real estate, #300 in personal estate, born in Maryland [this is Tom Harbin's youngest brother]

John W. Harbin, 46, grocer, born in Maryland [this is Tom Harbin's brother]

Julia Harbin, 48, born in Maryland [this is Tom Harbin's sister]
Sarah Harbin, 32, born in Maryland [this is Tom Harbin's sister]
Jas Harbin, 14, born in Maryland [this is Tom Harbin's son]

1871 City Directory
509 Eighth Street southeast
Washington, D.C.

Chas E. Joyce, clerk

1872 City Directory
724 Seventh Street southeast
Washington, D.C.

Philip W. Harbin, policeman

1872 City Directory
National Hotel
Washington, D.C.

Thomas H. Harbin [sic], cashier

Evening Star, Aug. 28, 1873: "On Wednesday, 6th inst., by the Rev. Charles Andrews, James B. Silcott of Loudoun Co., Va., to Miss Joanna Harbin of Washington, D.C."

Washington Post, March 6, 1878: "Last night a musical and dramatic entertainment was given in aid of St. Peter's Parochial School."

Washington Post, May 25, 1878: "St. Peter's Reading Room Association last night made another effort to advance the interest of their society. St. Peter's Schoolhouse was crowded with a large and appreciative audience to witness 'Shandy Maguire.' The entertainment opened with a variety performance in which Messrs Harbin, Mawdsley, Lenman and Pic took prominent parts. 'Shandy Maguire' was well represented by Messrs Pic, Harbin, Foley and Lenman, and Misses McCaffrey, Maginnis, Darr and De Barry."

Washington Post, Sept. 5, 1878: "William I. Russell, an old resident of East Washington, and for many years an employee of the Navy Yard, died at his residence, 1005 G Street southeast, yesterday. His remains will be interred at Congressional Cemetery Friday afternoon [Sept. 6]."

1879 City Directory
627 L Street southeast
Washington, D.C.

James Harbin, laborer [this is Charlie Russell's step-nephew]

1879 City Directory
706 I Street southeast
Washington, D.C.

James Harbin, machinist [this is Charlie Russell's stepbrother]

1879 City Directory
724 Seventh Street southeast
Washington, D.C.

Philip W. Harbin, police [this is Charlie Russell's stepbrother]
Samuel P. Harbin, carpenter [this is Charlie Russell's step-nephew]

1879 City Directory
National Hotel
Washington, D.C.

Thomas H. Harbin, clerk

1879 City Directory
223 Eighth Street southeast
Washington, D.C.

George F. Harbin (dry goods, 333 Pennsylvania Avenue southeast) [this is Tom Harbin's youngest brother]
James T. Harbin, clerk [this is Tom Harbin's eldest son]
John W. Harbin, clerk [this is Tom Harbin's brother]
Julia A. Harbin [this is Tom Harbin's sister]
Sarah P. Harbin [this is Tom Harbin's sister]

1880 Census
909 I Street southeast
Washington, D.C.

Rebecca Russell, 57, widow, born in D.C.; parents born in Maryland [this is Charlie Russell's sister-in-law, the widow of William Ignatius Russell]

Julia Russell, 29, daughter, tailoress, born in D.C. [this is Charlie Russell's niece]

Martha Russell, 22, daughter, at home, born in D.C. [this is Charlie Russell's niece]

Agnes Russell, 16, daughter, tailoress, born in D.C. [this is Charlie Russell's niece]

Mary Burroughs, 22, cousin, tailoress, born in D.C.; parents born in Maryland [it is clear from the term "cousin," that it was Julia or Martha or Agnes who attended to the census taker when he came around. Mary Burroughs is Charlie Russell's niece]

1880 Census
Washington, D.C.

John Wesley Stant, 30, laborer, born in D.C., as were his parents
Jane Stant, wife, 27, born in Virginia, as were her parents [this is Charlie Russell's niece]
John W. Stant, son, 7, born in D.C. [this is Charlie Russell's grandnephew]
Chas E. Stant, son, 5, born in D.C. [this is Charlie Russell's grandnephew]
George F. Stant, son, 3, born in D.C. [this is Charlie Russell's grandnephew]

1880 Census
Washington, D.C.

Chas Brooks, 49, laborer, born in Ireland, parents born in Ireland [this is Charlie Russell's brother-in-law, Charles W. Brooks Sr.]

Sarah Brooks, 43, born in Maryland, parents born in Maryland [this is Charlie Russell's sister, "Sally"]

John Russel Brooks, 17, born in D.C., apprentice to plumber [this is Charlie Russell's nephew, "Russell"]

Chas W. Brooks, 14, born in D.C., at school [this is Charlie Russell's nephew, Charles W. Brooks Jr.]

1880 Census
Clarksville
Mecklenburg County
Virginia

Charles H. Russell, 47, born in Maryland, parents also born in Maryland, wagon manufacturer

Virginia P. Russell, wife, 37, born in Virginia [this is
Jennie, Charlie Russell's second wife]

Willie H. Russell, son, 21, born in D.C., wagon painter [this is Charlie Russell's son]

Anne E. Russell, daughter, 19, born in D.C. [this is Annie, Charlie Russell's elder daughter]

Alice L. Russell, daughter, 15, born in Virginia [this is Charlie Russell's younger daughter]

1880 Census
704 I Street, SE
Washington, D.C.

James Harbin, widower, 58, machinist, born in Maryland, as were his parents [this is Charlie Russell's stepbrother]

Daniel Harbin, son, 16, single, clerk in store, born in D.C., father born in Maryland, mother born in Virginia [this is Charlie Russell's step-nephew]

John Harbin, son, 20, single, sailor, born in D.C., father born in Maryland, mother born in Virginia [this is Charlie Russell's step-nephew]

1880 Census
627 L Street southeast
Washington, D.C.

William Worthan, 70, engineer, born Maryland, father born Maryland, mother born in Virginia

Mary A. Worthan, wife, 64, born Maryland, father born in England, mother born in Virginia

John L. Worthan, son, 29, proprietor of restaurant, born in Virginia

James S. Harbin, son-in-law, 25, brassfounder, born in D.C., father born in Maryland, mother born in Virginia [this is Charlie Russell's step-nephew]

Midie Harbin, daughter, 24, born in Virginia
Mary E. Fugit, niece, 11, at school, born in D.C., father born in D.C., mother born in Virginia

1880 Census
724 Seventh Street northeast
Washington, D.C.

Philip W. Harbin, 56, policeman, born in Maryland, as were his parents [this is Charlie Russell's stepbrother]
Sarah Harbin, wife, 55, born in D.C., father born in Massachusetts, mother born in England [this is Charlie Russell's step-sister-in-law]
Isabelle, daughter, 27, at home, born in D.C. [this is Charlie Russell's step-niece, Mary Isabelle]
Samuel, son, 25, furniture dealer, born in D.C. [this is Charlie Russell's step-nephew, Samuel Philip]

1890 City Directory
724 Seventh Street southeast
Washington, D.C.

Philip W. Harbin, police [this is Charlie Russell's stepbrother]

1880 Census
138 East Capitol Street
Washington, D.C.

Charles E. Joyce, 33, born in Ireland, clerk in Post Office, parents born in Ireland
Alice Joyce, wife, 31, born in D.C., parents born in Maryland
Alice Joyce, daughter, 8, born in D.C., at school
Daisey Joyce, 6, born in D.C.
John Russell, father in law, 64, carpenter, born in Maryland, both parents born in Maryland
Jennie Russell, sister in law, 25, teacher, born in D.C.

1880 Census
Seventh Ward
Baltimore
Baltimore County
Maryland

Thomas A. Jones, 61, officer house of correction, born in Maryland, as were his parents [this is Tom Harbin's brother-in-law]
Maggie Jones, 22, wife, born in Maryland, as were her parents [this is Tom Jones's second wife]

Appendix B

1880 Census
Piscataway
Prince George's County
Maryland

Adam Weschler, 30, farmer, born in Pennsylvania, parents born in Germany [this is Tom Harbin's nephew]
Margaret J. Weschler, wife, 29, born in Maryland, as were her parents
Alice A. Weschler, daughter, 6, born in Maryland
Agnes M. Weschler, daughter, 4, born in Maryland
Andrew A. Weschler, daughter, 2, born in Maryland
Joanna Howell, mother-in-law, 53, born in Maryland, as were her parents [this is Tom Harbin's sister]

1880 Census
718 First Street northwest
Washington D.C.

Thos H Harbin, 44, born in Maryland, as were his parents. Clerk in hotel
Ella A. Harbin, wife, 28, born in Virginia, as were her parents
Mary B. Harbin, daughter, 6 months, born in D.C.
Mary McCarty, 13, servant, born Ireland

1880 Census
223 Eighth Street
Washington, D.C.

George F. Harbin, 38, single, dry goods dealer [this is Tom Harbin's youngest brother]
Sarah Harbin, sister, 40, single, clerk in dry goods store [this is Tom Harbin's sister]
James T. Harbin, nephew, 23, single, clerk in dry goods store [this is Tom Harbin's son]
Samuel Howell, nephew, 21, single, clerk in dry goods store [this is Tom Harbin's nephew]
Alice Jones, 24, niece, 24, single [this is Tom Harbin's niece]
Harriet Mills, servant, 55, black widow
Note: everyone, including their parents, was born in Maryland.

Washington Post, April 21, 1881: "The Olivette Club gave a pleasant sociable at Washington Hall, corner of Third Street and Pennsylvania Avenue southeast, last night." James T. Harbin was one of the group.

Washington Post, June 9, 1881: "The bower is made attractive by the presence of Misses Mary E. Kealey, Annie Mitchell, Annie Kealey, Jennie Mitchell, Mary Oyster."

Washington Post, May 18, 1882: "J.T. and T.H. Harbin were given a permit yesterday to build two buildings on Seventh Street between East Capitol and A Street southeast, for $5,000."

Washington Post, July 18, 1882: "The Washington Electrotyping Company [sic], Tapley W. Young and James T. Harbin, promoters, was formed last evening at the National Hotel."

Washington Post, Sept. 7, 1882: "The Washington Electro-Plating Company has leased the building opposite the Norfolk Steamer's wharf foot of Sixth Street southwest with steam facilities included, and will begin operations the first of next week."

Washington Post, Aug. 20, 1883: "Captain C.E. Joyce, of the Post Office department, is quite sick."

Washington Post, Dec. 9, 1883: "Captain Charles E. Joyce, Post Office Department, is dangerously ill at his residence, 224 East Capitol Street."

Washington Post, Feb. 17, 1884: "Mrs. Lucy Joyce died at 8.15 o'clock yesterday morning at her late residence No. 2120 K Street northwest, in the sixty-seventh year of her age. Mrs. Joyce came to this city from New York in 1861 when her three sons were serving in the United states Army. She was the mother of Charles E., Edward W., and Miss Mary Joyce, Miss Lucy Russell and Mrs. John P. Simonton. Two of her sons were killed in the service. Her husband died of disease contracted from exposure during Early's raid on this city. She was woman of remarkable energy and bore the sacrifice of the members of her household with great fortitude. The funeral will take place on Monday at 8.45 A.M."

Washington Post, Feb. 18, 1884: "Mr. Charles Brooks, a well-known citizen of the eastern section of the city, dropped dead yesterday afternoon about 3.30 o'clock, at his home, 1105 New Jersey Avenue southeast. Dr. J.W. Bayne was immediately summoned but life was extinct before he arrived. Mr. Brooks served in the First United States Infantry during the war, and was, at the time of his death a member of John A. Rawlins Post No. 1, Grand Army of the Republic."

Washington Post, April 27, and June 15, 1884: Just two of many display and classified ads run in the *Post* by Harbin's Dry Goods Store. The ads give a flavor of what George sold.

Evening Star, Dec. 18, 1884:

> Death of Charles Joyce. Mr. Chas E. Joyce, a clerk in the contract division, Post Office department, died yesterday afternoon at his home, 224 East Capitol Street, after a lingering illness of consumption. Mr. Joyce, who was 38 years of age, entered the Army in 1861 and served in the Irish Brigade with great gallantry during the War, having been promoted at Gettysburg to a lieutenancy for bravery in action. After the War he went to Ireland where he was arrested and imprisoned for alleged participation in the Fenian movement, but through the intervention of the U.S.

authorities, was released. He was a prominent member of J.A. Rawlins, Post No. 1, G.A.R., of this city. He leaves a widow and two little daughters. The funeral will take place at 3.30 P.M. Before his death Mr. Joyce named the following to serve as pall-bearers: M.E. Urell, Dennis O'Connor, J.M. Keogh and N.B. Fithian, of John A. Rawlins Post, Grand Army of the Republic, and Mr. H.E. Weaver, Col. Trott, J.I. Porter, and G.M. Severing, of the Post Office Department.

Washington Post, December 18, 1884:

Death of Chas E. Joyce. A well-known grand Army man dies of consumption. Mr. Charles E. Joyce, a clerk in the Post Office department, and a well-known member of the Grand Army of the Republic, died yesterday at his residence, after a lingering illness of six months duration. He was conscious to the last moment, and shortly before his death gave full directions for his funeral, and selected Maj. Urell, Dennis O'Connor, J.M. Keogh and N.B. Fithian of John A. Rawlings Post, Grand Army of the republic; and Mr. H.E. Weaver, Col. Trott, J.I. Porter, and G.M. Severing of the Post Office Department, to act as pallbearers. The funeral takes place tomorrow afternoon and will be attended by the different Grand Army posts in this city in a body. Mr. Joyce entered the service of the United States in September 1861, in Company A, Eighty-Eighth New York Volunteers (Irish Brigade) and served through the War. At the Battle of Gettysburg he was promoted to the rank of second lieutenant for gallantry, and shortly after was wounded and taken off the field in the same ambulance with General Hancock. He received his discharge in 1864 and was appointed a clerk in the war Department. In 1869 he was appointed a cadet to west Point by Gen. Grant but failed to pass the examination on account of physical defects resulting from the wounds he received during the War. On his return to this city he was appointed to a clerkship in the Navy Department and subsequently changed to the Post Office Department, where he remained up to the time of his death. He was one of the oldest members of Rawlins Post, and had held the position of Post Commander for several years, and that of quartermaster until his death. He had been connected with several of the local papers in this city, and was well-known in newspaper circles, where he had a host of friends.

Washington Post, Dec. 20, 1884:

The funeral of the late Charles E. Joyce yesterday was very largely attended. The G.A.R. services were performed by Post Commander Dennis O'Connor, assisted by chaplain Theodore L. Lamb. The floral offerings included a column surmounted by a dove from the fellow clerks of the deceased in the Post Office department, a cross from the Choral Union, and a wreath from the department of the Potomac, G.A.R. The pallbearers selected by the deceased before his death officiated in that sad capacity. The remains were interred in the Congressional Cemetery.

Tom Harbin's will, 1885:

In the presence of God. Amen! I, Thomas H. Harbin, of the City of Washington, in the District of Columbia, declare this to be my last will and testament.

I bequeath absolutely to my dear wife, Ella A., all my personal estate after the payment of all my just debts, my funeral expenses, and the cost of marking my grave with a tombstone. I devise to my said wife for her life the use and usufruct of all my real estate with the remainder ever in fee simple, [?] to my children begotten of her, excluding from all benefits hereunder my son James who is doing well, while my children begotten or that may be begotten by me, are, or will be, quite young.

I hereby appoint my said wife the sole executrix of this will, revoking all former wills by me made.

In testimony whereof I, Thomas H. Harbin, have hereunto set my hand and set my seal this sixteenth day of December in the year of our Lord eighteen hundred and eighty four. Signed Thomas H. Harbin. [Seal]. Signed, sealed, published and declared by the above named testator Thomas H. Harbin as and for his last will and testament in the presence of us who, at his request, in his presence and in the presence of each other, have hereunto subscribed our names as witnesses—Daniel P.G. Callaghan, 1135 7th St., NW; James McKenzie, ditto; Richard P. Jackson, 3036 Q Street.

Callaghan & McKenzie were Tom's attorneys.

Washington Post, Dec. 18, 1885: "The Late John H. Harbin's will [sic]. John H. Harbin, by his will, bequeathed his personal estate to his widow, Ella A. Harbin. His real estate he also leaves to her, and, at her death to be divided among their children, excluding James who is considered not in want of anything."

Washington Post, April 18 and April 23, 1887, classified ads: "Annie A. Russell, stenographer and typewriter. Pupils desired. Terms moderate. Highest references. 515 14th Street, Occidental Building."

1890 and 1891 City Directories
Washington, D.C.

George F. Harbin, 223 Eighth Street, southeast (home)
319 Pennsylvania Avenue, southeast (business)

This is Tom Harbin's youngest brother. This business address was next door to Ann Virginia Smoot Coleman's house at 323, the one she inherited from her mother. James Coleman was still there, still a jail guard.

1890 City Directory
1713 Seventh Street northwest
Washington, D.C.

John Stant, laborer
Jane Stant, charwoman [this is Charlie Russell's niece]
Jane Stant, mail bag rep [there are two Jane Stants here with different occupations, yet only one Jane Stant existed. This is hard to explain]
Charles Stant, laborer [this is Charlie Russell's grandnephew]
Julia Russell, sewing [this is Charlie Russell's niece]
Agnes Russell, sewing [this is Charlie Russell's niece]

1890 City Directory
18 Seventh Street southeast
Washington, D.C.

Sarah Brooks, widow of Charles [this is Charlie Russell's sister]

John R. Brooks, plumber [this is Charlie Russell's nephew]
Charles W. Brooks, clerk, Pension Office [this is Charlie Russell's nephew]
Annie A. Russell, typewriter [this is Charlie Russell's elder daughter]

1891 City Directory
18 Seventh Street southeast
Washington, D.C.

Sarah A. Brooks, widow of Charles [this is Charlie Russell's sister]
John R. Brooks, plumber [this is Charlie Russell's nephew]
Charles W. Brooks, clerk, Pension Office [this is Charlie Russell's nephew]
Lydia Russell, tailoress [this is Charlie Russell's cousin]

1890 City Directory
712 I Street southeast
Washington, D.C.

James Harben, laborer [this is James S. Harbin, Charlie Russell's step-nephew]

1890 City Directory
715 Virginia Avenue southeast
Washington, D.C.

John H. Harbin, machinist [this is Charlie Russell's step-nephew]

1890 City Directory
1831 Sixth Street northwest
Washington, D.C.

Daniel W. Harbin, engineer [this is Charlie Russell's step-nephew]

1890 City Directory
224 East Capitol Street
Washington, D.C.

Alice R. Joyce, widow of Charles E., Pension Office, clerk [this is Charlie Russell's niece]
John H. Russell, engineer [this is Charlie Russell's eldest brother]

Washington Post, Feb. 22, 1890: "Order appointing George F. Harbin guardian of minor children, bond $18,000."

Washington Post, Sept. 25, 1890: "A pension of $20 a month has been granted to Mrs. Sarah Harbin, the widow of Policeman Harbin."

1891 City Directory
444 Q Street northwest
Washington, D.C.

Julia Russell, sewing [this is Charlie Russell's niece]
Agnes Russell, sewing [this is Charlie Russell's niece]

1891 City Directory
1805 Wiltberger Street, NW
Washington, D.C.

John W. Stant, laborer [this is the husband of Charlie Russell's niece]
John W. Stant Jr., butcher [this is Charlie Russell's grand nephew]

1891 City Directory
724 Seventh Street southeast
Washington, D.C.

Sarah Harbin, widow of Philip [this is Charlie Russell's step-sister-in-law]
Samuel P. Harbin, carpenter [this is Charlie Russell's step-nephew]

1891 City Directory
712 I Street southeast
Washington, D.C.

James S. Harbin, machinist [this is Charlie Russell's step-nephew]

1891 City Directory
1314 Eleventh Street southeast
Washington, D.C.

Daniel Harbin, notions [this is Charlie Russell's step-nephew]

1891 City Directory
224 East Capitol Street
Washington, D.C.

Alice R. Joyce, widow of E. Charles [sic], Pension Office, clerk [this is Charlie Russell's niece]
Alice O. Joyce, Census Office, clerk [this is Charlie Russell's grandniece]
John H. Russell, engineer [this is Charlie Russell's eldest brother]
Annie A. Russell, typewriter [this is Charlie Russell's elder daughter]

Washington Post, June 28, 1891: "Mrs. Thomas Harbin and her children leave for Burlington, Kansas on Tuesday, to be gone until October 1." This is Ella, Tom's widow

Washington Post, Feb. 5, 1892: "The Washington branch of the Bichloride of Gold Club met last night at 207 C Street southeast and effected an organization. Mr. James T. Harbin was elected temporary chairman and Mr. WFM Bolies temporary secretary."

Washington Post, Feb. 9, 1892: "The reception to Dr. Keeley, of Dwight, Ill., given by the Bichloride of Gold Club at the Arlington last night was a successful and pleasant affair."

Washington Post, Dec. 27, 1893: "Some time ago A. Richards secured a permit to construct a wharf on land claimed by him on the bank of the Eastern Branch at the foot of South Capitol Street. It has developed that this same land is claimed by George F. Harbin. Yesterday, these two gentlemen, accompanied by their attorneys, were given a hearing by the Commissioners."

Washington Post, Sept. 26, 1895: "Mr. George Harbin and Mr. Adam Gaddis of East Washington, were given a hearing before the Commissioners yesterday at which the visitors favored the project of moving the center parking from Pennsylvania Avenue southeast."

Washington Post, Dec. 9, 1895: "At 2 o'clock Sunday morning Dec. 8, 1895, Agnes M. Russell, aged thirty one years. Funeral Tuesday afternoon, December 10, at 2 o'clock, at 444 Q Street northwest. Friends are invited to attend."

Washington Post, Aug. 2, 1896:

"Portland"

You may tell again of the beautiful black
That Sheridan rode that day;
How he nobly, gallantly bore the man
Who was "twenty miles away"
But there ne'er was a horse like Portland
You may paint with an artist's delicate touch,
The white, silky mane of the steed
On which Napoleon upright sat,
And proudly, lordly, decreed;
But there ne'er was a horse like Portland
You may tell with an orator's valued gift
How, with genuine lack of fear,
That faithful, dear old sorrel bore
True, brave, Paul Revere;
But there ne'er was a horse like Portland
You may quote from the lines of your history book,
The marches Washington made;
Of the sturdy steeds that carried him,
And their lives for his country paid;
But there ne'er was a horse like Portland
So, Sheridan's black and Bonaparte's white,
Revere's and Washington's too,
Just look to your laurels, hold to them tight,
Or you'll find yourselves minus a few;
For there ne'er was a horse like Portland

Daisy Isabel Joyce, of 127 Maryland Avenue northeast

Washington Post, Oct. 4, 1896:

"Semper Fidelis"

I wonder if in after years
I ever shall forget you

I marvel how I ever lived
Before the time I met you
I ask for no companionship
Save yours, nor do I heed
The world and all its pleasures, which
To most men is their creed
Joys and sorrows come and go,
But you I'll have forever;
Ah, could you, would you doubt my love
For you, my meerschaum, never

Washington Post, Jan. 3, 1897:

"Dot Dog of Mine"

So many people what has dogs
Will dell you how dey make you laf
Und so I want to get not left
I'll dell you of de one I haf
My leetle dog is werry wise
Und cute und schus as good as any
He do schus like de dago's monk
If you will show dot dog a penny
Dis leetle dog does lof me much
He follows me all over once
Und sits up on de baby's schtool
Schus like a boy in school a dunce
He schleeps so nice de fire by
Und listens for a noise aboud
Und if he hears a ting he flies
So sudden to de back yard oud
His name you tink already yet
Is Schneider or von Bismarck, too
I call my dog not one of dem
He's schus plain "Dog" to me and you
by Daisy Isabel Joyce

1900 Census
319 43rd Street
Washington, D.C.

Richard A. O'Brien, 41, born May 1859 in Virginia, parents born in Virginia, plumbing inspector

Mary E. O'Brien, wife, 40, born in Aug. 1859, born in D.C., parents born in Maryland, had five children and five alive [this is Charlie Russell's niece, the former Mary E. "Molly" Burroughs]

Louise R. O'Brien, daughter, 16, born April 1884 in D.C., at school
Gertrude K. O'Brien, daughter, 14, born Oct. 1885 in D.C., at school
Ralph B. O'Brien, son, 12, born Dec. 1887 in D.C., at school
Howell V. O'Brien, son, 9, born March 1890 in D.C., at school
Richard A. O'Brien, son, 4, born Sept. 1895 in D.C.

1900 Census
1113 M Street
Washington, D.C.

John W. Stant, 49, born July 1850 in D.C., married 30 years, parents born in D.C., laborer

Jane Stant, wife, 47, born Jan. 1853, 9 children and 4 alive, born in Virginia, parents born in Maryland [this is Janie, Charlie Russell's niece and daughter of William Ignatius Russell]

John W. Stant Jr., 26, born Sept. 1873 in D.C., married 2 years, blacksmith [this is Charlie Russell's grandnephew]

Charles E. Stant, son, 25, single, born May 1875 in D.C., carpenter [this is Charlie Russell's grand nephew]

Geo. F. Stant, son, 22, born Dec. 1877 in D.C., single, blacksmith [this is Charlie Russell's grandnephew]

Wm. H. Stant, son, 16, born July 1883 in D.C., moulder [this is Charlie Russell's grandnephew]

Sally Stant, daughter-in-law, born Jan. 1876, married 2 years

Mary L. Edelin, niece, 5, born Jan. 1895 in D.C., parents born in D.C.

1900 Census
Clarksville
Mecklenburg County
Virginia

C.H. Russell, 67, born in Sept. 1833 [incorrect], in Maryland, manufacturer, parents born in Maryland

V.P. Russell, wife, 49, born in Virginia, married 29 years [this is Charlie Russell's second wife, Virginia P. (Jennie) Moss]

A.L. Russell, daughter, born in Sept. [should say April] 1865 [this is Alice, Charlie Russell's younger daughter]

They lived next door to Charlie's son, Willie, and his family.

W.H. Russell, 40, born in Sept. 1859 [incorrect], in Maryland [incorrect], wagon manufacturer, parents born in Maryland [half right] [this is Willie, Charlie Russell's son]

Kate Russell, wife, 37, born Dec. 1862 [incorrect], Virginia.
Parents born in Virginia [this is Charlie Russell's daughter-in-law]

G.G. Russell, 10, born Oct. 1889 [incorrect], Virginia [this is Charlie Russell's grandson, his namesake Charles H. Russell]

C.M. Russell, daughter, 9, born Oct. 1890 [incorrect], Virginia [this is Charlie Russell's granddaughter, Carrie]

M.P. Russell, daughter, 9, born Oct. 1890 [incorrect], Virginia [this is Charlie Russell's granddaughter, Minnie]

Katie Russell, daughter, 7, born Sept. 1892 [incorrect], Virginia [this is Charlie Russell's granddaughter, Sallie Kate]

J.W. Russell, son, born April 1896 [incorrect], Virginia [this is Charlie Russell's grandson, John W.]

W.H. Russell Jr., son, 3, born April 1896 [incorrect], Virginia [this is Charlie Russell's grandson]

Arthur D. Russell, son, 1, born May 1899 [incorrect], Virginia [this is Charlie Russell's grandson]

1900 Census
636 C Street
Washington, D.C.

William J. McGee, 38, born April 1862 in Michigan. Married 8 years, 4 children with 4 alive. Father born in Ireland. Mother born in Maryland. Government clerk [this is Charlie Russell's son-in-law]

Anna A. McGee, 39, born Aug. 1860 in D.C. Father born in Maryland; mother born in Virginia [this is Annie, Charlie Russell's elder daughter]

Charles R. McGee, son, 7, born Sept. 1892 in D.C. At school [this is Charlie Russell's grandson, Charles Russell McGee]

William J. McGee, 6, born Sept. 1893 in D.C. At school [this is Charlie Russell's grandson, William James McGee Jr.]

Isabel J. McGee, daughter, 5, born Feb. 1895 in D.C. [this is Charlie Russell's granddaughter, Isabel Jarboe McGee]

Mildred J. McGee, daughter, 1, born July 1898 in D.C. [this is Charlie Russell's granddaughter, Mildred Jarboe McGee]

Alice E. [?], boarder, 35, born July 1865 in Michigan. Father born in Ireland. Mother born in Maryland. Government clerk [this may well be William J. McGee's sister]

1900 Census
505 L Street between 1st and 2nd Streets
Washington, D.C.

James Harbin, 45, born in Feb. 1855 in D.C., father born in Maryland, mother born in D.C., instrument manufacturer [this is James S. Harbin, Charlie Russell's step-nephew]

Miriam Harbin, wife, 46, born May 1856, married 22 years, 2 children with one alive, born Virginia, parents born in Maryland [this is Midie]

John Worthan, boarder, 47, born Jan. 1853 in Virginia, married 18 years, parents born in Maryland, bartender [this is Midie's brother]

Lelia Harbin, boarder (daughter crossed out), 11, born Dec. 1888 in D.C., parents born in D.C., at school [this is Charlie Russell's step-grandniece]

1900 Census
1328 Eleventh Street
Washington, D.C.

John H. Harbin, 38, born Dec. 1861, born in D.C., as were his parents, machinist [this is Charlie Russell's step-nephew]

Mary A. Harbin, wife, 36, born Dec. 1863, married 15 years, 5 children and 5 alive, born in Maryland, parents born in Virginia

James W. Harbin, son, 14, born Oct. 1885 in D.C., at school Annie R. Harbin, 11, born Oct. 1888 in D.C., at school
John E. Harbin, son, 8, born Nov. 1891 in D.C., at school
Eva May Harbin, daughter, 4, born Feb. 1896 in D.C.
Mary E. Harbin, daughter, 1, born Feb. 1899 in D.C.

1900 Census
915 Eighth Street
Washington, D.C.

Daniel W. Harbin, 35, born July 1864 in D.C., both parents born in D.C., machinist's helper [this is Charlie Russell's step-nephew]

Elizabeth Harbin, wife, 32, born Feb. 1868, married 12 years, 6 children and 6 alive, born in D.C., parents born in Germany

May Harbin, daughter, 10, born Aug. 1889 in D.C., at school
Wilmer Harbin, son, 9, born Dec. 1890 in D.C., at school
George Harbin, son, 8, born May 1892 in D.C., at school
Eugene Harbin, son, 6, born Jan. 1894 in D.C.
Ethel Harbin, daughter, 4, born Oct. 1895 in D.C.
Willie Harbin, son, 3, born Oct. 1896 in D.C.

John W. Nokes Jr., lodger, 24, born April 1876 in D.C., parents born in Maryland, painter

John W. Nokes, lodger, 63, born Aug. 1836, widower, married 42 years, born in Maryland, as were his parents, painter

1900 Census
724 Seventh Street southeast
Washington, D.C.

Samuel P. Harbin, head, 44, born April 1856, D.C., single, born Washington D.C., as were his parents [this is Charlie Russell's step-nephew, the late Officer Philip Harbin's son]

Mary E. Harbin, sister, 46, born Aug. 1853, D.C., single, born in D.C., as were her parents [this is Charlie Russell's step-niece, Mary Isabelle Harbin]

Sarah Harbin, mother, 76, widow, born Aug. 1823, married 35 years, 4 children with 2 alive, born Massachusetts, father born in London, mother born in D.C. [this is Charlie Russell's step-sister-in-law and the late Officer Philip Harbin's widow]

1900 Census
623 East Capitol Street, SE
Washington, D.C.

R. Joyce, 57, head, born July 1848, D.C., widow, parents born in Maryland, clerk in Pension Office [this is Mary Alice (Alice) Joyce, Charlie Russell's niece]

John H. Russell, father, 84, born Feb. 1816, Maryland, widower, parents born in Maryland [this is Charlie Russell's eldest brother]

Jennie Russell, sister, 48, born Sept. 1851, D.C., parents born in Maryland [this is Charlie Russell's niece, Janette Alice (Jennie)]

Sarah Brooks, aunt, 71, born Oct. 1828, Maryland, parents born in Maryland [this is Charlie Russell's sister, "Sally"]

Alice A. Joyce, daughter, 28, born July 1871, D.C., parents born in Maryland [this is Alice O. Joyce, Charlie Russell's grandniece]

Isabella Joyce, daughter, 26, born Dec. 1873, D.C., parents born in Maryland [this is Daisy Joyce, Charlie Russell's grandniece]

1900 Census
11 Seventh Street southeast
Washington, D.C.

Ella A. Harbin, 44, born in Virginia in Sept. 1856, married 21 years, parents born in Virginia, 2 children, owned home free and clear [this is Tom Harbin's second wife]

Mary B. Harbin, daughter, 19, born in Nov. 1880 in D.C., father born in Maryland, mother born in Virginia, at school [this is Tom Harbin's only daughter]

George F. Harbin, son, 17, born in Nov. 1882, in D.C., father born in Maryland, mother born in Virginia, at school [this is Tom Harbin's younger surviving son]

1900 Census
223 Eighth Street
Washington, D.C.

George Harbin, 60, single, born Feb. 1840 in Maryland, as were his parents, buyer of dry goods [this is Tom Harbin's youngest brother]

Sarah P. Harbin, sister, 62, single, born April 1838 in Maryland, as were her parents, clerk courts [this is Tom Harbin's sister]

James T. Harbin, nephew, 43, born Sept. 1856 in Maryland, married 17 years, his parents born in Maryland, stenographer [this is Tom Harbin's son]

Jennie A. Harbin, niece, 41, born Jan. 1859 in D.C., married 17 years, 4 children with 3 alive [this is Tom Harbin's daughter-in-law, whom he never knew]

Margaret A. Harbin, grandniece, 9, born Jan. 1891 in D.C. [this is Tom Harbin's granddaughter]

Percival F. Harbin, grandniece, 5, born Jan. 1895 in Maryland [this is Tom Harbin's grandson]

Marie A. Harbin, grandniece, 16, born Sept. 1883 in D.C., at school [this is Tom Harbin's granddaughter]

Washington Post, Jan. 6, 1904: "Mr. Charles W. Brooks died yesterday morning, at his residence, 416 Second Street northwest, after an illness of two days. Mr. Brooks had been identified with the Pension Bureau for the past twenty-two years, having entered as a boy. He was a son of the late Charles W. Brooks, who served with distinction in the Mexican and Civil Wars. Mr. Brooks leaves a widow. The funeral will occur tomorrow at 9 o'clock from St. Patrick's Church."

Washington Times, July 25, 1905:

John H. Russell Dies at Home of Daughter. Veteran Resident of Washington Has Passed Away After Long and Useful Career. John H. Russell, one of the oldest and best known citizens of Washington, died this morning at the residence of his daughter, Mrs. Alice R. Joyce, 626 East Capitol Street, after a long illness. Mr. Russell was born in Charles County, Maryland, in 1816. When he was twenty one years of age he came to Washington and had resided here ever since. He was active in politics, being always a staunch Democrat. He represented the old Sixth Ward in the city council under the administration of Mayors Magruder, Wallach and Bowen. His health failed twenty years ago and since that time he has been an invalid. Mr. Russell is survived by his two daughters, Mrs. Alice R. Joyce and Miss Jennie Russell, of Washington, and a brother Charles H. Russell of Virginia. Funeral services will be held at St. Joseph's Church, corner of Second and C Streets, Northeast, Thursday morning, at 9 o'clock.

Washington Post, July 26, 1905:

John H. Russell Dead. Aged Resident of Capitol Hill Yields to Grim Reaper. John H. Russell, an aged resident of this city, died yesterday morning at the home of his daughter, Mrs. Alice R. Joyce, 626 East capitol Street. Mr. Russell had been long in failing health and was confined to his bed for many months suffering from a complication of diseases incident to old age. Mr. Russell was born in Charles County, Md., in 1816, and took up his residence in Washington in 1837. he entered the field of local politics and was a member of the City Council for the Sixth ward under the administrations of the mayors of the city. Mr. Russell had a wide acquaintance with Washingtonians and his reminiscences of "ancient days" in the District were particularly accurate and interesting. He is survived by two daughters, Mrs. Alice R. Joyce and Miss Jennie Russell, both of this city. A brother, Charles H. Russell, lives in Virginia. The funeral services are to be held Thursday morning at 9 o'clock in St. Joseph's Church.

Washington Times, July 27, 1905:

Late J.H. Russell is Laid to Rest. The funeral of the late J.H. Russell, who died at the home of his daughter, Mrs. Alice R. Joyce, at 626 East Capitol Street, Northeast, last Tuesday morning, took place this morning from St. Joseph's Church, Second and C Streets, Northeast, at 10 o'clock. A short service was held at the home before the remains were taken to the church. The Rev. George B. Harrington of Buckeystown, Md, officiated at this service. At the church requiem mass was said by the Rev. Ignatius Fealy, assistant pastor of the church. The funeral sermon was preached by the Rev. James A. Smyth. The pallbearers were Alexander McKenzie, Charles S. Price, James Hutchinson and John J. Higgins. Many beautiful floral tributes were received from friends of the deceased. The remains were interred in Congressional Cemetery.

Washington Post, Dec. 17, 1905: "Died Saturday, Dec. 16, at the residence of her brother, George F. Harbin, 223 8th Street, southeast, Sarah P. Harbin. Funeral on Monday, Dec. 18, from St. Peter's Church." She was buried in Mount Olivet Cemetery, in D.C.

Washington Post, Aug. 19, 1909: "Miss Daisy Isabel Joyce, daughter of Mrs. Alice Joyce, of 628 East Capitol Street, and Jackson S. Elliott of the

Associated Press, were married yesterday afternoon at Philadelphia. The ceremony was performed by the Rev. Father Cavanaugh, chancellor of the Cathedral."

New York Times, Aug. 19, 1909, from a Washington Correspondence of the previous day: "Miss Daisy Isabel Joyce, daughter of Mrs. Alice Russell Joyce of this city, and Jackson S. Elliott, a Washington newspaper man, were married this afternoon in Philadelphia by the Rev. Father Kavanaugh [sic]. They met as reporters on a Washington newspaper soon after Mr. Elliott came her from Iowa several years ago. Mr. and Mrs. Elliott will soon make an extensive tour through the South."

1910 Census
317 B Street northeast
Washington, D.C.

Richard O'Brien, 49, married 26 years, born Maryland as were his parents [incorrect], plumbing inspector

Mary O'Brien, wife, 47, born in D.C., parents born in Maryland, 6 children, 5 alive [this is Charlie Russell's niece]

Gertrude O'Brien, daughter, 23, single, born in D.C., stenographer in an insurance office Howell O'Brien, son, 18, architect, born in D.C.

Richard A. O'Brien, son, 15, born in D.C.

1910 Census
Main Street
Clarksville
Mecklenburg County
Virginia

Charles H. Russell, 77, born in Maryland, manufacturer of farm wagons, parents born in Maryland Virginia Russell, wife, 48, married 36 years [this is Jennie, Charlie Russell's second wife]

Alice L. Russell, daughter, 44, single [this is Charlie Russell's younger daughter]

Although it was called Main Street in the census, it was really Virginia Avenue, originally Virginia Street. Also on Main Street was Charlie's son, Willie, with his family.

William H. Russell, 51, born in Washington, D.C., married 22 years, father born Maryland, mother born in Washington, mfr of wagons, employer [this is Willie, Charlie Russell's son]

Kate G. Russell, 48, born in Virginia, as were her parents Charles H. Russell, son, 21, single, born in Virginia [this is Charlie Russell's daughter-in-law]

Carrie M. Russell, daughter, 20, single, schoolteacher in public school [this is Charlie Russell's granddaughter]

Minnie P. Russell, daughter, 20, single, born in Virginia [this is Charlie Russell's granddaughter]

Sallie Russell, daughter, 18, born in Virginia [this is Sallie Kate, Charlie Russell's granddaughter]

John W. Russell, son, 16, born in Virginia [this is Charlie Russell's grandson]

William H. Russell, son, 12, born in Virginia [this is Charlie Russell's grandson]

Arthur D. Russell, son, 11, born in Virginia [this is Charlie Russell's grandson]

Thomas J. Russell, son, 4, born in Virginia [this is Charlie Russell's grandson]

1910 Census
155 E Street southeast
Washington, D.C.

James S. Harbin, 54, born D.C., father born Maryland, mother born D.C., instrument maker Navy Yard [this is Charlie Russell's step-nephew, James Samuel Harbin]

Miriam S. Harbin, wife, 53, married 32 years, one child and one alive, born Virginia, parents born Maryland [this is Midie]

Lealya [sic] Harbin, daughter, 20, born in D.C. [this is Charlie Russell's step-grandniece]

1910 Census
747 Eleventh Street southeast
Washington, D.C.

John H. Harbin, 50, born in D.C., as were his parents, machinist at the Navy Yard [this is Charlie Russell's step-nephew, John Henry Harbin]

Mary A. Harbin, wife, 46, married 25 years, 5 children and 5 alive, born Maryland, parents born in Virginia

Kath A. Harbin, daughter, 21, born in D.C.

Eva A. Harbin, daughter, 14, born in D.C.

Mary E. Harbin, daughter, 11, born in D.C.

1910 Census
1427 Potomac Avenue
Washington, D.C.

James W. Harbin, 24, born D.C., father born D.C., mother born Maryland, machinist at the Navy Yard [this is Charlie Russell's step-grandnephew, James Wilbur Harbin, the son of John Henry Harbin]

Susie E. Harbin, wife, 23, born Virginia, as were her parents

James W. Harbin Jr., born D.C.

1910 Census
724 Seventh Street southeast
Washington, D.C.

Mary B. [sic] Harbin, 58, born in D.C., father born in Maryland, mother born in D.C., stenographer at home [this is Charlie Russell's step-niece, Mary Isabelle, the daughter of the late Officer Philip Harbin]

Samuel P. Harbin, boarder, 55, born in D.C., father born in Maryland, mother born in D.C., house carpenter [this is the step-nephew of Charlie Russell and son of the late Officer Philip Harbin]

Minnie E. Fabers, boarder, widow, born in Pennsylvania, as were her parents, own income

1910 Census
1433 Tea Street, NW
Washington, D.C.

Jackson Elliott, married, newspaper reporter, refused to tell any information

Isabelle Elliott, married

1910 Census
628 East Capitol Street
Washington, D.C.

Alice R. Joyce, 58, widow, 3 children with 2 alive, born in D.C., parents born in Maryland, government clerk

Alice O. Joyce, daughter, 25, single, born in D.C., both parents born in D.C., government clerk

Jennie A. Russell, lodger, 52, single, born in D.C., parents born in Maryland, own income

1910 Census
11 Seventh Street southeast
Washington, D.C.

Ella A. Harbin, 49, widow, 2 children, born in Virginia, as were her parents, no occupation [this is Tom Harbin's second wife]

George F. Harbin, son, 26, single, born in D.C., father born in Maryland, mother born in Virginia, professor Catholic University [this is the younger of Tom Harbin's sons]

Blanche Harbin, daughter, 23, single, born in D.C., father born in Maryland, mother born in Virginia, music teacher [this is Tom Harbin's only daughter]

1910 Census
Middletown
Frederick County
Maryland

Jennie A. Harbin, 50, married 27 years, marital status very vague, 3 children and 3 alive, born in D.C., as were her parents, no occupation

Margarita A. Harbin, daughter, 19, born in D.C., father born in Md, mother born in D.C., no occupation [this is Margaret, Tom Harbin's granddaughter]

Frank P. Harbin, son, 15, birth details same as his sister, no occupation [this is Tom Harbin's grandson]

1910 Census
223 Eighth Street
Washington, D.C.

George F. Harbin, 70, single, born in Maryland, parents born in Maryland, merchant dry good, employer [this is Tom Harbin's youngest brother]

Thomas F. Maguire, lodger, 33, married 2 years, born in Massachusetts, as were his parents, engineer [this is Tom Harbin's grandson-in-law]

Marie A. Maguire, lodger, 26, born in D.C., as were her parents [this is Tom Harbin's granddaughter]

Marie E. Maguire, lodger, 1, born in D.C., as were her parents [this is Tom Harbin's great-granddaughter]

Washington Post, Sept. 18, 1914: "On Thursday, Sept. 17, 1914, at 5:00 P.M., at her residence, 1411 N Street northwest, Catherine M., beloved wife of Raymond T. Baker and daughter of the late Jeremiah and Catherine Costello. Notice of funeral later."

The will of Charles H. Russell, 1920:

I, Charles H. Russell, of Clarksville, Mecklenburg County, Virginia, do make this writing as and for my last will and testament, hereby revoking any and all former wills at any time made by me.

First, I will and direct that all of my just debts be paid by my executors hereinafter named, out of my estate.

Second, I give and bequeath to my daughter, Alice Lee Russell, the 'hall clock' now standing in the hall in my dwelling house in Clarksville, Va., and also all the furniture, beds and bedding of every kind and description in the room in my said dwelling house now occupied by her as a bed chamber.

Third, I give and devise to my said daughter, Alice Lee Russell, the house and lot now occupied by my cook, Mary Averett, situate in the town of Clarksville, Va, at the corner of Beauty Street and Main Street, and adjoining the lot on which I now reside, to beheld by her in fee simple.

Fourth, I give and devise to my wife, Virginia P. Russell, and my daughter, Alice Lee Russell, the house and lot in the town of Clarksville, Virginia, now occupied by me as a residence, together with the household and kitchen furniture therein of every kind and description (except that already given, in this my will, to my daughter Alice Lee Russell), to be held, used, occupied and enjoyed by them jointly as a home, for and during the life of my wife, Virginia P. Russell, and at the death of my said wife, Virginia P. Russell, I devise and bequeath said dwelling house and lot and all of said household and kitchen furniture therein to my daughter, Alice Lee Russell, as her absolute property and in fee simple.

Fifth, I give and bequeath to my wife, Virginia P. Russell, the sum of one thousand dollars to be paid to her out of my estate within sixty days after my death, said sum of one thousand dollars to be her absolute property.

Sixth. I give and bequeath to Mary Averett, who has been my faithful servant for many years, the sum of fifty dollars, to be paid to her out of my estate.

Seventh. I have heretofore given to my two daughters, Alice Lee Russell and Annie Alice McGee, the sum of fifteen thousand dollars each, in bonds secured on real estate, and have delivered said bonds to them some time past. I do now ratify and confirm said gift to each of them, and do will and direct that neither of my said daughters shall be required to account for said sums so received by them, or either of them, or to account for any other sum or sums of money received, by them, or either of them, from me in my life-time in the division of my estate; but that they shall each take their respective shares in my estate under this my will without accounting for said sums so received of me in my lifetime.

Eighth. I do give and devise to my son, William H. Russell, all of my right, title and interest in the property on Main Street, in the town of Clarksville, Virginia, now occupied by him as a residence, along with the house and lot in the rear now occupied by Mr. Stokes; it being all of my interest in all of the property situate on the North side of said Main Street between the lot of the Presbyterian Church and the cross street immediately to the West. And I do further give and bequeath to my said son, William H. Russell, fifteen thousand dollars in value of my two-thirds interest, in moneys and accounts due to the firm of C.H. Russell and son, and in stocks and material and machinery on land belonging to said firm, said fifteen thousand dollars in value to be set apart and delivered to him out of my said interest in the money and accounts due to said firm, and in the stock and material on land and machinery belonging to said firm, the property given him under this clause of my will to be his absolute property.

Ninth. I will and direct that my executors hereinafter named shall set apart from my estate the sum of fourteen thousand dollars, and that they shall invest and reinvest the same in good and solvent securities, or loans secured on real estate, and shall collect and receive the income received from said funds, they shall pay to my wife Virginia P. Russell so long as she may live, the sum of fifty dollars per month upon her request for the same; should said fund yield a net income of more than fifty dollars per month or six hundred dollars per annum which I wish paid to my wife Virginia P. Russell during her life, I direct that the excess of said net income over six hundred dollars per annum be equally divided by my executors between my three children, W.H. Russell, Alice Lee Russell and Annie Alice Magee [sic] at the ends of each year. At the death of my said wife I will and direct that said funds of fourteen thousand dollars and any accrued income thereon shall be equally divided between my said three children, William H. Russell, Alice Lee Russell, and Annie Alice Magee, and said fund shall be paid over to them in equal proportions by my executors.

Tenth. I will and direct that all the rest and residue of my estate of every kind not hereinbefore disposed of shall be equally divided between my three children, William H. Russell, Alice Lee Russell and Annie Alice Magee, and that they shall have and hold their respective shares thereof as their absolute property.

Eleventh. I do nominate and appoint my son, William H. Russell, of Clarksville, Va., and William Leigh, of Danville, Virginia, Executors of this my last will and testament. Witness my signature and seal this the 10th day of February, 1915. C.H. Russell [seal].

Signed and acknowledged by the said Charles H. Russell as his last will and testament in our presence, who, at his request and in his presence and in the presence of each other, have subscribed our names as witnesses thereto. [signed]. C.L. Doggett and J.N. Crowder.

At the Clerk's office at Mecklenburg Circuit Court, January 19th, 1920, the last will and testament of Chas. H. Russell, dec'd, late of the County, was this day produced before the clerk of said court in his office by W.H. Russell, one of the executors named in said will, and fully proved by C.L. Doggett, one of the subscribing witnesses thereto, under oath, and thereupon the said will was admitted to probate. Teste: H.J. Hutcheson, clerk.

Clerk's fee: $4.20

Transfer fee: $1.00
Tax: $101.50
Total costs of probate: $106.70

Charlie's obituary, written in Mecklenburg County on Feb. 18, 1920, and published four days later (presumably to coincide with his birthday) reads (with information supplied by Alice, his daughter):

> Charles H. Russell. Eighty-seven years ago today, in the old historic home known as Blenheim, Charles County, Maryland, Charles H. Russell, one of our county's oldest and best known citizens, first saw the dawn of a long and useful life, the greater part of which was spent in our midst. He was the son of William H. Russell, a veteran of the war of 1812, also a grandson of a soldier of the Revolution, his maternal grandfather, Thomas Cahill [sic], having come to this country with the British Army during the war with England and joined the colonists in their fight for independence. At the outbreak of the Civil War Mr. Russell held a position at the Washington Navy Yard, and was also a member of a prominent military company, Washington Light Infantry. When the said company was mustered into the United States service Mr. Russell refused to take up arms against the South. Stripped of his accoutrements and uniform and given one hour in which to leave the District of Columbia, with a hasty farewell to his family and friends he walked to Alexandria, Virginia, and from there made his way to Richmond, and offered his services to the Confederate Government. In consideration of his mechanical knowledge he was given control of the gun shops, which, at a later time, were moved to Clarksville, Virginia. He was a member of the "Home Guards," when that valiant handful of greybeards and boys checked Wilson's raiders and saved the railroad bridge over Stanton River [sic]. He was wounded in this engagement and bourned from the field in what was thought to be a dying condition. After the war he started life anew in Clarksville and for sixty years was a loved and familiar figure in our midst. The deceased was twice married, his first wife was Miss Mary Ann Jarboe of Fairfax, Virginia, who died shortly after the Civil War. He afterwards married Miss Virginia P. Moss, of Mecklenburg Co., who survives him. He leaves one son, William H. Russell, of Clarksville, and two daughters, Mrs. William J. McGee, of Washington, D.C., and Miss Alice L. Russell, of Clarksville. Industrious, earnest and generous, his daily life was a lesson to those about him. We shall all miss him; now advanced in years, his associates, with whom he always looked forward to a pleasant exchange of courtesies, and who will recall with sadness his gentleness and cheery smile. Wayward lads treasure his wise counsel, bringing sunshine and hope for the future when the way ahead seemed dark; the hearts of the little ones, whom he particularly loved, will ever remember his kindness and generosity and mourn because he will come no more. The husband and father has passed over leaving an enviable record—a well spent life, deeds of kindness, charity and love for his fellow man and a name and memory that will never be forgotten. The bereaved family have the sincere sympathy of sorrowing friends. To the widow, consolation will come with the memory of the long years and happy days spent with such a helpmate; to the son, the sample of industry, unquestioned honesty and [next line missing] will be an incentive to follow in the footsteps of the greatest father that ever lived, his own. To the daughters, who watched with him so untiringly during the hopeless days and nights of pain and suffering, peace and consolation will come, with heartfelt thanks that such a privilege was granted them and of a duty fulfilled.

1920 Census
Main Street
Clarksville
Mecklenburg County
Virginia

William H. Russell, 60, born Virginia. Both parents born D.C. Mfr of wagons. Owned his house free and clear [this is Willie, Charlie Russell's son]
Kate Russell, wife, 57 [this is Charlie Russell's daughter-in-law]
William Russell, son, 24 [this is Charlie Russell's grandson]
Arthur Russell, son, 20 [this is Charlie Russell's grandson]
Thomas Russell, son, 17 [this is Charlie Russell's grandson]
They lived just down the road from....
Jennie P. Russell, 78, widow, born in Virginia, as were her parents. Owned her own house, free and clear [this is Charlie Russell's second wife]
Alice Russell, daughter, 54, born in Virginia. She says her parents were born in Virginia, but only her mother was [this is Charlie Russell's younger daughter]

1920 Census
1810 Lamont Street
Washington, D.C.

William J. McGee, 59, Chief Government, born Michigan, father born in Ireland, mother born in NY; owns house on mortgage [this is Charlie Russell's son-in-law]
Anne A. McGee, wife, 56, born in D.C., father born in Maryland, mother born in D.C. [this is Annie, Charlie Russell's elder daughter]
Charles R. McGee, son, 27, automobile salesman, born in D.C. [this is Charlie Russell's grandson]
Isabel C. McGee, daughter, 24, born in D.C., clerk Relief Society [this is Charlie Russell's granddaughter]
Mildred McGee, daughter, 11, born in D.C. [this is Charlie Russell's granddaughter]

1920 Census
724 Seventh Street southeast
Washington, D.C.

Samuel P. Harbin, 64, born in D.C., father born in Maryland, mother born in D.C., city carpenter [this is Charlie Russell's step-nephew, the son of the late Officer Philip Harbin]
Isabelle Harbin, sister, 68, born in D.C., father born in Maryland, mother born in D.C. [this is Charlie Russell's step-niece, Mary Isabelle Harbin, the daughter of the late Officer Philip Harbin]
Eugene Campbell, boarder, 30, born in North Carolina, as were his parents, machinist at the Navy Yard
Valentina C. Poppescu, lodger, 24, born in Rumania, as were her parents, telegraph operator at a telegraph company

1920 Census
967 East 18th Street
Brooklyn
Kings County
New York

Jackson S. Elliott, 44, born in Illinois, father born in NY, mother born in Canada (English-speaking), manager newspaper

Isabelle Elliott, wife, 40, born in Washington, D.C., father born in Ireland (Irish-speaking), mother born in Washington, D.C. [this is Daisy Elliott, formerly Joyce, Charlie Russell's grandniece]

Jackson S. Elliott, son, 7, born in Washington, D.C.

Joyce Elliott, daughter, born in NY

1920 Census
1811 Wyoming Avenue, NW
Washington, D.C.

Alice R. Joyce, 70, widow, born in D.C., parents born in Maryland, civil clerk in the Pensions Office [this is Charlie Russell's niece]

Alice O. Joyce, daughter, 45, born in D.C., father born in Ireland (English-speaking), mother born in D.C., civil clerk in the Mayor's office [this is Charlie Russell's grand niece]

1920 Census
Company F Barracks
National Home for Disabled Volunteer Soldiers
Washington County
Tennessee

James T. Harbin, member, 63, born in Maryland, as were his parents, on furlough [this is Tom Harbin's eldest son]

1920 Census
217 12th Street
Washington, D.C.

Jennie A. Harbin, 60, born in D.C., as were her parents, no occupation [this is Tom Harbin's daughter-in-law]

Francis P. Harbin, son, 25, single, born in Maryland, father born in Maryland, mother born in D.C., retail salesman [this is Tom Harbin's grandson]

James B. Griffin, lodger, 25, single, born in New York, parents born in USA, Government clerk

1920 Census
11 Seventh Street southeast
Washington, D.C.

George F. Harbin, 32, single, born in D.C., father born in Maryland, mother born in West Virginia, consulting electrical engineer [this is Tom Harbin's son]

Blanch Harbin, 34, single, same birth details for her brother, no occupation [this is Tom Harbin's granddaughter]

1930 Census
Clarksville
Mecklenburg County
Virginia

Kate G. Russell, 68, born in Virginia, as were her parents, no occupation [this is Willie Russell's widow]

Arthur D. Russell, son, 30, born in Virginia, as were his parents [partially incorrect; his mother was], President of wagon factory [this is Charlie Russell's grandson]

1930 Census
1810 Lamont Street
Washington, D.C.

William J. McGee, 68, married at 29, born in Michigan, father born in Northern Ireland, mother born in New York, lawyer, general practice [this is Charlie Russell's son-in-law]

Annie A. McGee, wife, 69, married at 30, born in D.C., father born in Maryland, mother born in Virginia, no occupation [this is Charlie Russell's elder daughter]

C. Russell McGee, son, 37, single, born in D.C., real estate salesman [this is Charlie Russell's grandson]

Isabel J. McGee, daughter, 34, single, born in D.C., artist, painting [this is Charlie Russell's granddaughter]

Alice L. Russell, sister-in-law, 65, single, born in Virginia, father born in Maryland, mother born in Virginia [this is Charlie Russell's younger daughter]

1930 Census
724 Seventh Street
Washington, D.C.

Mary I. Harbin, 75, single, born in D.C., father born in Maryland, mother born in D.C., no occupation [this is Charlie Russell's step-niece, Mary Isabelle, the daughter of Officer Philip W. Harbin]

1930 Census
967 East 18th Street
Brooklyn
Kings County
New York

Jackson S. Elliott, 54, aged 32 when he married, born in Illinois, both parents born in Canada (English-speaking), Assistant General Manager, Associated Press

Isabel Elliott, wife, 48, aged 28 when she married, born in Washington,

D.C., father born in Ireland (Irish-speaking), mother born in Washington, D.C. [this is Daisy Joyce, Charlie Russell's grandniece]
Jackson S. Elliott, son, 17, born Washington, D.C.
Joyce Elliott, daughter, 15, born NY

1930 Census
National Soldiers Home
Elizabeth City
Virginia

James T. Harbin, member, 73, born in Maryland, as were his parents, veteran of the Spanish—American War [this is Tom Harbin's eldest son].

South Hill Enterprise, March 10, 1976:

Farm Wagon Manufacturer. C.H. Russell and Son Closes after 120 years. By John Kline, *Enterprise* reporter. Back in the 1850s, C.H. Russell left a job with the U.S. Navy in Washington, D.C., and moved his family and belongings to Clarksville to start to start his own blacksmith and general repair shop. In the early days of the business he built a few wooden wagons by hand for local tobacco growers.

Eventually he brought in his son, William H., named the business C.H. Russell and Son, Inc., and became a leading manufacturer of farm wagons. The business was to prosper greatly spanning three generations of Russells.

C.H. Russell and Son had a long and eventful past. There were numerous setbacks and bad times economically during the Depression days of the 30s. But they also made great improvements and grew as a company as the wagon industry grew nationally. In their best years they employed as many as 45 or 50 people and turned out as many as 4,000 wooden farm wagons a month. Over the years they were hit by two warehouse fires that destroyed a large part of the operations. But in each instance the Russells re-built the warehouses and continued the business.

From the early days, when the first wagons were built by hand, C.H. Russell and Son took on new inventions to increase their productivity. They advanced from manual to steam-powered machinery when steam energy became more efficient, then to diesel power, when diesel oil could be had for three or four cents a gallon, then to electric power after a fire that originated in the diesel room back in 1933 all but destroyed the operation.

In the early days of the company the first wagons were made and sold on an individual basis as a supplement to Russell's repair and blacksmith work. In the years following the Civil War wagon orders increased as the economy of the Reconstruction South improved. Eventually C.H. Russell devoted full time to the manufacture of farm wagons. Fire destroyed the first shop and Russell's son, William H., who had taken over the company by that time, moved the plant to a location in what is now downtown Clarksville. By the turn of the century W.H. Sr. decided the company needed more room to expand. In 1907 a brick warehouse was built on a hill in the northwest part of town, a block up from what is now Clarksville Elementary School. C.H. Russell and Son has been at that location ever since.

A.D. Russell joined the company around 1921 after studying at VPI. He and his brother W.H. Jr., who is the president of the company, are the third generation of Russells to operate the business. By 1921 the farm wagon business was booming.

Russell and Son was one of the last farm wagon manufacturers to go out of business in the 1950s when the tractors took over.

Bibliography

Blackburn, Ethel Silcott. *Silcott Family History, 1735–1792*. Privately printed, ca. 1994.
Bracey, Susan. *Life by the Roaring Roanoke*. Mecklenburg Co., Va.: Privately printed, 1977.
Centenary of St. Peter's Church and Golden Jubilee of Rt. Rev. Monsignor James M. O'Brien, Pastor of St Peter's Church. Privately printed, date unknown.
Chamlee, Roy Z. *Lincoln's Assassins*. Jefferson, N.C.: McFarland, 1990.
Jones, Thomas Austin. Autobiography. Included in John M. Wearmouth and Roberta J. Wearmouth, *Thomas A. Jones: Chief Agent of the Confederate Secret Service*. Port Tobacco, Md.: Stones Throw, 2000.
Kauffman, Michael. *American Brutus*. New York: Random House, 2004.
MacManus, Seumas. *The Story of the Irish Race*. Old Greenwich, Conn.: Devin-Adair Company, 1921.
Mahoney, Ella V. *Sketches of Tudor Hall and the Booth Family*. Bel Air, Md.: Tudor Hall, 1924.
Quisenberry, Anderson Chenault. *Genealogical Memoranda of the Quisenberry Family and Other Families*. Washington, D.C.: Hartman & Cadick Printers, 1897.
Singer, Jane. *The Confederate Dirty War*. Jefferson, N.C.: McFarland, 2005.
Slater's Commercial Directory of Ireland, 1846.
Spies, Scouts and Raiders. Alexandria, Va.: Time-Life Books, 1985.
Stone, Charles P. *Washington on the Eve of the War*. New York: Century Magazine, 1883.
Tidwell, Bill. *April '65*. Kent, OH: Kent State University Press, 1995.
Steers, Edward, Jr. *Blood on the Moon*. Lexington: University Press of Kentucky, 2001.
United States. *The War of the Rebellion*. Series 2. Vol. 2. *Treatment of Suspected and Disloyal Persons North and South*. Washington, D.C.: 1897.
Walker, Homer A. *Historical Court Records of Washington, District of Columbia*. Publisher unknown, 1955.
Washington, DC. New York: Mercantile Illustrating Company, 1894.
Wearmouth, John M., and Roberta J. Wearmouth. *Abstracts from the Port Tobacco Times and Charles County Advertiser*. 3 vols. Bowie, Md.: Heritage Books, 1990–1993.
_____ and _____. *Thomas A. Jones: Chief Agent of the Confederate Secret Service*. Port Tobacco, Md.: Stones Throw, 2000.
Weaver, Jeffrey C. *The Virginia Home Guards*. Lynchburg, Va.: H. E. Howard, 1996.

Newspapers

Charlotte Gazette (Charlotte Co., Va.)
Cincinnati Enquirer, 1884 and 1892
Evening Star (Washington, D.C.)
National Intelligencer (Washington, D.C.)
New York Times
Planter's Advocate (Upper Marlboro, Md.)
Port Tobacco Times (area of coverage includes Charles County, St. Mary's County, and Prince George's County, Md.)
Roanoke Valley
South Hill Enterprise (South Hill, Mecklenburg County, Va.)
Times [of London]
Torchlight. Oxford, N.C.
Washington Post
Washington Times

Other Sources

Charles County Court Proceedings
Chicago Historical Society
Maryland Provincial Court Proceedings
Washington, D.C., City Directories, 1836, 1843, 1847, 1853, 1860, 1868, 1870.

Also of great importance was the truly prodigious output of Wesley E. Pippenger, author of countless valuable books concerning the history of the District of Columbia.

Index

Abercrombie, Robert (Irish landlord) 26
Acton, Samuel G. (Old Capitol prisoner) 109, 111
Adams, Austin (Maryland hotel keeper) 118
Adams, E.A. (D.C. politician) 71
Adams family (of Charles County) 101
Allen, E.J. *see* Pinkerton, Allen
Allen's Fresh (Maryland) 16, 20–22, 99–100, 103, 114, 157, 160
Anacostia Fire Company 36
Anderson Guards (Rifles) 43, 45
Andrew Johnson Guards 48
Andrews, Charles (Reverend) 74, 166
Andrews, W.R. (D.C. attorney) 146
Antietam (battle) 50, 78
Anti-Know Nothing Party 36–39, 41
Appomattox Court House 64
April '65 (book) 61–62
Arsenal explosion 54
Arthur, Chester Alan (president) 131
Asbury, Herbert (author) 37
Ashland (Virginia) 122
Ashton, Henry 34
Associated Press 93, 95
Atwater, Elizabeth A. 138–139
Atwater, Samuel T. 139
Atzerodt, George (assassin) 118
Averett, Mary (cook) 186
Averett family (of Clarksville) 53, 80, 82

Baden, Joseph (Confederate agent) 116, 118, 120–121
Baker, Colonel (of Machodoc Creek, Va.) 120
Baker, Lafayette C. (assassin hunter) 56, 59–60, 121, 138
Baker, Lieutenant (Union officer) 121
Baker, Raymond T. (2nd husband of Kate Costello) 89, 186
Balback, Captain (of the Washington Rifles) 43
Bayne, J.W. (D.C. doctor) 78, 83, 133, 171
Beauregard, P.G.T. (Civil War general) 52
Beauregard Rifles 49
Bedlam Neck (Maryland) 18
Beecher, Captain (Fenian) 69
Beers, Mr. (D.C. politician) 32
Bellew, James (D.C. undertaker) 84
Beltsville (Maryland) 41, 160
Bench, Benjamin (Piscataway carpenter) 106
Benedict (Maryland) 104, 105
Berry, John (private) 78, 79
Bichloride Club of Gold 144, 175
Blanche, Sister (of the Orphan Asylum) 55
Blanks, Walter D. (of Clarksville) 89
Blenheim (the Lee estate in Maryland) 20, 22, 188
Blount, H. (Captain of the Tenallytown Rifles) 43
Bohrer, George (politician) 39
Boisseau, James Thomas (politician) 35–37, 41
Bokel, A. (Reverend) 78
Bolies, W.F.M. (D.C. alcoholic) 144
Bond, William (Revolutionary War lieutenant) 18

Booth, John Wilkes (assassin) 33, 58, 114, 117–122, 125, 137–138
Boteler, Edward M. (D.C. undertaker) 85
Boteler, Lieutenant (D.C. policeman) 87
Bowen, Mayor (of D.C.) 182
Bowman family (of Charles County) 117
Boyle, Francis E. (Reverend) 55, 119, 123–124, 129, 133, 140
Bradfield, Emma V. (James B. Silcott's 2nd wife) 74
Bradley, Jane Eliza *see* Harbin, Jane Eliza
Bradley, William A. (of the National Hotel) 125
Bragg, Braxton (Civil War general) 52
Branch, Len (Reverend) 115
Brawner, Mary L. (citizen of East Washington) 141
Breckinridge, Major (Artillery officer) 78
Brennan, Florence (friend of Alice O. Joyce) 95
Briscoe, John H. (Revolutionary War officer) 18
Britton, Lloyd L. (of the National Hotel) 136
Brooke, Andrew (D.C. drunkard) 141
Brooks, Charles W., Jr. (Charlie Russell's nephew) 42, 88, 153, 163, 168, 174, 181
Brooks, Charles W., Sr. (Charlie Russell's brother-in-law) 20, 27, 42, 70, 83, 153, 163, 168, 171, 181
Brooks, Gustavius Adolphus (of N.C.) 150
Brooks, John Russell (Charlie Russell's nephew) 42, 89, 163, 168, 174
Brooks, Kate (Mrs Charles W. Brooks, Jr.) 89, 186
Brooks, Sally (Charlie's sister) 20–22, 24, 40, 42, 65, 66, 83, 86, 89, 153, 156, 163, 168, 173, 174, 181
Brough (plantation) 16
Bruce, Edwin (married into the Quesenberrys) 128
Bryant, William L. (Confederate agent) 59, 108, 120, 121
Bryantown (Maryland) 98–105, 107, 117, 138, 155
Buchanan, Franklin (commandant of the Navy Yard) 33
Buffalo Springs (Virginia) (spy camp) 56–58
Bunn, Winfield A. 85
Burch, John A. (of Charles County) 104
Burke, Denis F. (Union Army colonel) 56
Burroughs, Mary E. "Molly" (Charlie Russell's niece, married to Richard A. O'Brien) 40, 54, 66, 77, 79, 94, 159, 167, 177, 183
Burroughs, Mary Eliza (Charlie Russell's sister) 19–20, 22, 40, 54, 156, 159
Burroughs, Philip Hezekiah (Charlie Russell's brother-in-law) 19, 28, 39, 40, 156, 159
Burroughs family 28, 156
Byrd, Smith and Tiffany (Baltimore jobbers) 104

Cahill, J. (of the Washington Light Infantry) 47
Cahoe family (Charlie Russell's mother's family) 18–19, 114, 188
Callaghan, Daniel P.G. (witness to Tom Harbin's will) 173
Callahan, John C. (D.C. boarding house owner) 126
Calvert family 125–126
Calwell family 92
Camden (Revolutionary War battle) 19
Campbell, Eugene (boarder) 189
Canter, Henry (of Charles County) 104
Carraher, John Victor (D.C. doctor) 142
Carrico, Thomas (of Charles County) 101, 117
Carrington, E.C. (general) 45
Carrington Home Guards 45
Carrington sisters (of Sunnyside Academy) 76
Carroll, Ralph (boarder) 157
Catholic Club 141
Catholic Knights 132, 136, 141
Cavanaugh, Mr. (Reverend) 93, 183
Cawood, Charles H. (Confederate agent) 59
Cedar Springs (Florida) 51
Centreville (Maryland) 99
Chain Bridge (in D.C.) 41, 56, 161
Chamberlin, Georgette A. (of the National Hotel) 135, 142
Chamlee, Roy Z. (author) 119
Champion, Samuel (Navy Yard foreman) 35–37
Chancellorsville (Civil War battle) 50
Chapel Point (Maryland) 17
Chaptico (Maryland) 18, 28
Charles County (Maryland) 16–24, 28, 34, 65, 76, 94, 98–100, 102–104, 108, 117–119, 155, 157–158, 160, 182, 188
Charlotte Hall Military Academy (Maryland) 58
Chunkers (a D.C. gang) 38

Cincinnati Enquirer (newspaper) 137, 138, 139
Clarke, P.J. (friend of Capt. Joyce in NY) 71
Clarksville (Virginia) 52, 56–58, 64–66, 76, 80–82, 88, 94, 96, 162, 178, 183, 186–189, 191–192
Clarksville Volunteers 54, 188
Clay, Henry 126
Clerklee, Alice 20
Cleveland, Grover (president) 131
Coakley, Emma (married into the Quesenberrys) 128
Cochran, Sallie (James H. Harbin's 2nd wife) *see* Harbin, Sallie
Cold Harbor (Civil War battle) 54
Coleman, Ann Virginia (born Ann Virginia Smoot) (wife of James Coleman) 40, 130–131, 141, 148, 173
Coleman, Henry Eaton (Confederate colonel) 55
Coleman, James (D.C. blacksmith/jailer) 35, 38, 40, 130, 173
Coleman family 130
Colliflower family 79, 94
Collinsworth family 38
Come Retribution (book) 61–62
Confederate Dirty War (book) 62
Confederate Secret Service 114
Congressional Cemetery (D.C.) 27, 31, 64, 74–76, 84, 85, 87–89, 134, 166, 172
Connolly, Patrick (Fenian) 70, 162
Conrad, Thomas Nelson (Confederate spymaster) 58–60, 76
Contee, Philip A.L. (overseer) 20
Cooper, Peter (of Clarksville) 94
Corydon *see* Cullen, John Joseph
Costello, Kate *see* Brooks, Kate
Costello family 89, 186
Cox, Samuel (Confederate agent) 101, 108, 117, 120
Crandell, James (D.C. magistrate) 33–34, 157–158
Cread, Ella A. (Tom's 2nd wife) *see* Harbin, Ella A.
Crosby, William H. (of the National Hotel) 126, 135–137, 142
Crowder, J.N. (of Clarksville) 187
Cuba 66, 124, 138, 145
Culbertson, William W. (congressman) 134–135
Cull, Justice (D.C. judge) 55
Cullen, John Joseph (alias Corydon) (informer) 69

Curtis, E.H. (alias Ray) (D.C. rapist) 126
Dahlgren, John (commandant of the Navy Yard) 33
Daily National Hotel Reporter (newspaper) 137, 138, 139
Dalton, J.L. (D.C. politician) 71
Darr, Nellie (D.C. actress) 129, 166
Davis, A.D. (of the National Rifles) 44
Davis, A.W. (the Spanish Spy) 67
Davis, Arthur Lee 83
Davis, Charles W. (D.C. politician) 41
Davis, James Y. (of the Washington Light Infantry) 43, 47
Davis, Jefferson (Confederate president) 65, 108, 117, 137
Davis, Katie *see* Davis, Sarah K.G.
Davis, M. (D.C. politician) 71
Davis, Mr. (John H. Russell's partner) 65
Davis, Sarah K.G. "Katie" (Willie Russell's daughter, and wife of Arthur Lee Davis) 82–83, 178, 184
Dawkins, Margaret (born Margaret Harbin) (James T. Harbin's daughter, and 1st wife of Robert Brooks Dawkins, Jr.) 102, 143, 147, 151–152, 181, 185
Dawkins, Robert Brooks, Jr. (D.C. lawyer) 149–151, 181, 185
Dawkins family (of Louisiana) 149, 150–151
De Barry, Katie (D.C. actress) 129, 166
Deep Bottom Run (Civil War battle) 54
DeJarnette, Daniel Coleman (Virginia politician) 76, 82
DeJarnette, Joseph Spencer (asylum keeper) 76, 82
Dement, Walter (of Charles County) 99
Dements Enlargement (plantation) 99, 104–106
Democratic Jackson Association 48
De Neal, George (witness at James T. Harbin's wedding) 133
Dent, George, Jr. (Confederate agent) 109, 111–113
Dent, George, Sr. (Confederate agent) 109, 111–113
Dilworth, Dan (Reverend) 26
District Militia 48
Doggett, C.L. (of Clarksville) 187
Doheny, Michael (Fenian) 67, 69
Donnelly, James A. (Old Capitol prisoner) 109
Donohue, Frank (D.C. doctor) 84

Dooley, F.X. (D.C. pharmacist) 136, 141
Dooley, Michael & Ann (citizens of Capitol Hill) 140
Dot Dog of Mine (poem by Daisy Joyce) 177
Doughty, Francis (witch hunter) 16
Downer, Mrs (D.C. boarding house owner) 40, 161
Dubant, Peter M. (of the Washington Light Infantry) 43
Duncanson, Miss (Quesenberry governess) 116, 120
Dunne, Captain (Fenian) 69
Dwight (Illinois) 143, 144, 175

Early, Jubal (Civil War general) 56, 171
Eastern Dispensary 141, 142
Eaton, Joseph (servant) 163
Ebbs, H.J. (of the Washington Light Infantry) 47
Ebert, Harry L. (ice cream king) 149
Ebsen, Christian (Illinois hoofer) 58
Ebsen, Rudolph "Buddy" (actor) 58
Edelin, Mary L. (related to the Stants) 178
Edelin, Philip (Piscataway doctor) 106
Edelin, Stanislaus (Navy Yard smith) 35
Edinburgh (ship) 41
Elliott, Daisy *see* Joyce, Daisy
Elliott, Jackson S (Daisy Joyce's husband) 92–93, 95, 182–183, 185, 190–191
Elliott family 92–93, 190, 192
Emmet, Robert (Irish patriot) 25, 68
English, William Hayden (vice-presidential candidate) 131
Ennis, Philip J. (of the Washington Light Infantry) 47
Europa (ship) 41
Ewing, Thomas (Revolutionary War colonel) 18

Fabers, Minnie E. (boarder) 185
Farinholt, Benjamin (hero of Staunton River Bridge) 55
Farrar, Officer (D.C. policeman) 134–135
Fealy, Ignatius (Reverend) 90, 182
Federal Trade Commission 150–151
Fenians 67–71, 162
Fenwick, Ignatius, Jr. (Revolutionary War officer) 18
Fermoy (Cork, Ireland) 26–27, 41
Ferrell family (of Charles County) 103
Fighting 69th (New York regiment—the Fighting Irish) 49

Financial and Mining Record (magazine) 67
Fithian, Napoleon B. (Union soldier) 84, 172
Floyd, John B. (secretary of war) 44
Foley, Mr. (D.C. actor) 129, 166
Ford's Theatre (in D.C.) 118–119, 138
Forrest, Uriah 18, 114
Forrest family 18, 115
Foxwell, Captain (of the Anderson Guards) 43
Frazier family (of Piscataway) 21
Fredericksburg (Civil War battle) 50
Fugit, Mary E. (related to the Worthans) 169

Gaddes, Bill (Navy Yard smith) 35
Gaddis, Adam (citizen of East Washington) 176
Gaddy, David (author) 61, 108
Gadsby, John (of the National Hotel) 125
Gallyon, Frances *see* Russell, Frances
Gangs of New York (book) 37
Garfield, James A. (president) 131
Garrett's barn (Caroline County, Virginia) 121
Gaskin, Elizabeth *see* Harbin, Elizabeth
Gates, General (Revolutionary War) 19
Gath *see* Townsend, George Alfred
Georgetown Mounted Guard 44–45
Gerhardt, Captain (of the Turner Rifles) 43
Getty, William F. (Old Capitol prisoner) 109
Gettysburg (Civil war battle) 53–54, 56, 63, 74, 77, 171
Gladstone, William Ewart (British prime minister) 70
Gleanings (plantation) 98
Goode, Thomas F. (of Buffalo Springs) 57
Gordon, James A. (D.C. politician) 39
Grant, Ulysses S (president) 30, 70, 77, 131, 172
Graves, Maria (Charlie Russell's grandmother) *see* Russell, Maria
Green, John (the widow Quesenberry's father) 115
Green family (of Rosedale) 115, 127–128
Greenfield, Henry (D.C. protester) 55
Greenhow, Rose O'Neale (Confederate agent) 52, 58–59, 109, 113
Greenwood (the slick swindler) 133–134
Griffin, James B. (boarder) 190
Griffin, Kate *see* Russell, Kate

Index

Griffin, Zed (Willie Russell's father-in-law) 82
Griggs, Mamie (born May Harbin) (daughter of Daniel W. Harbin) 89
Grimes, Mary Louise (connected to the Colliflowers) 79
Grymes, Ben (Confederate agent) 108
Grymes family (of Mont Chene, Va.) 116
Guilford Court House (Revolutionary War battle) 19
Guimaro (Cuban battle) 66
Guinand sisters (both Mrs Alexander McKenzie) 75, 154
Guiteau, Charles J. (assassin) 131

Hagerstown (Maryland) 144–145
Hall, James O. (author) 61, 108, 139
Halsey, Bull (World War II admiral) 150
Hancock, Winfield Scott (Civil War general) 53, 77, 131, 172
Hands, John (of the Washington Light Infantry) 47
Harbin, Blanche (born Mary Blanche Harbin) (Tom's daughter) 126, 139, 149, 151, 170, 181, 185, 191
Harbin, Catherine (born Catherine Langley) (Tom's mother) 99–101, 104, 155
Harbin, Catherine (Tom's sister) 100–101, 105, 107, 155
Harbin, Corrine Marie (born Corrine Marie Lothrop) (wife of Francis P. Harbin) 149
Harbin, Daniel W. (son of James H. Harbin) 25, 75–76, 85, 89–92, 154, 164, 168, 174–175, 180
Harbin, Edward Villers (Tom's great grandfather) 98
Harbin, Eliza (looked after Charlie Russell's sister Sally) 21, 24, 40, 156, 161
Harbin, Eliza Janette *see* Steiner, Lula
Harbin, Elizabeth (born Elizabeth Gaskin, later Mrs Mammel, and later still Mrs Daniel Harbin) 85, 90–91, 154, 180
Harbin, Elizabeth (of Charles County) 102
Harbin, Ella A. (Tom's 2nd wife) 126–127, 135, 137, 139, 149, 151, 164, 170, 172, 175, 181, 185
Harbin, Ethel (daughter of Daniel W. Harbin) 92, 180
Harbin, Eugene (son of Daniel W. Harbin) 92, 180
Harbin, Eva (daughter of John Henry Harbin) 180, 184

Harbin, Francis Percival "Frank" (James T.'s son) 145–149, 151, 181, 185, 190
Harbin, Gene *see* Harbin, Eugene
Harbin, George (Daniel Harbin's son) 92, 180
Harbin, George Francis (Tom's brother, the dry goods merchant) 77, 100–101, 104–105, 107–113, 126–136, 139–149, 165, 170–171, 173–174, 176, 181, 186
Harbin, George Francis (Tom's son, the professor) 127, 139, 146, 151–152, 155, 181, 185, 190
Harbin, George William (son of Naylor Harbin) 21
Harbin, Harry Wilmer (son of Daniel W. Harbin) 91–92, 180
Harbin, Horace (of Charles County) 40, 98
Harbin, James (son of Naylor Harbin, and Janette Russell's 1st husband) 21–22, 24, 40
Harbin, James Alexander (Tom's brother) 100–101, 103–104, 155
Harbin, James H. (Charlie Russell's stepbrother) 21–22, 24–25, 39, 73, 75, 84–85, 95, 154, 156, 158–159, 163, 166, 168
Harbin, James Samuel (son of James H. Harbin) 25, 75, 84–85, 92, 95, 160, 164, 168, 174–175, 179, 184
Harbin, James T. (Tom's son) 93, 106, 108, 126–129, 131–133, 136–137, 143–147, 149, 166–167, 170–172, 181, 190, 192
Harbin, James Wilbur (son of John Henry Harbin) 84, 92, 95, 180, 184
Harbin, James Wilbur, Jr. 95, 184
Harbin, Jane (Tom's sister) *see* Jones, Jane
Harbin, Jane Eliza (born Jane Eliza Bradley) (Mrs James H. Harbin) 25, 75, 154, 156, 160, 163
Harbin, Janette *see* Russell, Janette
Harbin, Jennie (born Jane Adele Mitchell) (wife of James T. Harbin) 132, 133, 143, 146–149, 181, 185, 190
Harbin, Jesse (of Charles County) 102
Harbin, Joanna W. *see* Silcott, Annie
Harbin, Johanna (Tom's sister) *see* Howell, Johanna
Harbin, John (Naylor Harbin's son) 21
Harbin, John E. (son of John Henry Harbin) 180
Harbin, John Henry (son of James H. Harbin) 25, 76, 84, 92, 95, 160, 164, 168, 174, 179, 184

Harbin, John Walter (Tom's brother) 99, 101, 105, 107–108, 130–131, 155, 165, 167
Harbin, Joseph (Tom's elder son) 106
Harbin, Joseph B. (Tom's brother) 99–101, 103–104, 105–106, 155
Harbin, Julia (Tom's sister) 99, 101, 103–105, 107, 129, 155–156, 166–167
Harbin, Katharine (daughter of John Henry Harbin) 184
Harbin, Katherine "Kate" (daughter of James H. Harbin) *see* Robinson, Kate
Harbin, Lelia (daughter of James S. Harbin) 75, 85, 95, 179, 184
Harbin, Lula *see* Steiner, Lula
Harbin, Lydia (Tom's great grandmother) 98
Harbin, Mamie *see* Harbin, May
Harbin, Margaret (of Charles County) 102
Harbin, Margaret (daughter of James T. Harbin) *see* Dawkins, Margaret
Harbin, Marie (James T. Harbin's daughter) *see* Maguire, Marie
Harbin, Martha V. (daughter of James H. Harbin) 25, 34, 157
Harbin, Mary (born Mary McNea) (Tom's grandmother) 98
Harbin, Mary (born Mary Villers) (wife of William Harbin) 98
Harbin, Mary Ann (Mrs John Henry Harbin) 84, 92, 95, 179, 184
Harbin, Mary Blanche *see* Harbin, Blanche
Harbin, Mary Elizabeth (born Mary Elizabeth Stewart) (Tom's 1st wife) 102, 105
Harbin, Mary Isabelle (Philip W. Harbin's daughter) 31, 74, 88, 154, 160, 164, 169, 180, 184, 189, 191
Harbin, Mary Jane (John H. Russell's wife) *see* Russell, Mary Jane
Harbin, May (daughter of Daniel W. Harbin) *see* Griggs, Mamie
Harbin, Miriam S. "Midie" (Mrs James S. Harbin) 75, 85 92, 95, 169, 179, 184
Harbin, Mitchell (son of Philip W. Harbin) 31, 154
Harbin, Nannie (daughter of Philip W. Harbin) *see* McKenzie, Nannie
Harbin, Naylor 21
Harbin, Philip W. (Charlie Russell's stepbrother) 21–22, 24, 29, 31, 54–55, 75, 86–90, 154, 160, 162, 164, 166–167, 169, 174, 184–185, 189, 191
Harbin, Rezin, Jr. (Tom's uncle) 98, 102

Harbin, Rezin, Sr. (Tom's grandfather) 98–99
Harbin, Richard (of Charles County) 102
Harbin, Roswell 98
Harbin, Sallie (born Sallie Cochran) (the 2nd Mrs James H. Harbin) 84
Harbin, Sally (of Charles County) 102
Harbin, Samuel P. (of Charles County) 98
Harbin, Samuel P. (son of Philip W. Harbin) 88, 154, 164, 167, 169, 175, 180, 185, 189
Harbin, Sarah (born Sarah Nesmith) (wife of Philip W. Harbin) 31, 86–88, 154, 160, 164, 169, 174, 175, 180
Harbin, Sarah A. (daughter of Philip W. Harbin) *see* McKenzie, Nannie
Harbin, Sarah Priscilla (Tom's sister) 100–101, 105, 107, 142, 146, 155, 166–167, 170, 181–182
Harbin, Susie (formerly Susan Eugene King) (wife of James Wilbur Harbin) 92, 184
Harbin, Thomas Henry "Tom" (Confederate agent) 21, 48, 59, 77, 98, 100–101, 103–108, 114, 116–118, 120–127, 130–139, 142–143, 146, 149, 152, 155, 157, 161, 164–167, 169–170, 172, 175, 181, 185, 190–191
Harbin, Virginia "Vergie" (Daniel W. Harbin's daughter) 89, 92, 153
Harbin, Walter (Tom's father) 21, 99–101, 104–105, 117, 155
Harbin, William (son of Daniel W. Harbin) 92
Harbin, William (Tom's ancestor) 98
Harbin, Wilmer *see* Harbin, Harry Wilmer
Harbin family in England 98
Harrington, George B. (Reverend) 90, 182
Harris, George (Piscataway doctor) 106
Harris, John B. (of Piscataway) 106
Harris, R.E. Kennon (Virginia lawyer) 81
Hartranft, John (Civil War general and jailer) 122–123
Hawkins, Colonel (War of 1812) 98
Hayden, B.L. (Maryland killer) 39–40
Hayes, James J. (D.C. dry goods dealer) 149
Hebb, John Wise (Confederate spymaster) 57–59
Hebb family 58
Heffernan, Sarah A. (D.C. bride) 158
Hendley, Matthew (Irish land agent) 26

Herold, Adam G. "George" (father of David Herold) 33
Herold, David (assassin's helper) 33, 58, 110, 118–124
Herrell, John E. (citizen of Capitol Hill) 140
Herring, Mike 96
Higgins, John J. (pallbearer) 90, 182
Hill, Charles B. (Maryland asylum keeper) 148
Hitz, Justice (D.C. judge) 148
Holt, Martha (of Piscataway) 106
Hoover, Herbert (president) 151
Hotel Reporter see *Daily National Hotel Reporter*
Hough, George (D.C. killer) 140
Howard, Clement W. (D.C. company president) 133
Howell, Gustavius (of Charles County) 102
Howell, Johanna (born Johanna Harbin) (Tom Harbin's sister) 99, 101–102, 107, 127, 146–147, 155–156, 161, 165
Howell, John H. (Tom Harbin's brother-in-law) 99, 101–102, 161
Howell family 102, 161, 165, 170
Howerton, Evelyn see Russell, Evelyn
Hubbard, Lt. (of the Gatling gun episode) 79
Hughes, Margaret (boarder with the Prestons) 156
Hunter, Elizabeth see Russell, Elizabeth
Hutcheson, H.J. (clerk, of Clarksville) 187
Hutchinson, James (pallbearer) 90, 182
Hutchinson, William (D.C. politician) 39
Hutton family (of Piscataway) 107

Interstate Commerce Commission 75
Irish Brigade 49–50, 161, 171
Irish Republican Brotherhood see Fenians
Ivins, H.R. (boarder) 164

Jack the Slasher (D.C. robber) 142–143
Jackson (D.C. police capper) 87
Jackson, Richard P. (witness to Tom Harbin's will) 173
Jackson, Stonewall (Civil War general) 58
Jackson Democratic Association 131
Jacksonville (Florida) 145
Jarboe, Benedict (Navy Yard smith/guard) 36
Jarboe, Daniel W. (D.C. killer) 35–37
Jarboe, Mary Ann (born Jane) (Charlie Russell's 1st wife) see Russell, Mary Ann
Jarboe family 38–40, 154, 158–159
Jenkins, John "Grindingstone" 16
Jenkins family 41, 101–102
Jensen family 151
John Kerr Lake (Virginia) 58
Johnson, John (D.C. lawyer) 31, 33–34
Johnstown Flood 141
Jones, Jane (Tom Harbin's sister, and wife of Thomas Austin Jones) 99, 100, 101, 113–114, 155–157, 160, 165
Jones, Thomas Austin (Confederate agent) 59, 99–101, 108–111, 113–114, 117, 120, 127, 128, 135, 157, 160, 165, 169
Jones family 100, 127, 157, 160–161, 165, 169, 170
Jordan, Thomas (Confederate spymaster) 51–52, 59, 66–67
Jordan family 51
Joyce, Alice (born Mary Alice Russell) (John H. Russell's daughter, and Capt. Joyce's wife) 27, 29–30, 34–35, 39, 48, 70, 73, 77, 84–85, 93, 95, 154, 158, 163, 169, 172, 174–175, 180, 182–183, 185, 190
Joyce, Alice O. (Capt. Joyce's daughter) 84, 95, 154, 169, 172, 175, 181, 185, 190
Joyce, Belle (Capt. Joyce's niece) 73
Joyce, Bridget (Capt. Joyce's sister-in-law) 73
Joyce, Charles Emmet 25, 27, 31, 41, 49–50, 53–54, 56, 67–71, 73–74, 77–79, 83–84, 95, 130, 154, 161–162, 164, 166, 169, 171–172
Joyce, Daisy (born Isabelle Daisy Joyce) (Capt. Joyce's daughter, and wife of Jackson S Elliott) 84, 92–93, 95, 142, 169, 172, 176–177, 181–183, 185, 190–192
Joyce, Edmond W. (Capt. Joyce's brother) 27, 171
Joyce, Isabel (Capt. Joyce's sister) 27
Joyce, James (Irish writer) 27
Joyce, James F. (of the National Hotel) 135
Joyce, John O'Connell. (Capt. Joyce's brother) 25, 27, 41, 49–50, 78
Joyce, Kate (Capt. Joyce's sister) 27
Joyce, Katie (Capt. Joyce's niece) 73
Joyce, Lucy (Charles Emmet's sister) see Russell, Lucy
Joyce, Lucy (Capt. Joyce's mother) 25, 78, 83, 171
Joyce, Margaret (Capt. Joyce's sister) see Simonton, Margaret
Joyce, Mary (Capt. Joyce's sister) 74, 171

Joyce, Mary Alice *see* Joyce, Alice
Joyce, Michael (Capt. Joyce's brother) 27, 41, 49, 73, 77–79, 83
Joyce, Michael (stone mason) 26
Joyce, Michael R. (Capt. Joyce's father) 25, 41, 56, 78, 161
Joyce family in Ireland 26
Junior Potomac Rifles 45

Kane, John (Confederate officer) 54
Kautz, August V. (Civil War general) 55
Kealey, D.E. (D.C. politician) 32
Kealy, Annie & Mary E. 170
Keeley, James (Navy Yard smith) 35
Keeley, Leslie (of the alcohol cure) 143–144, 146, 175
Keeley Institute 93
Keeling, E. (connected to the Sansburys) 23
Kelly, Benson (of the National Hotel) 129
Kelly, James (colonel of the Irish Brigade) 50
Kelly, John (Fenian) 68
Kelly, Mr. (Irish court clerk) 69
Kennedy, Mary (Capt. Richard A. O'Brien's mother) 79
Kennedy family (married into the Snyders) 60
Keogh, John M. (Irish patriot) 84, 172
Keyes, Erasmus D. (Union Army colonel) 52
King, P. (Captain, National Rifles) 43
King, Susan Eugene "Susie" *see* Harbin, Susie
Kirby, Carrie Moss (Willie Russell's daughter, and wife of Thomas E. Kirby) 82, 178, 183
Kirby, Thomas E. 82
Kirby family 82
Kline, John (reporter) 71
Knight, Edward A. (Reverend) 39–40, 105, 119, 158
Know Nothing Party 35, 37
Koonce, Minnie Price (Willie Russell's daughter) 82, 178, 183
Koonce, R. Sidney 83
Krafft, Catharine (D.C. widow) 39
Kramer, Frederick (D.C. killer) 90–91

Laidler Ferry Farm (Maryland) 20
Lamb, Officer (D.C. policeman) 134
Landron House (Civil War battle) 54
Langley, Catherine (Tom's mother) *see* Harbin, Catherine

Langley family (of Charles County) 99, 102
Langster (D.C. police capper) 140
Latane, Dorothy *see* Russell, Dorothy
Lathrop, C.E. (D.C. politician) 71
Laurel Sanitarium (Maryland) 93
Lee, Robert E. (Civil War general) 20, 52, 55, 64–65, 99
Lee family 20, 22, 65, 99
Leech, A.D. (Maryland doctor) 145
Leigh, William (of Danville) 187
Leins, Lena (D.C. rape victim) 130
Leitch, Samuel Gooch (Confederate agent) 62
Lenman, Charles (D.C. actor) 129, 166
Leonard, Andrew (citizen of Capitol Hill) 140
Letcher, John (Virginia governor) 51
Lincoln, Abraham (president) 23, 32–33, 45, 48, 54, 59, 61, 63–64, 108, 113, 117, 118, 131, 135, 137–139
Lincoln, Mrs (president's wife) 139
Lincoln's Assassins (book) 119
Little, Mr. (D.C. politician) 32
Lloyd, Allen (D.C. dead body finder) 146
Lloyd, John (tavern keeper) 118
Lloyd, Lt. (of the National Rifles) 43
Longstreet, General (Civil War) 63
Lord, Lt. (Union officer) 47
Lothrop, Corrine Marie *see* Harbin, Corrine Marie
Luby, Thomas Clarke (Fenian) 67
Luxon, Thomas J. (D.C. night watchman) 31

MacManus, Seamas (Irish author) 70
Maddox, Samuel John (officer in the War of 1812) 17–18, 32–33, 158
Madigan, Officer (D.C. policeman) 87
Maginnis family (of D.C.; frog-vomiting boy) 134
Magruder, Alexander (Revolutionary War captain) 18
Magruder, George (colonel, War of 1812) 41
Magruder, Mayor (of D.C.) 38, 182
Maguire, Marie (James T. Harbin's daughter, and wife of Thomas F. Maguire) 143, 147, 152, 181, 186
Maguire, Thomas Francis 147, 186
Maguire family 147, 148, 186
Mammel, Elizabeth *see* Harbin, Elizabeth

Index

Manassas (Bull Run) (Civil War battles) 49, 52
Manila (Philippines) 145
Marbury family 86, 96, 114
Maryland Militia 17, 34, 158
Mason, Sgt. (of the Gatling gun episode) 78
Massey, Tom (of King George Co., Va.) 128
Mattawoman (Maryland) 99-100
Matthews, John (D.C. actor) 119
Mawdsley, Mr. (D.C. actor) 129, 166
Maximilian, Emperor 115
McCafferty (Fenian) 69
McCaffrey, Miss (D.C. actress) 166
McCarty, Mary (servant) 170
McClellan, George (Civil War general) 50, 112
McCool, Finn (legendary Irish hero) 67
McCullough, Ben (Texas Ranger) 46, 48
McDermott, Sgt. (of the Washington Light Infantry) 47
McDowell, Major (Union officer) 46
McGee, Annie Alice (Charlie Russell's daughter, and wife of William J. McGee) 17, 40, 64, 76, 83, 86, 94-96, 154, 163, 168, 173-175, 179, 186-189, 191
McGee, William James (Charlie Russell's son-in-law) 86, 95-96, 179, 188, 189, 191
McGee family 86, 96, 154, 179, 189, 191
McGrath, Thomas (D.C. politician) 42
McGuigan, Thomas E. (Reverend) 147
McKenna family 132, 141
McKenney family 105
McKenzie, Alexander 75, 154, 182
McKenzie, James (witness to Tom Harbin's will) 173
McKenzie, John Vincent (son of Alexander McKenzie) 75
McKenzie, Josie (born Josie Vann) (wife of J.V. McKenzie) 75
McKenzie, Nannie (born Sarah A. Harbin) (daughter of Philip W. Harbin, and wife of Alexander McKenzie) 31, 75, 90, 154, 160, 164
McKenzie, Sarah A. *see* McKenzie, Nannie
McKenzie family 75, 154
McKim, Samuel (D.C. doctor) 35, 110, 133
McMahon, William (D.C. murder victim) 140
McManus, Terence (Irish patriot) 68

McNamee, John (of the Washington Light Infantry) 47
McNea, Mary *see* Harbin, Mary
McNeir, William T. (D.C. bridegroom) 158
Meagher, Thomas Francis (Irish patriot) 31, 49-50, 67-68
Mechanics' Union Rifles 43, 48
Mecklenburg County (Virginia) 52, 54, 56-58, 76, 81, 163, 168, 178, 183, 186-189, 191
Medley Neck (Maryland) 28, 40
Meigs, Montgomery C. (Navy Yard boss) 35-37
Memphis Appeal (newspaper) 66
Menas de Tana (Cuban battle) 66
Metropolitan Livery (in D.C.) 65
Metropolitan Rifles 43, 45, 48
Meyenberg, S. & W. (D.C. dry goods dealers) 105, 108
Milburn, Nancy *see* Russell, Nancy
Milburn brothers (Confederate agents) 56-58
Miller, G.W. (D.C. politician) 71
Millett, John A. (boarder) 107
Mills, Harriet A. (George F. Harbin's slave) 113, 170
Minor, Charles L.C. II (educator) 60
Mitchell, Ann *see* Smoot, Ann
Mitchell, Jennie *see* Harbin, Jennie
Mitchell family (Mrs Jennie Harbin's family) 132, 146, 170
Mohun, Mr. (D.C. politician) 32
Monmouth (Revolutionary War battle) 19
Mont Chene (estate in King George Co., Va.) 116
Moore, Miss (D.C. teacher) 35
Moore, Sgt. (of the Gatling gun episode) 79
Moriarty, Bishop (Irish cleric) 68
Morris, Jules Andrew (Daisy Joyce's son-in-law) 93
Morro Castle (ship) 67
Moss, Virginia Price (Charlie's 2nd wife) *see* Russell, Jennie
Mount Hope (Maryland) 148-149
Mount Olivet Cemetery (in D.C.) 40, 107, 129, 131, 133, 137, 146, 148-149, 151, 182
Mountjoy Prison (in Ireland) 69, 70, 162
Mudd, Samuel Alexander (Confederate agent) 58, 107-108, 117-120, 138
Mudgett, Ann (Mrs Jackson Elliott, Jr.) 93

Index

Muller, Mr. (D.C. actor) 129
Murphy, Timothy (Reverend) 26
Murray, Charles (of the Washington Light Infantry) 47
Murray, James J. (married into the O'Briens) 79, 94
Myrick, Mary A. (D.C. teacher) 35

Nalley, Captain (of the Metropolitan Rifles) 43
Nally, John Rufus (D.C. fireman) 35–37
National Guard 43, 45, 79, 151
National Hotel (in D.C.) 117–118, 125–126, 131–137, 142, 166–167, 171
National Rifles 44–49
National Soldiers Home 149, 190, 192
Navy Yard *see* Washington Navy Yard
Neale, Hugh 16
Nesmith, Sarah *see* Harbin, Sarah
Nesmith, Sarah A. (Philip W. Harbin's mother-in-law) 41, 160
Nevitt, Coroner (the Elizabeth Harbin murder case) 91
Newport (Maryland) 17, 99, 118
Newton, Augustine (of the National Hotel) 125
Nibrah House 147, 149
Noe, Henry (of the Washington Light Infantry) 44
Nokes, John W. (boarder) 180
Norris, William (Confederate agent) 59, 114
North Anna River (Civil War battle) 54
Nova Scotia 28

Oakley, Catharine A. (sister of Janette Russell) 21, 27, 153, 162
Oakley, Charles 21
Ober, Franklin H. (D.C. politician) 39, 41–42
O'Brien, Captain (Fenian) 69
O'Brien, Molly *see* Burroughs, Molly
O'Brien, Richard A. (Molly Burroughs' husband) 77, 79, 88, 94, 177, 183
O'Brien family 79, 177, 183
O'Connell, Daniel (Irish patriot) 25
O'Connor, Dennis (Irish patriot) 84, 172
O'Donel, C.J. (Irish magistrate) 69
O'Donovan, Mike (Reverend) 26
Olcott, Horatio J. (NY land agent) 34
Olds, Rev. (D.C. Episcopalian minister) 123
Olin, Stephen 76
Oliver family (in Charles County) 101

Olivette Club (James T. Harbin's acting club) 129, 132, 170
O'Mahoney, John (Fenian) 67
O'Neill, John J. (congressman) 85
O'Toole, T.J. (Reverend) 119
Our American Cousin (play) 118
Owen, S.W. (Captain, President's Mounted Guard) 43
Owens family (married into the Burroughs family) 28
Oyster, Mary 170

Palo Alto (Mexican War battle) 51
Papal Zouaves 125
Pariz, Marcelano (boarder with the Russells) 25, 29, 158
Patterson, Coroner (in the Gatling gun episode) 78
Paxson, Timothy (of Buffalo Springs) 57
Peake, John H. (D.C. politician) 41–42
Peel Robert (British prime minister) 25
Percival, Frank (James T. Harbin's medical partner) 145
Peril (ship) 66
Petersburg (Civil War siege) 55, 56
Philippines 145, 146, 149
Pic, Mr. (D.C. actor) 129, 166
Pilgrim, James (playwright) 129
Piney Chapel (Maryland) 19
Pinkerton, Allen (detective) 52, 58, 109, 113
Piscataway (Maryland) 21, 23, 98, 105–107, 127, 147, 161, 170
Plater family 114
Plug Uglies 37, 38
Plummer family 150–151
Po River (Civil War battle) 54
Pollard, Isaac J. (Baltimore jobber) 106
Pomfret (Maryland) 17
Poole, Bill "the Butcher" (NY gangster) 37–38
Pope's Creek (Maryland) 100
Poppescu, Valentina "Bobbie" (boarder) 88, 189
Port Tobacco (Maryland) 20, 118
Porter, Andrew (D.C. provost marshal) 109, 111–112, 161
Porter, Joseph I. (pallbearer) 84, 172
Portland (poem by Daisy Joyce) 176
Potomac Light Infantry 44, 48
Prescott House (in D.C.) 110
President's Mounted Guard 43, 45, 48
Preston & Olin College *see* Virginia A & M

Preston family (of D.C.) 40, 156
Price, Caroline Belle (married into the Quesenberrys) 128
Price, Charles S. (pallbearer) 90, 182
Pride, Henry (Confederate officer) 52, 54–55
Prince George's County (Maryland) 18, 20–21, 23, 41, 98, 105–107, 127, 144–145, 148, 161, 170
Pryor, J.B. (author) 66
Putnam Rifles 43

Queen, William (Confederate agent) 108
Queen, Zephaniah 102
Quesenberry, Nicholas Austin 115–116
Quesenberry, Rose (the widow Quesenberry) 114–117, 120–122, 127–128
Quesenberry family 115–116, 121–122, 124, 127–128

Ragan, J.R. (D.C. alcoholic) 144
Randolph-Macon College 76
Rawlins, John A. (Civil War general) 70
Reams Station (Civil War battle) 54
Renehan, Frank (Old Capitol prisoner) 109
Resaca de la Palma (Mexican War battle) 51
Reynolds, Joseph (of the Washington Light Infantry) 47
Richards, A. (D.C. wharf builder) 175
Rip Raps (a D.C. gang) 38
Ripley, Edward H. (Union officer at Richmond) 61
Roberts, J.H. (D.C. politician) 42
Robertson, William B. (friend of Janette Russell's) 34
Robinson, J.C. 74
Robinson, J.W. (D.C. politician) 41
Robinson, Kate (daughter of James H. Harbin, and wife of J.C. Robinson) 25, 74, 160, 164
Rosedale (Green-Quesenberry home) 114–116, 122
Rousby family 114
Royster family (of Clarksville) 52–53
Ruff, George R. (D.C. politician) 32
Russell, Agnes M. (William Ignatius's daughter) 72, 77, 85, 153, 167, 173–174, 176
Russell, Alice (John H.'s daughter) *see* Joyce, Alice
Russell, Alice Lee (Charlie's daughter) 17, 50, 56, 65, 76, 94–95, 163, 168, 178, 183, 186–188

Russell, Annie Alice (Charlie's daughter) *see* McGee, Annie
Russell, Arthur Davidson (Willie's son) 83, 179, 184, 189, 191–192
Russell, Carrie Moss (Willie's daughter) *see* Kirby, Carrie
Russell, Charles (Charlie's great uncle) 17
Russell, Charles H. II (Willie's son) 82, 178
Russell, Charles Henry "Charlie" (Confederate agent) 15–17, 19–22, 24–25, 27–28, 31, 33, 35–45, 47–52, 54–57, 59–62, 64–65, 70–74, 76, 79, 81–83, 85–88, 90, 93–95, 105, 114, 130, 141, 156–159, 161, 163, 167–168, 173–175, 178–192
Russell, Charles Henry, Jr. (Charlie's son) 71
Russell, Charles Lewis (Charlie's uncle) 17–18, 83
Russell, Christopher (Charlie's ancestor) 16
Russell, Dorothy (born Dorothy Latane) (wife of Thomas Joseph Russell) 83
Russell, Edward (Capt. Joyce's nephew) 74
Russell, Elizabeth (born Elizabeth Hunter) (wife of Willie Russell, Jr.) 83
Russell, Elizabeth (Mrs. Thomas Cahoe) 18
Russell, Ella Louise (born Ella Louise Watkins) (wife of Charles Henry Russell II) 82
Russell, Evelyn (born Evelyn Howerton) (wife of Arthur Russell) 83
Russell, Frances (born Frances Gallyon) (wife of John William Russell) 83
Russell, Henry Jackson (Charlie's son) 50
Russell, Ignatius (Charlie's great uncle) 17
Russell, James (Charlie's grandfather) 17, 19, 83
Russell, James, Jr. (Charlie's uncle) 17
Russell, Jane Eliza (Charlie's cousin, and wife of Benedict Wise) 58
Russell, Janette (Charlie's stepmother) 20–25, 27, 29, 31–34, 39, 47, 48, 50, 65, 76, 77, 130, 153, 157–158, 162, 163
Russell, Janette Alice (John H.'s daughter) *see* Russell, Jennie
Russell, Janie (William Ignatius's daughter) *see* Stant, Janie
Russell, Jennie (born Virginia Price

Moss) (Charlie's 2nd wife) 72, 76, 94, 168, 178, 186, 187–189
Russell, Jennie (born Janette Alice Russell) (John H.'s daughter) 27, 34, 48, 77, 79, 84–85, 93, 153, 158, 163, 169, 180, 182, 185
Russell, Jeremiah (Charlie's uncle) 17
Russell, John (British prime minister) 25
Russell, John Alexander (Charlie's cousin) 83, 93
Russell, John Baptist (Charlie's cousin) 58
Russell, John Baptist (Charlie's great uncle) 16
Russell, John H. (Charlie's brother) 19, 22, 24–25, 27–30, 32–33, 37, 39, 41–42, 47–48, 50, 65, 71, 73, 75, 77, 79, 84–86, 89–90, 153, 158, 161–162, 169, 174–175, 180, 182
Russell, John William (Willie's son) 83, 178, 184
Russell, Julia E. (William Ignatius's daughter) 28–30, 72, 85, 154, 159, 167, 173–174
Russell, Kate (born Kate Griffin) (wife of Willie Russell) 82, 96, 178, 183, 189, 191
Russell, Lewis *see* Russell, Charles Lewis
Russell, Lucy (Capt. Joyce's sister, and wife of Patrick Russell) 27, 41, 73–74, 171
Russell, Luke (Charlie's ancestor) 16
Russell, Lydia Rose (Charlie's cousin) 83, 86, 93, 174
Russell, Margaret Alice (John H.'s eldest daughter) 27
Russell, Margaret Rebecca (wife of William Ignatius Russell) 28, 31, 39, 72, 77, 85, 153, 159, 167
Russell, Maria (born Maria Graves) (Charlie's grandmother) 17
Russell, Martha (William Ignatius's daughter) 77, 153, 159, 167
Russell, Mary Alice *see* Joyce, Alice
Russell, Mary Ann (born Jane Jarboe) (Charlie's 1st wife) 35–36, 38–40, 48, 50, 56, 64–65, 71–72, 94, 105, 158–159, 162, 188
Russell, Mary Elizabeth (Charlie's cousin, married George William Hebb) 58
Russell, Mary Jane (born Mary Jane Harbin) (John H. Russell's wife) 21–22, 24–25, 27, 29, 33, 153, 157
Russell, Mary "Mamie" (Capt. Joyce's niece) 73–74

Russell, Minnie Price (Willie's daughter) *see* Koonce, Minnie Price
Russell, Mrs. (D.C. boarding house keeper) 24
Russell, Nancy (born Nancy Milburn) (wife of John Baptist Russell) 58
Russell, Patrick (Capt. Joyce's brother-in-law) 73–74
Russell, Philip (Charlie's brother) 20, 22, 24–25, 27, 77, 153
Russell, Philip (Charlie's great uncle) 20
Russell, Sarah (born Sarah Cahoe) (Charlie's mother) 18–20, 22
Russell, Sarah (Charlie's sister) *see* Brooks, Sarah
Russell, Sarah K.G. (Willie's daughter) *see* Davis, Sarah K.G.
Russell, Thomas Joseph (Willie's son) 83, 184, 189
Russell, Walter (Charlie's ancestor) 16
Russell, William (Charlie's great grandfather) 16
Russell, William B. (Charlie's father) 17–20, 22, 24, 31–34, 157–158
Russell, William Horace "Willie" (Charlie's son) 40, 57, 60, 64–66, 72, 76, 80, 82, 94, 96, 159, 163, 168, 178, 183, 187, 189, 192
Russell, William Horace, Jr. (Willie's son) 83, 179, 189
Russell, William Ignatius (Charlie's brother) 19–20, 22, 24, 27–28, 31, 33, 38–39, 42, 55, 66, 72, 77, 85, 94, 153, 159, 162, 178
Russell, William, Jr. (Charlie's great uncle) 16, 17
Rutherford, Captain (of the Mechanics' Union Rifles) 43
Ryan, Edward F. (Reverend) 133
Ryan, James P. (Fenian) 71

Saint Ignatius's Church (Maryland) 17, 19, 21
Saint Joseph's Church (D.C.) 90, 92
Saint Mary's County (Maryland) 16–21, 28, 58, 156
Saint Peter's Church (D.C.) 22–24, 36, 39–40, 74, 94, 113, 119, 123, 129, 131–133, 136–137, 140–141, 146, 151, 166
Saint Vincent's Orphan Asylum (D.C.) 55
Sanderson, Nicholas G. (Navy Yard smith) 35
Sansbury family 23, 153, 154, 157
Santa Anna, General 57

Savage, Frances (Jackson S Elliott's 2nd wife) 95
Schaeffer, Frank B. (of the National Rifles) 44–46, 48–49
Scott, Winfield (general) 57
Scott Rifles 45
Sears, James W. (D.C. dry goods dealer) 105
Secret Service Bureau 59
Seminoles 51
Semper Fidelis (poem by Daisy Joyce) 176–177
Sessford, John, Jr. (D.C. politician) 39
Seven Days Battles (Civil War battles) 50
Severing, G.M. 172
Seward, Frederick W. (assistant secretary of state, son of William Seward) 111–112, 161
Seward, William (secretary of state) 110–112
Shandy Maguire (play) 129, 166
Shea, Mr. (D.C. actor) 129
Shelton, David (of Buffalo Springs) 57
Shelton, Officer (D.C. policeman) 54–55
Sherman, William Tecumseh (Civil War general) 51
Shiloh (Civil War battle) 52
Silcott, Annie (born Joanna W. Harbin) (Mrs Silcott) 25, 34–35, 39, 74, 153, 157, 160, 163, 166
Silcott, James B. 74, 166
Silcott family 74
Siler, F.A. (of the Washington Light Infantry) 47
Simonton, Margaret (Capt. Joyce's sister) 27, 73
Simonton family 73, 171
Singer, Jane (author) 62–64
Sisters of Charity 148
Skinner, Mary Ann *see* Harbin, Mary Ann
Smallpox 89
Smallwood's Maryland Brigade 19
Smead, John R. (of the National Rifles) 45–46
Smith, James C. (Baltimore jobber) 106
Smith, Richard (D.C. dead body) 146
Smollen, Inspector (British policeman) 69
Smoot, Ann (born Ann Jenkins, later Ann Mitchell, and then wife of George A. Smoot) 40–41
Smoot, Ann Virginia *see* Coleman, Ann Virginia
Smoot, George Arthur 40–41
Smoot family (of Charles County) 40

Smothers, Tom (D.C. rapist) 130
Smyth, James A. (Reverend) 90, 182
Snyder, Nicholas (D.C. blacksmith) 27–28, 32, 60–61, 153
Snyder, William H. (D.C. blacksmith) 27, 61–64, 154
Snyder family 27–28, 32, 60–61, 63–64, 153, 154, 156
Soltedo Murder Case 140
Sotterley (estate) 114
South Mountain (Civil War battle) 50
Spanish Spy *see* Davis, A.W.
Speiden, William (D.C. blacksmith) 27–28, 39, 156
Spencer, John W. (Clarksville justice) 81
Spotsylvania Courthouse (Civil War battle) 54
Spy camps 56, 57, 58
Stamps, Fred 151
Staniels, Rufus P. (Union officer) 61, 62
Stansbury *see* Sansbury
Stant, Janie (born Jane Russell) (daughter of William Ignatius Russell, and wife of John Wesley Stant) 65–66, 72–73, 85, 94, 154, 159, 167, 173, 178
Stant family 72–73, 94, 153, 154, 167, 173, 175, 178
Stanton, Edwin (secretary of war) 113
Staunton River Bridge (Civil War battle) 55–56, 188
Steele, A. Floridus (Reverend) 75
Steiner, Alie (Lula's daughter) 73
Steiner, Joseph (Lula's husband) 73, 85
Steiner, Lula (born Eliza Janette Harbin) (daughter of James H. Harbin, and wife of Joseph Steiner) 25, 73, 85, 154, 160, 163
Stephens, James (Fenian) 67–68
Sterns, Ed (D.C. druggist) 133
Stevens, R.C. (of the Washington Light Infantry) 43
Stewart, Captain (of the Georgetown Mounted Guard) 44
Stewart, Mary Elizabeth (Tom Harbin's 1st wife) *see* Harbin, Mary Elizabeth
Stokes, Mr. (of Clarksville) 187
Stone, Charles P. (inspector general) 42, 44–46
Storke, Henry D. 115
Story of the Irish Race (book) 70
Strawberry Plains (Civil War battle) 54
Stuart, Jeb (Civil War general) 59
Stuart, Richard Henry (Confederate agent) 108, 115, 121, 126

Sullivan, Mr. (Reverend) 136
Sulpician Fathers 23
Sunnyside Academy for Girls 76
Surratt, John, Jr. (Confederate agent) 118, 125
Surratt, John, Sr. 106
Surratt, Mary (Confederate agent) 23, 38, 41, 101–102, 106–107, 122–123
Surrattsville (Maryland) 106

Tait, Bill (Navy Yard smith) 35, 37
Talbert, William (D.C. politician) 41, 42
Tayloe family 115
Taylor, Annie E. (George F. Harbin's slave) 113
Tenallytown Rifles 43
Tenney, Franklin (of the National Hotel) 126, 135, 137, 144
Thistleton, Captain (of the Putnam Rifles) 43
Thompson, John (Confederate agent) 117
Thompson, John E. (Piscataway barkeep) 106
Three Brothers (plantation) 99, 104–106
Tidwell, William (author) 56–58, 61–62, 108
Tiffany, Edward (Baltimore jobber) 106
Tiger Tail (Seminole chief) 51
Tillion, Juliet (married a Sansbury in D.C.) 23
Torpedo Bureau 61–62
Totopotomoy Creek (Civil War battle) 54
Towers, Levi (of the Washington Light Infantry) 43
Townsend, George Alfred (journalist, nickname "Gath") 114, 117, 121, 124, 135, 137–139
Trott, Stanley T. (pallbearer) 84, 172
Truman, Alexander (Revolutionary War captain) 19
Tucker, James (Navy Yard boss) 35
Turner Rifles 43, 45
Tydings, Ella (D.C. rape victim) 126

Union Regiment 45
United States Census Bureau 29, 60
Upper Zachia (Maryland) 99–100
Urell, Michael Emmet (Irish patriot) 77, 84, 88, 172

Vanderdonck, Mary (daughter of Doughty, the witch hunter) 16
Van Horsigh, Joseph (Reverend) 22–24, 158

Vann, Josie *see* McKenzie, Josie
Vann, Livingston 75
Venable, William S. (friend of Janette Russell's) 34, 157
Venable family 157
Villers, Mary *see* Harbin, Mary

Waldorf (Maryland) 19
Walker, William J. (Old Capitol prisoner) 109
Wallach, M. (of the Washington Light Infantry) 47
Wallach, Mayor (of D.C.) 182
Waltemyer, Joseph (D.C. hatter) 133, 136, 141
Walter, Jacob Ambrose (Reverend) 119
Walton, Gertrude (connected to the Colliflowers) 79
Washington, George 53
Washington Electro-Plating Company 133, 143, 171
Washington Light Infantry 43, 45–47, 49, 188
Washington Monument 37
Washington Navy Yard 24–25, 32, 35–36, 38, 41–42, 47, 84, 91–92, 95, 105, 117, 122, 159, 188
Washington Rifles 43, 45
Watkins, Ella Louise *see* Russell, Ella Louise
Watkins, George S. (Confederate agent) 109, 111–113
Watkins, L.D. (of the National Rifles) 44
Watkins, Rudolph (Confederate agent) 109, 111–113
Wayson, Israel (D.C. politician) 32
Wearmouth, John & Roberta (authors) 114
Weaver, Hanson E. (pallbearer) 84, 172
Weightman, Roger C. & Henry T. (of the National Hotel) 125
Weller, M.I. (pallbearer) 136
Welsh, Thomas J. (witness to murder) 90
Weschler family 142, 146, 149, 170
Western State Hospital (Staunton, Va.) 82
Westminster (ship) 27
Whaley, Mr. (Reverend) 76
Whig Party 101
Wicomico River (Maryland) 16
Wilderness (Civil War battle) 54
Willard, Emma (owner of an academy) 139
Williams, S. (D.C. assistant adjutant general) 113
Williamson sisters (both Mrs Royster) 53
Wilson, James H. (Civil War general) 55

Wilson, Lt. (Union officer) 108–109
Wilson, Riley J. (Louisiana congressman) 150
Wilson, Thomas A. *see* Harbin, Thomas Henry
Wise, Benedict (Captain Hebb's cousin) 58
Wood, Policeman (of D.C.) 91
Wood family (of D.C.) 72

Worthan family 75, 168, 179

Yates, Jack (of the Washington Light Infantry) 47
Young, Tapley W. "Tap" (James T. Harbin's partner) 171, 132–133
Young Ireland Movement (Young Irish Movement) 31, 67
Yturbide family 115, 127

www.ingramcontent.com/pod-product-compliance
Ingram Content Group UK Ltd.
Pitfield, Milton Keynes, MK11 3LW, UK
UKHW041959140426
5217IPUK00015B/881